A DISCOVERY OF OLD ESSEX

A Discovery of Old Essex

by
RICHARD PUSEY

Illustrated by
Rod Brown

ROBERT HALE · LONDON

Robert Hale Limited
Clerkenwell House
Clerkenwell Green
London EC1R 0HT

British Library Cataloguing in Publication Data

Pusey, Richard
  A discovery of old Essex.
  1. Essex—Description and travel
  I. Title
  914.26'704858   DA670.E7

ISBN 0-7090-2318-9

Photoset in North Wales by
Derek Doyle & Associates, Mold, Clwyd.
Printed in Great Britain by
St Edmundsbury Press, Bury St Edmunds, Suffolk.
Bound by Hunter & Foulis Limited.

Contents

Contents

List of Illustrations

Foreword

by Sir William Addison

Soil, says Wordsworth, 'has a secret and mysterious soul'. There is no doubt about Essex being a county of the soil. It was already so highly cultivated when Caesar came that he was able to feed four legions, their auxiliaries and seventeen hundred cavalry off the land, and after a short time to export a surplus from Colchester to the Continent. But a secret and mysterious soul? Where do we look for that? The answer has never been better given than by Richard Pusey in this book. Of all the scores of wide-ranging books on Essex that I have read, not one has given me more pleasure than this. There are surprises and delights on every page.

As a practised lecturer Richard Pusey knows the value of combining the element of expectation with the element of surprise. In his search for what he calls 'the phantom scenery of the past' he takes us to such secluded places as 'the Forest retreat of Bedesmens Berg' in the parish of Writtle where, to quote him, 'we can enjoy the peace and rustled silence of what S.L. Bensusan so beautifully called "the litany of green things growing" '. The best things are now to be found where nobody thought to look.

At this point I can imagine someone interrupting with, 'But there is no forest of Bedesmens Berg', which for all the charm of the alliteration only meant an anchorite's cell, and referred to a hermitage founded in 1135 of which nothing remains. That is true; but you must see what Richard Pusey makes of it! On reading his account I found myself reciting Kipling's most magical poem, 'The Road Through the Woods', which concludes with the line: 'But there is no road through the woods'.

The unexpected at nearby Norton Mandeville is of a different kind. We are mundane-minded folk in Essex. This tiny village is so sequestered that I should be surprised if half the people living in either of the Ongars have ever been there. And if they went they wouldn't find what, thanks to this book, I for one shall chuckle over whenever the name Norton Mandeville is mentioned. It is recorded that a sixteenth-century curate, Thomas Bainbrick, refused to read the burial service at the graveside on one occasion because a 'great Winde' was blowing. Although his name suggests that he was a Yorkshireman, and should therefore have been tough, he was afraid of catching cold.

Most Essex place-names trip off the tongue like those in Edward Thomas' lines:

> If I should ever by chance grow rich
> I'll buy Codham, Cockridden, and Childerditch.

All except a mere handful are Saxon and earthy: like Sluts Green, Shellow Bowells, and Little Rakefires, inhabited by old men 'dipping great thoughts in beer', and enlivened by young women like Agnes Sawen, 'a common enchantress of both men and beasts'. Such names came from the womb of language as lustily as Agnes Sawen's byeblows. But Essex has also several Norman names which sometimes produce clues to place names with interesting manorial origins: Molehill Green at Felsted and elsewhere refers not to 'the little gentlemen in black velvet', but to a feudal system of tenure. It is the alertness and scholarship which Richard Pusey brings to the interpretation of local names, as well as the fun he finds in them, that should give this book national as well as local appeal.

W.A.

Acknowledgements

I wish to thank those publishers who have kindly agreed to the use of copyright material: namely, Sheed and Ward for an extract from G.K. Chesterton's *The Coloured Lands*; and for lines from Vita Sackville West's *The Land* reprinted by permission of William Heinemann Ltd.

As intimated in the preface I owe a particular debt of gratitude to the staff of the Essex Record Office and to the editor of the *Essex Countryside* magazine. I am indebted, too, not only to the numerous authors, contemporary and of old, who have lightened my way but also to those who have aided my enquiries in the many places visited. If they were listed here there names would be legion.

Finally, my thanks to Sir William Addison for his generous foreword to the book. I have been little more than a name to him whereas for me his books on Essex down the years have been a constant sourse of pleasure and an education.

Preface

This is not another A to Z guide to Essex. There are a number of these already which cover the county well, though of necessity in a concise way. This book is more selective. Although some familiar and prestigious sites get my attention, this in the main is a celebration of little places and, above all, of things which have stayed obscure.

Much of Essex gone still remains a *terra incognita*. Each one of us who longs to go where 'the past is a foreign country' is in the position of that character in Chesterton's *The Coloured Lands* who wanted to discover America: 'His gay and thoughtless friends, who could not understand him, pointed out that America had already been discovered, I think they said by Christopher Columbus, some time ago ... But the Admiral explained to them, kindly enough, that this had nothing to do with it. They might have discovered America, but he had not.'

It is in this spirit of enquiry that I have set out to bring to light much that has not often reached the public eye, and some of it never at all. Dr Johnson remarked somewhere that in the making of books many another will be read. This is certainly true of histories and biography, and this book would have proved impossible without the prior investigations of others. So I have gone to many old volumes, some very rare and most long out of print. Some I have acknowledged by name in the text. But, as I have written for a wider circle than specialists in the field of local studies, I have avoided chapter and verse, and that *bête noire* of the common reader, the curse of footnotes.

There is much here, too, by way of archive research, and for this I am grateful to the Essex Record Office where I have oft been glimpsed 'a passing apparition'. I have gone as well to virtually all the places I've written up, and many have enticed me back time and again. They are richly varied, in both scene and associations, and in these pages they represent each quarter of the county.

Several of the chapters first appeared in the *Essex Countryside*, and I thank the editor for his approval to include them here. They have been revised and enlarged with new material.

Miller Christy, back in 1887, began his book on Essex trade-signs with this quotation: 'Prefaces to books (says a learned author) are like signs to public houses. They are intended to give one an idea of the kind of entertainment to be found within.'

This is perhaps truer of a table of contents but I hope this one, at the sign of old Essex, will induce you to step inside. My bill of fare awaits you.

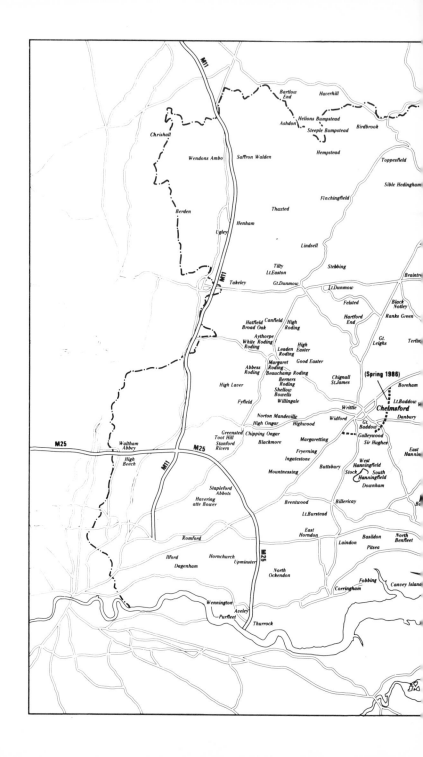

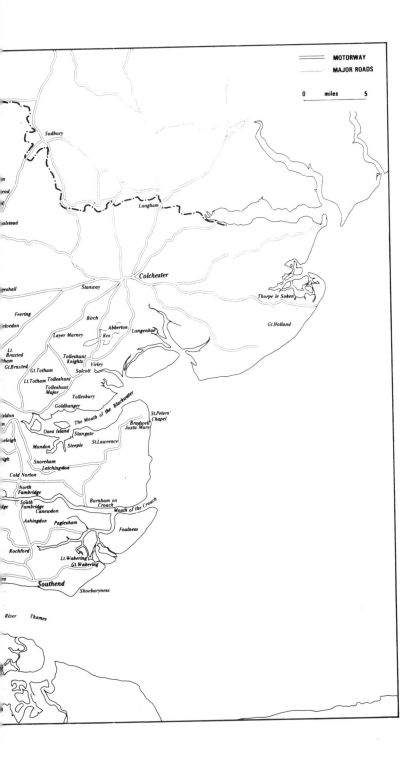

MOTORWAY
MAJOR ROADS

0   miles   5

Sudbury

Langham

alstead

Colchester

geshall   Stanway

Thorpe le Soken

Feering   Birch

eledon   Abberton   Langenhoe
            Layer Marney   Res

Gt.Holland

Lt.
Braxted   Tolleshunt
ham   Knights   Virley
Gt.Braxted Gt.Totham   Salcott
        Lt.Totham Tolleshunt
              Tolleshunt
              Major
                Tollesbury
            Goldhanger

aidon   St.Peters'
                The Mouth of the Blackwater   Chapel
n   Osea Island Stangate Bradwell
eleigh   Juxta Mare
        Mundon   Steeple St.Lawrence
igh
            Snoreham
            Latchingdon
Cold Norton

North
Fambridge
        South
dge   Fambridge
            Canewdon   Burnham on
                        Crouch   Mouth of the Crouch
Ashingdon   Paglesham
                        Foulness
Rochford
        Lt.Wakering
        Gt.Wakering
ea
    Southend
            Shoeburyness

River   Thames

We are drawn unto discourses of Antiquities, who have scarce time before us to comprehend new things, or make out learned Novelties. But seeing they arose as they lay, almost in silence among us, at least in short account suddenly passed over, we were very unwilling they should die again and be buried twice among us ...

'Tis opportune to look back upon old times, and contemplate our Forefathers. Great examples grow thin, and to be fetched from the passed world. Simplicity flies away and iniquity comes at long strides upon us.

Sir Thomas Browne: Urn Burial (1658)

Part I

Quiet Corners in the South

St Michael's, Fobbing

1

The Marshland Village of Fobbing

Along the reaches of the Thames there remain a few, a very few, enclaves of old Essex. One of these is Fobbing. Below the New Town of Basildon, the Five Bells and the A13, alias 'tanker alley', the village stands fifty feet above the river. Isolated, it clings like a limpet to its past, looking out across those lands once scathingly called by Waller

'cursed Essexian plains
where hasty death and pining sickness reigns.'

According to John Aubrey, that marvellous seventeenth-century gossip, seven of Fobbing's curates had succumbed to the vapours in the space of ten years, while Defoe was told even more extravagant tales of the treacherous ague. Today the marshes have long been drained, and the contemporary scene is very different.

This, then, is now the setting. To the south-east lie the Corringham Marshes, with Coryton and Shell Haven and the vast gleaming complex of the Mobile refinery. Coryton is no ancient name but commemorates the Cory brothers who in the last century set up oil installations here. Up to the 1870s no oil products could be taken further up the river than this point. It may also surprise you to learn that Shell Haven is not named after the petroleum company. In fact, it was known as such in the reign of Henry VIII. Samuel Pepys called it 'Shield-haven'. It really means a shelf-haven, for the 'shell' is a bank or slope. Shelley near Ongar derives its name in the same way.

Where the oil tanks now stand arrayed, looking like a science-fiction landscape, there were in centuries past great

19

flocks of sheep. The ewes were kept on the 'wicks' for their milk to make the celebrated Essex cheeses noted by the Elizabethan topographers Norden and William Camden. These were certainly not enjoyed by the poet John Skelton:

> A cantle of Essex cheese
> Was well a foot thick
> Full of maggots quick
> It was huge and great
> And mighty strong meat
> For the Devil to eat
> It was tart and punicate.

There were wicks, too, further east on Canvey Island. On the island Hole Haven is marked on a map of 1793 as 'Holy Haven', and here behind the sea wall is the Lobster Smack which figures in the closing stages of *Great Expectations*.

Two other curious marshland names are 'Fobbing Horse' and 'Oozedam'. The first has no equestrian associations but is most probably from the Old English for mud-hill. It is one of several 'Horses' to be found on Essex marshes. Oozedam means just what it sounds like, 'swampy'.

The chief attraction and most dominant building in Fobbing is the parish church. Like many another old hilltop church, it is dedicated to the Archangel Michael, the guardian of high places. Its silver-grey ragstone tower, more Kentish than Essex, has stood since the fifteenth century as a landmark to seamen and smugglers and has served as well as a watchtower. From its battlements the Dutch fleet would have been seen off Shell Haven when it ventured up the Thames in 1667. The view from the top is well worth the climb (the keys to both the church door and the tower are held at the modern rectory nearby), although the spiral ascent is a stern one and the steps are very narrow and well worn. Moreover, there is no handrail or rope to guide you up through the darkness.

Although the first known rector was Robert de Tong in 1345, there was a church on this spot long before then. The evidence lies in a late Saxon window blocked up in the north wall. One of the strangest inscriptions to be found in any Essex church can be seen here. Probably from the time of

Robert de Tong, it reads as follows:

X PUR LAMUR IESU CRIST
PRIEZ PUR SA ALME KI CI GIST
PATER NOSTER ET AVE
THOMAS DE CRAWDENE FUT APELLE.

In Lombardic capitals on a slab of Purbeck marble, this is an odd mixture of Norman-French and Latin. It begins 'For the love of Jesus Christ' and begs the reader to pray for the soul of Thomas of Crawdene.

Another fascinating rarity in St Michael's is a barrel organ, not to be confused with the hurdy-gurdy or the old street piano organ. The barrel organ in church was a popular instrument last century, taking over from the little village bands up in the musicians' gallery, and in turn being replaced almost everywhere in the late 1800s by the pipe organ. Fobbing's barrel organ was made by a Soho firm which started business in 1794. Now carefully restored, it is in full working order. It has three bands which can play thirty-six tunes, including such numbers as 'The Old Hundreth Psalm', 'Morning Hymn' and 'Hanover'. The tunes are listed by hand inside the door of the case, which stands at the west end of the nave. The organ is conspicuous, some twelve feet high and five feet wide.

The timber porch of the church has an interesting carving in a spandrel, a Neptune-like figure and a sea serpent. I like to think that this piece of marine mythology may have been carved by a sailor home from the perils of the sea. Herbert W. Tompkins in his book *A Companion into Essex* (1938) writes of a cannon ball found embedded in the east wall of the porch but of this I can find no other record.

The parish registers are of particular note, for the earliest date from 1539. The Dutch influence on the area comes through in several entries. Thus, among the burials recorded for 1623, we find that 'Powell a Dutchman dwelling in Ooze was buried Feb 18th' while the register for 1663 notes 'Bolding a Dutchman'. John Arnau 'a ffleminge' appears in 1641. And 'Brian the Dutchman who was killed by a fall from his horse was buried 29 July 1658'. Cornelius Vermuyden, who with his assistant Joos Croppenburgh embanked and reclaimed land on Canvey in the seventeenth century, was also responsible for enclosing marshes around Fobbing.

Canvey Island is written as 'Candy Island' in the register for 1653. Daniel Defoe styled it the same in 1724 in his *Tour through the Whole Island of Great Britain*. A truly strange annotation to an entry in the Fobbing registers reads 'This rote in portwine!'

The severity towards un-wed mothers is harshly expressed on a page of the baptismal register for 1758: 'Geoffrey – the bastard son of Sarah Crispe a young impudent whore of this parish July 26'.

A worthy of the church here was Dr John Pell, a mathematician of much repute in his day. He was an unwilling rector from 1661 until his death in 1685. He was also the vicar of nearby Laindon from 1663, in Aubrey's words 'the scurvey Parsonage of Laindon cum Basseldon in the infamous and unhealthy (aguesh) Hundreds of Essex'. Pell complained to the Archbishop of Canterbury about his benefice in these parts. 'I do not intend that you shall live there,' his Lordship is said to have remarked. 'No, sayd Pell, but your Grace does intend that I shall die there.'

The ancient parish of Fobbing extended as far north as Lee Chapel by Laindon. Three modern buildings, Basildon College of Further Education, the Sports Centre and the Hospital, stand upon the land of Fobbing Farm which was marked on Chapman and André's map of 1777. It ceased to be a farm in 1971. In a small parish, Fobbing's population until well into this century was also tiny. In 1821 it was 407. By 1938 it amounted to little more than a thousand. Today the population is still small compared with Corringham's twelve thousand plus.

Fobbing village has a few old houses worthy of note, all close to the church. Of these the pub, the White Lion, has pride of place. Thought to date from the 1400s, it has a central hall with cross-wings and a very fine fireplace. Wheelers House, too, is very distinctive, with white weatherboards. North-west of the church, Prosbus Hall has an eighteenth-century front but is much older at the rear.

But no short account of old Fobbing would be complete without some mention of what drew this modest place out of its rural obscurity and put it well and truly on the map in 1381. For it was here, and at Corringham and adjacent Stanford-le-Hope, that the great upheaval of the Peasants' Revolt began. It started as a protest against new taxation, the trigger for a long-smouldering discontent. In May 1381 peasants from these villages, incited by one Thomas Baker of Fobbing, gathered at Brentwood and defiantly refused to pay up.

The chroniclers of the Revolt, all of course Establishment men, recorded an inflammatory incident which fed the resentment of the people. In 'a certain village' hereabouts one of the commissioners called together the men and women and 'shamelessly lifted the young girls to test whether they had enjoyed intercourse with men'. By this means parents and neighbours were induced to meet the tax demands rather than endure further humiliation.

Thomas Baker remains but a name, a shadowy village hero. He does not appear again in the records. He was swept away by the great flood of events he helped to put in motion. The uprising spread to many parts of Essex and Kent and beyond, but after its initial success it was bloodily suppressed not far from where it started.

2

The Church at Thameside Wennington

Every year now there comes yet another sad announcement of the demise of one of our old Essex churches.

The list of redundancies grows. Mundon, Latchingdon, Langdon Hills, Shellow Bowells, East Horndon – these places among others have seen their ancient sanctuaries close their doors for regular worship, and several have been sold off as churchyard homes, making unlikely domiciles. Others lie under the shadow. The latest at risk include West Hanningfield, Mountnessing and, as I write, Thameside Wennington.

The small village of Wennington near Rainham lies just off the A13 on the old road and, as a consequence, is relatively unknown. It has also mercifully escaped the worse scars of the industrial and residential development across the flatlands of riverside Essex. 'London over the border' is shunned by most in search of countryside and relics of the past, but Wennington like Fobbing is a lone survivor in all that and will reward the diversion.

On the very edge of the marshes there is barely a rise in the landscape here. Writing in the eighteenth century the Essex historian Philip Morant noted that East Hall was 'Easthull' in 1518, the 'hull' meaning a hill although a mere fifteen feet above sea-level! The parish covers nearly thirteen hundred acres, mainly farmland, and stays lightly populated. Only in very recent years have the numbers been augmented. In the eighteenth century there was actually a decline, there being only twelve or thirteen houses in the parish, a striking contrast to the thirty or so in the century before that. The ever-watchful constable of the day, in his little world bounded by ditches, would have known everyone well, empowered as he was to report by name all

St Peter's, Wennington

'Common Poachers, Drunkards, Swearers, Night Walkers, Evesdroppers' and 'all those that Profaned the Lord's Day'.

The church is just inside the parish, a short way from the Lennard Arms, an Aveley pub which takes its name from the Barrett-Lennard family. (Gone now, their large Belhus estate once included Wennington.) As at the Norman church upstream at Rainham the dedication is a dual one, to St Mary and St Peter. A fifteenth-century stone shield on an outside wall is carved with crossed keys, the emblem of Peter, and he is also depicted in a stained glass window.

The church has much to offer of antiquarian interest. According to Pevsner, the little doorway on the south is Norman. There is characteristic work in its rounded head. Worley, in his *Dictionary of the County* (1915), describes it as diaper work and star pattern; Pevsner gives it as bands of saltire crosses. It is the only thing of its period in the fabric of the church, the remainder of the oldest parts being of the thirteenth century. The doorway looks very out of place, for at one time the original south side was taken down and the arcade bricked in. But in the general restoration of 1866 the aisle was rebuilt on the old foundations.

Pevsner's account does not do full justice to the church. He fails to mention the old font of Purbeck marble, whitewashed over, and the lovely little memorial wall tablet to the rector Henry Bust and his son which with its kneeling figures has survived from 1626. The furnishings of the church include a thirteenth-century 'hutch' chest with three locks and a Jacobean pulpit still with its wrought-iron stand for the preacher's hourglass. In an age of sermons, 'It did not state time with precision: it stifled it in powdery particles.' A curiosity is a square of lead bearing initials and the date 1740. That the roof was formerly leaded seems to be established by the fact that in 1568 four sheets valued at £3 were removed from there. The thief was punished by being sent to the pillory.

There are other good things in store for the visitor inside the church, but the most impressive part of its structure is the fourteenth-century three-stage tower, built of Kentish ragstone. The rugged appearance is due not only to the material but also to its exposure to the raw elements of the marshes. It is now badly worn and constitutes a major item in the estimated costs for the church's restoration.

I understand there is a fine view from the top. I have managed the tower at Fobbing but, not having a head for unenclosed heights, I became anxious on the ladders here, ladders with narrow treads and steeply rising into space, and reached no further than the second stage the day I was taken up. One bell hangs in the tower, bearing the date 1662. There was formerly a ring of two or three.

Back on *terra firma*, the churchyard as well has its interest. Here is the remarkable little monument to Sir Henry Perigal, who died in 1898 at the age of ninety-seven. He was an outstanding mathematician and astronomer. Cremated at Woking, his ashes were brought to rest here on native soil. The inscriptions on his memorial, although well worn, should be looked at closely for they include mathematical formulae and geometrical figures, strange hieroglyphics to those untutored in that science. The stone is by the east window.

A few yards away lies his second cousin, the Rev. Nicholas Brady, who was rector from 1874 to 1907 and who did so much for the church in his day. He was the son of Sir Antonio Brady, a noted archaeologist and philanthropist.

Another who can perhaps be regarded as a 'worthy' of this place was the Elizabethan rector William Asheton. He was in continuous trouble for refusing to wear a surplice. This sounds a trivial matter today but then it was held a sure mark of Puritan tendencies. Asheton was finally deprived of the living in 1590.

What then is to be the fate in our time of this simple church? It is going to cost thousands to put it right. The local clergy, I am told, are not enthusiastic; by 'local' is meant Rainham, for there is no resident pastor in the village. The move to save SS Mary and Peter is coming from the laity, from the sheep rather than from the shepherds. In February 1982 'The Friends of Wennington Church' formed after a public meeting. At present they number parishioners from Rainham as well as Wennington itself, with not a few well-wishers from places further afield. Fund-raising events are organized and the church is opened to visitors the first Sunday in every month throughout the afternoon.

In a time of ever-rising costs, the church faces grave financial problems, especially in rural areas, with a decline in church attendance and the patronage of the old estates. Yet it can be cogently argued that the closure of churches is an answer which lacks historical perspective, a short-term solution which could have bad long-term results. The ancient parish churches are part of the heritage of believer and non-believer alike. They are 'numinous' places, with a setting, ritual and atmosphere which can lift us above our mundane everyday selves and environment. They give a much-needed continuity with the past in a radically changing landscape. And it is in these churches, too, that we can have a sense of the past which is not dead and embalmed but in the living stream of history. Above all it is here in their encapsuled silence that we can become receptive to that which lies beyond mortality and time. There can be no adequate substitute for such experience in the more domestic arrangements of hut and front-room Christianity.

The nave of a church, from the Latin *navis*, is said to be so called because the old rounded roof-vaults resembled the upturned hull of a boat. This, I feel, makes every church a kind of Noah's Ark. For those of us who cherish them in this new Dark Age, what this vessel symbolically represents is full of hopeful implications.

3

Little and Great Sir Hughes

Coming inland from Essex by the Thames, there is one of the most interesting areas in the southern districts of the county. Scenically varied, it forms a rural triangle, its base along the broken ridge between Wickford and Billericay, with its apex being Chelmsford. This is green-belt land and so has stayed as yet immune from high-density development, an area of farming and commuter havens off the two main thoroughfares which serve as corridors linking the county town with the burgeoning populations of lower Essex.

Sir Hughes is the first of the places off the beaten track I want to lead you to in these fair parts.

When you come along the road from Great Baddow to West Hanningfield, the signpost raises expectations of something rather grand. In fact, Sir Hughes today is little more than an unusual and prestigious name upon the map. The lane takes you to a surprisingly modest place. Here there are but several houses of no great age screened by trees. There is now nothing but the name to suggest antiquity.

And yet Sir Hughes should be seen if only in passing. It is an unlikely survival, with the sprawl of Chelmsford absorbing Baddow only fields away. Moreover, its peace and isolation are very much at risk. It is now directly threatened by the building of the southern route around the county town which is scheduled for completion in 1986. The hamlet will then be perched on the edge of a virtual motorway.

Judging from old maps, Sir Hughes has always been small in scale. This was an estate, never a village. It takes its name from Sir Hugh de Badew, knighted in the reign of Edward III. The manor originated in the late twelfth or early thirteenth century when a Robert Marschall or Mascall was, in the words of Morant, 'the most ancient holder of the

Great Mascalls at Sir Hughes

manor on record'. In 1211 he held a hide of land (that is, between 60 and 120 acres) in return for maintaining King John's palfrey, his saddle horse. This was just three years before the signing of Magna Carta, so perhaps Robert Mascall attended on his monarch at Runnymede. He must certainly have been away from home a great deal in those turbulent years.

The family was of more than local standing. From the obscurity of its history one figure emerges of major cultural importance. In 1326 Richard de Baddow had the distinction of being the first founder of University Hall, Cambridge. It had only around ten scholars for the first few years, but in 1338 Richard, himself a notable scholar, gave it by deed to a granddaughter of Edward I, Elizabeth, Countess of Clare. So it was that the college became Clare Hall.

The name 'Mascall' is perpetuated by two properties on either side of Sir Hughes: Little Mascalls Farm and Great Mascalls. The latter is a white brick house of Georgian date. Set amid ornamental trees, it looks every inch an estate residence.

The designations 'Little' and 'Great' for Sir Hughes distinguished its two principal sites. At Great Sir Hughes, the further from the highway and noted in our time for its orchards, there was a fine Caroline mansion until between the wars. Bennett Bamford's watercolour of the house has been reproduced in postcard format along with four other Essex views, and the set is on sale at county libraries.

Sir Hughes had a succession of owners down the years. At one time it was in the hands of one of the most distinguished of South Essex families, the Tyrells. A map of 1787 shows that Little Sir Hughes then belonged to John Tyrell.

The place has also undergone several changes in name. In the sixteenth century it was called 'Shenges'. Across country in Little Baddow 'Shingay' had the same name in 1558. 'Shenges alias Sir Hughes.'

There was once some speculation, which has not been renewed in our day, on a possible connection between Sir Hughes and the exceptional oak effigies in Little Baddow church. The two figures, companion pieces of a man and a woman, lie in recesses in the south wall. It is odd that time and again in the past these effigies were both described as women, perhaps because the face of the man is so graceful and refined. By tradition they represent the founders of the church or rather patrons of its rebuilding in the fourteenth century, for the north wall is Norman. Pevsner dates the sculptures from around 1320.

A correspondent writing to the *Gentleman's Magazine* in 1853 quotes from a letter of Mr Joseph Strutt, the antiquarian, in which he mentions the opening of a grave beneath the effigies which revealed two bodies, 'women' apparently of the thirteenth century. Unfortunately, he gives no further details. It looks as though their sex was simply assumed to be female.

By tradition, too, one of the figures is that of Anne de Badew, the first wife of Sir Hugh. She was the sister of Sir John de Berners, whose son, Sir James, was executed in the reign of Richard II. Joseph Strutt thought he had found confirmation of her identification with the effigy in a manuscript pedigree of the Berners family seemingly compiled in 1616. The key line is: 'This Anne lyeth bureyed in an arch of the wall at Little Badew church, in Essex, with the monkey at her face'. 'The monkey at her face' is very curious, for the figure has no such animal. A monkey was apparently part of the crest of Anne's father, and an image of one may of course have disappeared from the tomb. Joseph Strutt surmised that the dog at her feet (and there is one for the other effigy) had been mistaken for a little ape. He thought, as well, that 'face' was a copyist's error for 'feet'. Yet if the lady does mark the resting place of Anne, the other must surely be Sir Hugh himself, buried beside his first wife.

Although the documentary sources are scattered and fragmentary, I suspect that Sir Hughes would repay closer study by an enthusiast for little places.

4

Hanningfield Under the Water

Of the many scenic attractions to be found in Essex, the reservoir at Hanningfield is one of the most impressive. Every year it draws hundreds of visitors throughout the spring and summer, lured by that magic attraction of an inland 'sea'.

Especially from the southern end of Middlemead there are fine views out across the water. It covers a gentle valley some 870 acres in extent and spreads across the invisible boundaries of four parishes. Seen from the road below the little church of St Peter's and the Hall, it is easy to tell why the water has been likened to a lowland loch or Swedish lake, for the resemblance is due largely to the conifer plantations around it. Those who like myself are fortunate to pass it frequently will know that the view is never quite the same from day to day. Hanningfield Water with its wide vistas and expanse of sky has an ever-changing aspect. Sometimes shrouded in mist, sometimes rough and lashed like an open sea, it can also look like a giant mirror with flocks of birds resting on its glassy surface. And the sunsets to be seen here often beggar description.

But initially the coming of the reservoir in the 1950s was regarded by local people with alarm. They saw the rich farmland slowly disappear, the old road between the villages of South and West Hanningfield vanish and the encroaching waters rise above properties with ancient names and histories. There was no danger, but as they watched, the landscape became a memory, a place of 'old effaced images of more than half-forgotten names'. Later, they heard with relief that plans to inundate a second valley, between Elms Farm and Tanfield Tye, had been abandoned. Had this happened, I would today be living by a lake.

33

Hanningfield Water was on the drawing-board as far back as the thirties, but the war delayed its construction until 1952. The huge operation of flooding so much land, building the great banks and the pumping stations took four years to complete. The main dam alone is one mile long and over sixty feet high. The maximum depth is fifty-five feet. Up to five hundred permits for trout-fishing are available each season, the water being re-stocked every year. The fish, along with the swallows which dominate the summer sky, often in spectacular numbers, keep the swarms of insects down to a tolerable level. It is singularly appropriate that the fishermen here cast their lines within sight of a church dedicated eight centuries ago to their patron saint.

The water is pumped overland from the Chelmer and the Blackwater. The basin provides the growing population of south Essex with 24 million gallons a day. In exceptional conditions, as in the great drought of 1976, extra can be drawn in from the Ely-Ouse scheme.

The reservoir must rank as an outstanding alliance of service industry and ecological art. Even the blatant modernity of the waterworks is being progressively softened by imaginative landscaping around the plant. Much of the land surrounding the water is under the care and protection of the Essex Water Board and is not accessible to the general public. However, there has been some discussion with the county on the feasibility of providing viewing facilities. Perhaps the time may yet come when something modestly similar to the walks and hides of Minsmere in Suffolk will be created.

But impressive as all these facts and figures may be, it is what lies under the reservoir which excites the greatest curiosity.

The belief is widespread among 'outsiders' that it covers a lost village, a North Hanningfield perhaps. The three compass-point parishes, South, East and West, do seem incomplete and appear to suggest another. There is even the belief, as widely held, that there is a church beneath the water, the bell of which rings when the water is low. Both of these romantic notions are incorrect, as a look at the older maps of the area will soon disclose. Yet the former, at least, is close to the truth.

St Peter's by Hanningfield Water

Under the reservoir at the very southern end lies the farmland of Giffords. It is close to South Hanningfield Tye and is just off the submerged lane. The first few yards of the old road are still above water. 'Cobblestones', a charming weatherboarded house, stands where it joins the main highway. Only a short walk away is the very popular old Windmill pub and restaurant. What remains here of the old lane is, of course, a no-through road, and its final length to the water's edge is closed to the public. The road re-appears at the other end, in West Hanningfield. Part of it can be followed from the corner by the fishermen's pub, the sixteenth-century Three Compasses, where it links with the Lower Stock Road. But much of what is left of the road is here, too, out of bounds, being on land held by the Water Authority. Closed as well on this route is the old way through to Seamans Lane in Stock.

The earliest mention of the pub by name occurs in a

weights and measures inspection return of 1758 when it was styled 'the 3 Cumpas'. But my research makes it virtually certain it was an alehouse two centuries before that. There is even evidence to suggest it may have been called 'the 3 Elms' in the seventeenth century. It is a small house and was smaller still until more recent years, and is known to have once had a cockpit inside. Until the last century a cage or lock-up stood near the pub on a piece of waste ground. Late in the reign of Victoria, the Compasses was the rustic meeting place for the short-lived Sparrows Club. Its members had to produce twelve heads of sparrows once a month!

Also to be seen just inside the old lane are the former village bakery, 'Tarlings', and a fine house of around 1500 called 'Gascoignes'.

Getting back to Giffords, the farm appears on a number of old maps held at the Essex Record Office. The earliest of these is an estate map drawn up for a Richard Honeywood Esquire in 1736. Giffords is also marked on Chapman and André's map of Essex of 1777. Another estate map, dated 1799, shows the farm to be in the same family, owned by a Honeywood with the very unusual Christian name of Filmer. He also had land at Great and Little Totham, and his accounts book for the 1780s still exists.

By 1829 Giffords belonged to Sir John Tyrell. The Tyrells were a prominent Essex family whose line went back well beyond Tudor times. As we have seen, they once held Little Sir Hughes.

Another of the farms which was flooded was Little Prestons. This lay within Stock, close to Great Prestons, which has survived. Little Prestons is under the northern end of the reservoir, where the banks provide a home for a wide variety of water birds including herons and the magnificent Canada goose. In fact, as a bird sanctuary the reservoir rivals that at Abberton.

Prestons is marked on John Norden's map of Essex which he drew in 1594. The common here was the scene of a great affray in 1580, a riotous and armed assembly in which well over sixty men from nearby parishes were hotly involved. The land was part of the manor of Downham Hall, at that time owned by the earls of Oxford. The clash seems to have been caused by a row over local rights to the use of the common. Most of those in the two groups which confronted each other were fined 6d each.

Also under the northern end of the water lies 'Pinnings', a property which had kept its name since William Pinning was here in the thirteenth century. A survey of the three Hanningfields taken in 1628 showed it as then belonging to Sir Henry Clovile. He was the last major figure of a family which had settled in West Hanningfield with a grant of land in the reign of William II. Nearby, too, was 'Peadown'. This had the name at least from 1677, when it was mentioned in Quarter Session Rolls.

But of the demolished houses beneath the water by far the most impressive was 'Fremnells' in Downham. This, too, is shown on the Norden map. The house which bears the name today stands just a little to the west of the submerged mansion.

Fremnells is a good example of how a place-name can change its form down the years. The very earliest mention of the place occurs in records of 1376. It was then 'Hemenales' and took its name from John de Hemenale in 1285. By the year 1544 it was known as 'Hemallys', alias 'Fremanallys'. Then by 1768 the house was called 'Tremnells'.

In the reign of the first Elizabeth it was held by Sir Henry Tyrell as 'Fremingnalls'. Sir Henry was an outstanding Justice of the Peace. Like the rest of his family he was a Roman Catholic, and his house at Downham had its own oratory, or chapel, though his main residence was Heron Hall at East Horndon. Although perhaps too notable a figure to be prosecuted for his outlawed faith, he knew that discretion was the better part of valour and outwardly conformed. He was very friendly with the Petres of Ingatestone Hall, home of the eminent Tudor secretary to the Crown, for Sir William Petre had connections with the Tyrells through both his marriages. Sir William's second wife, the Lady Anne, was also a very cautious Catholic.

The Elizabethan house was very largely changed by Benjamin Disborough or Disbrowe. Its most celebrated link in the seventeenth century was with his father, John Disbrowe, who had married one of Oliver Cromwell's four daughters. A member of Parliament, he commanded the

Roundhead cavalry at Bristol. Later he was appointed Major General of the Fleet by Cromwell and received over £3,000 a year for his services to the Protector. John Disbrowe was one of those who opposed the idea that Cromwell should be crowned king, and he also advised Oliver's son and successor, Richard, to rule without Parliament. Upon the return of Charles II to England, Disbrowe was accused of conspiring to take the life of the King and his Queen, Catherine of Braganza. He was cleared, however, and was released from prison.

Fremnells was re-fashioned in 1670 but much was left of earlier years. Writing before it went under the water, Nikolaus Pevsner thought it 'the best house of its date in Essex'. The impressive two-storey building had walls of brick and plastered timber framing. One of its main attractions was the hall, with panelling of the sixteenth century. The gateposts of the house dated from 1676. A further link with the family, a house called 'Disbrowe's Folly', could be seen last century at Downham on Crows Heath. But in the early 1800s this distinguished family came to an abrupt and stunning end. Smallpox broke out at Fremnells, and every member of the household perished. From then until its eventual disappearance the house was in less conspicuous hands.

A circular walk around the Water and its adjacent land will take you through a kaleidoscope of scenes all richly imprinted with the past. One good spot to start from is the top of Brock Hill, but if you want to cover it in one go, you should brace yourself, as this lovely circuit, part of it through the wooded backs of Stock, is nigh on eight miles. However, there are two pubs at which to pause a while. The rest of the journey gives a refreshment of another kind.

5

Tanfield Toy and the Manor of Peverels

Tanfield Toy, or Tye as it is sadly now called, lies just to the north of the ridge straddled by the linear village of West Hanningfield. Rising from the valley, it is a richly productive arable farm of some five hundred acres, presently owned by a Dane, its second European owner this century. The farmland here is of great antiquity and must have seen the plough long before the Normans came.

Making my home there now for ten years, living on the hillside in a modest cottage which was described as 'new' in 1919, I have acquired a special feeling for the place, a green-belt oasis with lovely views of gently undulating countryside. Just as importantly for me, it was here I received my first real stimulus to decipher the landscape and to read the past.

On the surface there is nothing too special about Tanfield Tye, apart from its air of remoteness and seclusion: few houses of particular note, no obvious excursion sights. And yet, like many another rural spot tucked well away, it quietly conceals its unique secrets. Among these are a long-lost and forgotten mansion and a remarkable link with prehistoric times.

Since boyhood I have been curious about the meanings of place-names, and it was the names here which first intrigued me.

Until well into this century the farm was known as Tanfield Toy. The 'Toy' is very unusual, at least in Essex today, for the only other I can trace in the county lay nearby in South Hanningfield, listed in Waller's *Essex Field Names*. It occurs as well in Gilbert White's *Natural History of Selborne*, in Letter II, where he refers to 'the bridge at the Toy, near Hampton Court'. Tanfield Toy was known as

From a window at Tanfield Toy

such to Philip Morant in 1768, while on the parish Tithes Award of 1844 there is shown a 'Tanfield Toy Field'. The farm continued to be marked with the old name on Ordnance Survey maps up to 1960.

It seems clear the 'Toy' is a rare dialect variant of 'Tye'. Other forms to be found are Tay, Tey and Tie. According to Charnock's *Glossary of the Essex Dialect*, published in 1880, the word 'Tye' has a dual derivation. In Old English it means an enclosure but it also comes from a Norse word meaning a strip of pasture. It is frequently employed to signify a green. So one way or the other we have here an expression which not only takes us back to an extremely remote past but in a form which comes close to being a solitary survivor. And this is why I find it such a pity that the delightfully archaic 'Toy' has been dropped.

As for 'Tanfield', this can be traced in the later stages of the manor of Peverels. It was from this medieval manor that the present farm arose, the manorial name enduring in 'Peveril Hall' and also in 'Little Peverels', the name of the lone house on the most westerly part of the farmland.

The foremost authority on Essex place-names, Dr P.H. Reaney, traced the origin of Peverels from Assize rolls and early Chancery proceedings. In the thirteenth century there is mention of a Hamo Peverel here. The name, of course, is Norman-French and occurs elsewhere in the county. Hatfield Peverel is the most prominent place to bear the name, but there is also Peverels Wood near Debden airfield.

Hatfield Peverel belonged to Ralph Peverel in 1086. Hamo was probably a descendant of Ralph, who had over thirty properties in the shire which he held from the Conqueror.

'Peverel' is a name of curious interest, the diminutive in Old French for pepper. It came to be used as a personal name, used either for a small, rounded man, 'peppercorn size', or for one with a fiery, peppery temperament. It is probably no more than an odd coincidence but in the seventeenth century the rent paid by Peverels to the holding manor of East Hanningfield was augmented annually by 'a pounde of pepper'.

John Peverel, who died about 1311, held land which had shortly before belonged to the Templars. On the western edge of the parish their presence is marked by a series of Temple names: Temple Wood and Farm, Temple Grove and Templeton Park, now a caravan site.

The age-old aura of mystery and romance around the Knights Templars shows no sign of fading. In fact, two best-sellers in recent years have served to deepen their legendary status still further. They play a cardinal role in the daring speculation of *The Holy Blood and the Holy Grail* and in Ian Wilson's book *The Turin Shroud*, in which he develops the hypothesis that they were the guardians of this most enigmatic of relics during its missing years. The religious, military order of the Templars founded after the First Crusade of 1099 was particularly favoured in England by Henry Plantagenet. The full name of the order was 'The Poor Knights of Christ and the Temple of Solomon', an ironic title as it proved, for in the course of two centuries they were to amass great wealth which gave rise to intense envy. In England, after being prohibited abroad, all the Templars were arrested in 1308. They were subsequently suppressed four years later, and their property was seized by the Crown, when they were charged with a whole catalogue of heinous crimes which included heresy, idolatry, black magic, child murder and homosexuality.

The belief persists that they hid much of their treasure, and *The Holy Blood* seems to have encouraged not a few enthusiasts to follow every remote possibility as to its whereabouts. Locally, there have been enquiries about the likelihood of a crypt on the Templar land in Hanningfield.

But although 'Templeton' indicates a manor, there was never a preceptory, a chapel, on the spot. The depressions to be seen within the woods are not evidence of ancient buildings but the remains of old gravel pits worked in Tudor times and probably later for the repair of the nearby highways.

John Peverel held the Templars' land under the name of 'Newlands', a name by which the manor was known as early as 1277. (There was another Templar estate called Newlands at Witham.) This almost certainly indicates land newly asserted – that is, taken in from the waste for cultivation. 'Waste' does not imply a lack of trees but simply means it was not farmed. On John Walker's map of 1611 the woods are marked 'Temple Ground' and 'waste'. In John Peverel's day part of the manor was also held from the powerful Hugh de Vere. The combined holding came to 205 acres, just fourteen acres short of that of Temple and Peverel Farm when it was sold by auction early this century.

When all the Templar lands were alienated, they were later granted to that other great military order, the Hospitallers or 'Order of the Friars of the Hospital of St John of Jerusalem'. They acquired the Hanningfield estate and may have run it from Little Maplestead where their round church remains.

Both monastic associations are reflected in the name 'Old Orders' which appears on Chapman and André's map of Essex. The site is now occupied by 'Gay Bowers' at the far end of Bakers Lane. The present owners also own The Grove, which is noted for badger setts and woodpeckers. By its purchase they saved twenty-eight acres of beautiful and ancient woodland from being levelled and 'developed', an act of preservation which fully deserves to be recorded. Incidentally, there is a Gay Bowers in the parish of Danbury as well.

It is at this point in the history of the manor that the name 'Tanfield' makes its appearance.

From the fifteenth century and possibly before, the ancient manor of Peverels was held by the Clovile family, in part from the Hospitallers and from a Lord Abergaveny. Then in the sixteenth century the marriage of William Tanfield of Coptfold Hall, Margaretting, to Elizabeth Clovile was to lead eventually to the name Tanfield being applied to part of the estate. William came from Harpelo in Northamptonshire. By 1597 the manor had passed to his son, John, and was 320 demesne acres in extent. He held one half from Peter Whetcombe 'of his manor of Temple-Parages' and the other half from William, Lord Petre.

John Tanfield died in 1625, aged seventy-eight. He is commemorated in a beautiful wall tablet in Margaretting church. The colourful gilded memorial now sited above the north door dates from shortly after his decease. It has small kneeling figures diminishing in size of John, his wife Katherine and their seven children. The couple face each other at a prayer-desk, with John's three sons behind him and Katherine's four daughters behind her. Each figure is displayed in fine Jacobean costume. The monument bears various coats of arms, representing the Tanfields' connections with other notable families.

With John's death, Peverels passed to his son and heir, Clovile Tanfield. Samuel Walker, in his survey of the Hanningfield manors in 1628, mentions him as holding it from the manor of East Hanningfield and gives its size as 208 acres. But more correctly Sam Walker's reference is to the manorial land of New Peverel Hall, which was to become Tanfield Toy in the next century. Old Peverels and its fields were leased out. In this way the estate developed into two farms.

When I began to research the history of the Toy at the Essex Record Office, I was delighted to find it had been surveyed and mapped by John Walker the Younger in 1611. He lived with his father at the charming cottage known as Kents just outside the village. Together they formed a partnership whose eminence and importance has at last been recognized in our own time. The map measures about sixteen by thirty-eight inches and, although the wording is faded in one or two places, it is in a good state of preservation. In the top right-hand corner there is a panel headed 'The Table'. Abbreviated, and with some words modernized, it reads as follows:

A Trew Plan of the Capital Messuage or Manor of Peverells with all the demesne lands thereunto belonging situate in the Parish and fields of Westhanningfield in the Hundred of

Chelmsford ... In which Plan you shall find the mansion houses set in their trew places and properties with the barns, stables, yards, orchards and gardens to the same belonging and also every field, close, meadow and wood likewise set in their trew proportion with their most known names written on every one of them ... And further you shall find in the said Plan the chaseways or highways passing through or by ... with every gate, stile and pond in their due place ...

A large photograph of this fine old map hangs in my parlour and, allowing for certain changes in the landscape since John Walker trod the fields, it has proved a reliable and revealing guide to the farm's topography today.

Walker shows two manorial houses on his plan: 'olde Peverel Haule' on the site now occupied by Little Peverels, and New Peverel Hall, where Tanfield Tye farmhouse stands today.

Old Peverels was a very modest establishment, a single-storeyed house with a close. Its total land came to 108 acres, mostly arable and pasture and with nine acres of woods and 'sprynges', the old Essex dialect word for copses. Old Peverels was on lease to an Arthur Petchey.

In complete contrast and truly a 'capital messuage' was the New Hall, which could not have been built long before 1611 and was doubtless the occasion for Walker's commission. A magnifying glass is needed to bring out the details of his tiny elevation drawing of the house. It depicts a mansion with six bays, of two floors and with a dormer window to each bay. There are three chimneystacks. In front of the house is a courtyard with a gateway. To the left a two-square space represents an ornamental garden with paths. Beyond this, at the rear of the house and dwarfing it, a very substantial orchard is drawn: four square plots surrounded by walks and measuring over two acres. Until a year or so ago a few fruit trees occupied the same position. The Tithe-Rent Award map of last century shows a field behind the farmhouse marked 'old orchard-arable', as does the sale catalogue for the farm in 1919.

Alas, there is no vestige of the fine house today. Moreover, there seems to be a complete absence of any documents which could throw light on its subsequent fate.

Hearth Tax returns for the parish do nothing to resolve the puzzle. That such an impressive house should vanish without trace, so much so that even the oral traditions of the locality are totally silent about it, strongly suggests it went at an early date, most probably early in the seventeenth century. The presumption must be it was destroyed by fire.

With its manorial halls the Walker map makes explicable the name of the present Peveril Hall, built earlier this century on the West Hanningfield Road but to the north of the original site. Under the terms of its sale in 1961 by the farmer of that time, it should really have been styled 'Peverel House'. The triangular plot it stands on is shown as such on John Walker's plan.

When compared with the map, the sale catalogue referred to above shows a marked persistence of some of the field names and little change in their acreage over three hundred years. The sheer longevity of so much detail in the countryside never ceases to amaze me, although our age threatens to erase it in a more thoroughgoing way than was ever witnessed by previous generations. As hedgerows disappear between the fields, their ancestral names must be among the chief victims. Among the field names of old which lasted here till the twentieth century are Sheepcote or Shipcote on Walker's map; Wreathy Lease, which became River Ley; Dunsted, formerly Dunstalle; and Harrow Croft, its spelling unchanged.

There are many other absorbing features on the map. The house marked 'Hoppers' appears to be the one now called 'The Cottage', a narrow miniature house which stands by the road to the east of Peveril Hall. The once numerous hop pits and grounds also shown have long vanished from the landscape, although it was not until around 1800 that hop cultivation finally declined in the Chelmsford area.

A seven-acre field abutting New Peverel Hall on the west is given as 'The Shotts'. A shott was a division of land, the course of a plough, and frequently occurs in Elizabethan wills to denote a furlong. Used in the plural, it often indicates the much earlier open-field system of farming in which the land was cultivated in strips. This was by no means the universal practice, but this field-name on the manor of Peverels seems to point to it here.

The Shotts long ago ceased to be a field with an identity of its own. But just a few yards away the soil concealed something from a much more distant past.

In 1976 Mr Alan Clarke, then my next-door neighbour and the farm worker on the Tye, uncovered while he was ploughing two shiny objects which were later authenticated at the British Museum as a pair of Late Bronze Age bracelets. Although slightly damaged, either by the plough or from pressure in the subsoil, they were otherwise in good condition. Estimated as being from between 900 and 600 BC they are made of eighty per cent British gold with a mixture of silver and copper.

That they should have lain here in the dark undisturbed for more than twenty-five centuries is incredible enough, but the circumstances of their chance discovery are equally remarkable. Only one of the bracelets appeared at first, and Alan then ceased ploughing for the day, mystified as to what he had found. The following morning he returned to his tractor in the field. When he started up and was barely moving forward, the second of the pair came glinting to the light.

The bracelets are unequal in size, oval rather than round, which makes them particularly rare. Although described as bracelets, they probably served as armbands, 'torques'. It is likely they were cast with hammered ends, and on one of these the ornamentation is very unusual, a tiny engraved circle.

Solitary finds of bracelets like these seem to have been very infrequent, for such articles are usually unearthed as part of a hoard. Judging from the *Victoria County History of Essex*, the Hanningfields are conspicuously lacking in any remains or finds which date from before the medieval period.

The torques were judged by the coroner's court to have been 'hidden' and were declared treasure trove. Their bullion value was initially fixed at £400 but £1,700 was later awarded. At first the farmer laid claim to their possession, the objects being on his land, and he is reported to have said to his farmhand, but no doubt jokingly, that he wanted to display them on his mantelpiece. However, their brief dispute was amicably resolved and the impressive cheque went to the finder. The bracelets can be seen at the

Chelmsford and Essex Museum.

For weeks after the news, strangers appeared on the farm questing for further treasure, including one elderly lady with a metal-detector. The exact location of the find remains undisclosed but was apparently close to a prehistoric trackway which runs across East Anglia. Extensive professional examination of the area has revealed nothing further, and there is no evidence of a Bronze Age settlement.

But let us return now across a mere three centuries to the Tanfields.

Their sojourn here proved relatively brief. After Clovile Tanfield the succession to the manor passed through William and then Edmund Tanfield. And then sometime between 1711 and 1716 the estate was bought from Daniel Tanfield by Dr Daniel Williams.

Daniel Williams was a celebrated Nonconformist divine and benefactor, born about 1643. Little is known of his earliest years, until he became a preacher while still a very young man. He seems to have been a controversial figure among his fellow dissenters. He was noted for his many theological works and sermons, but his memory today rests upon his remarkable library, much enlarged after his death, housed in Gordons Square: a collection of over twenty thousand books and five hundred volumes of manuscripts. It contains several very rare items including a death mask of Oliver Cromwell. One of the provisions in his will instructs his trustees to reprint his works at given intervals for two thousand years! Such self-esteem, or downright vanity, was noted by a contemporary who found him 'the greatest bundle of pride, affectation and ill manners I have ever met with'.

He had two wives, marrying the second, Jane, in 1701. She was a widow and the daughter of a merchant, a Huguenot refugee. Dr Williams acquired much of his wealth through these marriages. On his death his total estate was worth about £50,000, the greater part of which went to charity. Among his endowments was one to the Presbyterian chapel at Burnham. He seems to have been much taken with the time-span of two thousand years for he stipulated that after that time the income from all his properties should revert to the universities of Glasgow and Cambridge.

Daniel Williams died childless in 1716, after being a very sick man for some years, and he was buried in London at Bunhill Fields. His trustees still care for his tomb. Mrs Jane Williams died on 1 January 1739–40.

In accordance with his will, his estate was administered by his trustees, the Society for New England. In Essex, in addition to Tanfield Toy and Hanningfield Temple, his adjacent property, Dr Williams had the manor of Tolleshunt Major, otherwise styled 'Beckinghams'. His lands were held by the trust to finance various benefactions, including preaching the Word in the English plantations of the Caribbean 'for the good of what pagans and blacks lie neglected there'. The trusteeship of the Hanningfield estate lasted for two hundred years, until 1919. It was then put on the market, being auctioned as five lots. With its sale Tanfield Tye as it is today came quickly into being. For just a few years Temple and Peverel Farm, formerly Old Peverels, remained in other hands but then was joined to the Toy. Two other small farms on its perimeter, Hill Farm and Boards, were also added, both now ploughed out of recognition.

There is so much more that could be written. I could tell of what was clearly a fine plantation, two solitary Scots pines remaining on the lane; of the ancient ponds; of the days when horse shows were a great attraction here, and those years in the thirties when a Belgian converted all to one vast chicken farm.

But in no brief chronicle of the Tye's land and its legacy could one omit old 'Bawds', even though for long it was just a little neighbour.

Looking southwards down the valley, beyond our garden with its aged apple tree, there lies 'Nine Acre Croft', one time 'Marlpit 9 Acres', taking its name from when the fields were 'chalked' with marl unearthed nearby. It slopes away to a green lane, or rather what survives of it, a tattered, broken line of trees and shrubs denoting the ancient way to Boards. A vanished homestead, once it was part of Charvelles, another manor with a history all its own. I have partially tracked the owners and the residents of both back to the Elizabethan age. Often, after the harvest, little relics of the house appear, fragments of pottery, tile and brick peeping from the stubble. But these grow less and less.

I had the good fortune a few years back to meet a man who had lived in the house in its final days, his father being the shepherd hereabouts. The place was rat-infested, and one of his more gruesome tales was how, when he was lying in bed, the rats would scamper across the quilt, and once one even nipped a piece from his brother's ear!

Maps of the last century show a 'Garden Field', and when I first knew the site, a few garden shrubs could still be seen among the wild ones and the nettles. Since then the spot has further been eroded by the ruthless plough. Even the lane is shorter than it was.

Forlorn, it is a place now solely for night tenants, a place for owls and lovers. 'So all things pass, and become as a tale which is told.'

6

Clovile Hall and its Family

Long lost to sight, the Cloviles of West Hanningfield were the most outstanding family here from the reign of William Rufus to that of James I. They finally passed into complete obscurity in the late 1600s.

Unlike the Petres of Ingatestone and Thorndon, who came into Essex much later, the Cloviles never became of major importance in the county. As a consequence records are sparse and fragmentary. There are no revealing portraits, letters, diaries or even accounts books to which the historian can turn. Yet no matter how shadowy most of the family are now – and this is especially so for the long medieval period – they obviously loomed large in the daily life of the parish for over five centuries. Their history spanned the reigns of more than twenty monarchs. No other Hanningfield family came anywhere near them in this respect.

For much of that time their residence was Clovile Hall, the sole visible and public reminder of their presence here. As it stands, the substantial brick and timber house, although much renovated and enlarged, dates from the second half of the sixteenth century. Its present appearance is very different from that in Bennett-Bamford's painting of 1911 which can be seen at the Chelmsford and Essex Museum. The subsequent changes, which included the removal of an outer shell of weatherboards, must have been made between 1911 and 1923. In the latter year it was described mainly as it is now by the Royal Commission on Historical Monuments. From the painting it is clear that the Hall had been converted to farm workers' cottages, as was another fine old home in the village, Gascoignes near the Three Compasses.

The restoration of the Hall must have been a costly undertaking. Recently I heard from a man in Canada who

Clovile Hall, West Hanningfield

had lived as a boy in the parish back in the 1930s. He recalled the owner of the house then as an old gentleman who had been a tea-planter. This could well explain where the money came from.

Clovile Hall is close to the western extremity of the parish on the Ship Road. The site was well chosen. On a slight rise in the land, it has a rather commanding look when viewed from the south from across the fields. There can be little doubt it marks the location of an even earlier dwelling, the 'Cloviles' of 1412, when Henry IV was king, although some time before then the family may have lived closer in to the village where their original holdings lay. They were to move back in that direction in the opening years of the seventeenth century. It is likely that the present spot was chosen when they acquired the manor of Peverels. Just a few hundred yards to the west of the Hall were two historic properties: the Hanningfield estate of the Templars and a little further on Old Crondon Park owned by the bishops of London.

The Royal Commission gives a short description of the Hall when it was called 'The Meeting House', along with photographs of its most remarkable feature, the wall paintings in the attic rooms. These murals are on plaster panels between beams. The proportions of the south attic and the symmetry of its paintings are especially pleasing to the eye. Those in the north-facing room bear the date '1615'. Several of the murals here extend over curved timbers. Arabesque in style, the series was extensively restored by a Czech specialist in the 1960s, commissioned by the present owner, the solicitor Mr. M.J. Cullen; but one section in the south attic had deteriorated too far to be saved. For a country house guest, this room in particular must be a rare experience to sleep in, with its bizarre paintings and its leaded windows looking out into a wooded distance.

The paintings are in two tones, red and white. Mythological creatures – centaurs, mermen and serpents – are luxuriantly intertwined with fruit and flowers. This now obscure iconography, probably allusive to Vices and Virtues, also includes pelicans, fish, apes brandishing clubs, lions with coronets and heads of wolves. One of the strangest figures is the face of a man, in profile, with a serpent issuing from his forehead. The Jacobean artist who produced this macabre display is quite unknown.

In the painting in the north room there is also a faded coat of arms. These are not, however, the Clovile arms but those of a family called Skynner who were almost certainly responsible for the murals. The Clovile shield contains what are usually thought to be five gold nails, but they could be cloves, a rebus or punning device for the family name.

The Hall has undergone a change of name several times. Early in the seventeenth century, after being held by one Augustine Skinner, it became known as 'Fullers', from a family of that name who were its copy- or leaseholders. Then, reverting to its ancestral name for a while, it was again Fullers by the end of last century. Early this century it had become 'The Meeting House', which suggests a Nonconformist connection. Finally, by 1933 it was known as Clovile Hall once more. Up to the seventeenth century the house seems to have been known as Hanningfield Hall as well. This was certainly so for the Bramston family, of which more later. The house to its rear on Hall Lane acquired and has retained the title of West Hanningfield Hall, apparently from the time the Cloviles moved to another part of the parish.

The charming Hall Lane, barely the width of a car, is of great antiquity, being described in 1628 as a drift lane, a

drover's way. A species count along its hedgerows shows it
to be at least seven centuries old. Much of its length in the
summer is a leafy tunnel.

When I began to research the history of the Cloviles, I first
went to the one and only account of the family in print at
that time. Bare and concise and mainly genealogical, this is
Philip Morant's great two-volume *History and Antiquities
of the County of Essex*, first published in 1768.

Here we can read that the first of the Hanningfield
Cloviles, or Clonvill as it sometimes occurs in very early
records, was William de Clovill in the reign of Henry II. Yet
it seems the family were established in the parish before
then. In the now rare autobiography of Sir John Bramston
the Younger, written between 1683 and 1700, the year of his
death, he tells us the Cloviles were in Essex before the
Norman Conquest and had been granted land in Hanningfield by William II. Sir John's testimony is of particular
force, for his grandmother was a Clovile. Probably Morant
was using the first documentary evidence for their residence
here, whereas Bramston may have been relying on family
tradition. It is therefore very likely that the first Cloviles
came from France to settle in the county during the time of
Edward the Confessor; I have yet to trace from precisely
where. Edward had spent his early years in exile in
Normandy and after being crowned in 1043 encouraged
close links with northern France, as his Norman mother,
Emma, had before him. He is known to have allowed a
number of foreigners to settle in England, but only two
Frenchmen, Bretons, were given major holdings in Essex and
East Anglia.

Morant and the heralds Visitations name a long succession
of knights down the years in feudal Hanningfield. Most
remain but names, but several figures stand out for
comment. There was a William de Clovile, one of so many
Williams in the family tree, who in the time of Henry III
obtained permission to assart or clear the wood of Wideford
and convert it to arable. He held the manor there. By his day
and that of his son and heir Robert, the prestige and wealth
of the family in the area were clearly established. It was
Robert who 'received the gift of Warren de Montchensy of
all the lands in West Hanningfield called XX acres to hold of

the said Warren by 19s per annum'. The overlord Montchensys were for long the major landowners in the three Hanningfields. 'XX acres' is of topographical interest, for the name persisted for centuries. Situated at the far end of Blind Lane, formerly Twenty Acres Lane, it kept the name until the last century, eventually becoming what it is today, Tinsleys Farm.

Three other Cloviles are commemorated in the parish church of SS Mary and Edward. There is a small brass on the floor of the south aisle, but regrettably its inscription and a companion piece have gone. What remains is a head and shoulders of Lady Isabel Clovile which is said to be the second oldest brass of a woman to be found in Essex. It dates from the time of Chaucer. We know from Chancellor's *Ancient Sepulchral Monuments of Essex* (1890) that the inscription read as follows: 'Isabel Cloville and John her son lie here, which John died the 23rd day of October in the year of grace 1361. God have mercy on their souls.' Their England was that of the Black Death and the Hundred Years War. Isabel, whose date of death is unknown, was responsible for the addition of the south aisle, now in a sad way and threatening the church's redundancy. The fate of the inscription is one of the little mysteries of the parish. Late in the nineteenth century it was discovered 'in a black hole under the pulpit stairs'. A rubbing was taken but it vanished again, seemingly 'reaved' – that is forcibly deprived.

The third memorial in the church is the altar-tomb of the John Clovill who passed away on 5 July 1490. The Clovile arms can also be seen in a window of the south aisle.

With Francis Clovile, fuller biographical detail begins to emerge. In addition to the Hanningfield estate he held the manor of Wideford and had the advowson to the church there. This right to the presentation of the living was exercised from 1410 to 1597. In old Wideford church, ruthlessly rebuilt in 1862, the family coat of arms was displayed in the south window.

Francis was on good terms with his powerful neighbour Sir William Petre, who had the manor of Stock as well as Ingatestone. The Provision Accounts Book of Ingatestone Hall has several entries in which Francis and his wife figure. On the last day of 1551 'Maistress Clovell and her servant' were at Ingatestone for 'dyner' with six other 'strangers', the expression used in the accounts for guests who were not members of the family. She sat down to a menu of 'Boylde beiffe 6 peces, a legge of motton rosted, a conny [rabbit] and 2 humble pyes'. On Twelfth Day 1552 Mr Clovell was there for dinner with a larger gathering. The meal was much more ambitious, including venison, geese, partridges and larks. Sir William was no doubt present at this seasonal celebration, having returned from the Court of the young Edward VI.

Francis Clovile died on 3 May 1562. His will provides for interment in the parish church but there is no entry to this effect in the registers. Like many another will from the gentry of that age, it provides us with a cameo of a minor country squire. Francis was clearly a lover of riding. Although he had a year to live when he drew up his will, it reads like a reluctant farewell to 'Calton' and 'Saddleback' and all his other horses listed.

He left a son and two daughters, Anne and Priscilla. The heir, Eustace, distinguished himself as a JP. Priscilla first married Thomas Rush of Boreham, by whom she had a son. After the death of her husband in 1574 she wed Roger Bramston, who had come to Boreham from Whitechapel. This marriage was to prove of social importance for Essex and, indeed, for a short time, for all England.

The Bramston connection is one of great interest. The son and heir of Roger and Priscilla was the celebrated Sir John Bramston the Elder (1577–1654). Born in Maldon, he became Lord Chief Justice of the realm in 1635. Impeached by the Long Parliament, he was later asked by Cromwell to resume this high office but he declined. He and his family suffered much for their Royalist sympathies. Sir John settled at Roxwell, where his successors resided at the fine estate of Screens for the next two hundred years.

In Sir John Bramston the Younger's autobiography there occurs the following: 'Roger, by Priscilla Clovile, relict of Thomas Rushee, daughter of Francis Clovile, of Hanningfield Hall in Essex, Esq (an antient honourable family, and which had binn in that countie before, and remained there ever since the Conquest, possessinge lands of good value ...) Roger, I say, by the said Priscilla had issue, beside John my father, Mary, Margaret and William. John was born the 18th day of May 1577, at Maldon, whether his father and mother went on a visit to visit a sister Ann Bramston ...' Priscilla died in 1619, one year after her husband. The parish registers of Boreham show that both are buried there.

We know something of Priscilla's children and her grandchildren from the pages of Sir John the Younger; only a little, but what there is is colourful.

William, Priscilla's second son, fought on the side of the King at Edgehill (1642) and was in Colchester during the siege. Impoverished through his loyalty to the Crown, he passed his last years at Screens, where he died.

The registers of Little Baddow have revealed that Margaret and Mary were twins. Margaret never married. She lived at the parsonage in Boreham with Priscilla's son by her first marriage. She died in 1631, just short of being fifty-two. Mary married a Peter Stepkin, thought to be of German descent. Of their eleven children, three of the sons came to tragic ends. There was Thomas, who saw military service abroad and was killed in a duel in Sweden. Roger Stepkin died in the King's Bench prison before reaching the age of twenty-five, having 'wasted his estate'. Then there was Mary's son Peter, who seems to have been a hot-headed character. At first a Royalist, he was at Edgehill, like his uncle William, but he assaulted his commanding officer. Ordered to be shot, he escaped and went over to the Parliamentarians. But he was soon in trouble again, quarrelling with some officers, and he was killed resisting arrest. A fourth of Priscilla's grandsons, Charles, also fought for the King.

To return to the mainstream at West Hanningfield, Eustace Clovile, born in 1541, was twenty-one when he became the head of the family. More is known about Eustace and his offspring than any of the other Cloviles. He was a very diligent Justice of the Peace, unlike many in his day. He put in twenty-two attendances at Chelmsford Quarter Sessions from 1582 until his death seven years later, a record well above the average for the county. But he was an active JP as early as 1569 when he was still a young man of twenty-eight. In that year two Hanningfield women were jointly accused of living apart from their husbands, but a letter from Eustace cleared them of the charge.

When several years ago I was piecing together the histories of the old alehouses in the parish, I found at the Essex Record Office two 'recognizances [bonds] for victualling taken before Sir Thomas Mildemay, Knight, and Eustace Clovile, esq' dated 3 October, 24 Eliz., 1582.

Eustace died in London in 1589, the year following the great crisis of the Armada and after a period when the country was recovering from a grain shortage, both of which had strained the Justices to the utmost. Only forty-eight, he was brought to West Hanningfield for burial. His will, unlike his father's, is terse and concise, mainly one of monetary bequests. He left a very young family, his wife Jane having borne him twelve children over a period of fourteen years, seven being alive at the time of his death.

Of his sons there was George 'that came to an unhappy end'. Percival, the heir, was 'slayne, *sine prole*' (without issue). He was murdered at the age of twenty-three. At the coroner's jury in June 1598 it was found that he had succumbed to a deadly three-inch sword-thrust. The circumstances were not recorded. His assailant, one Robert Fryer, a Chelmsford man, had fled from the area, and there is no word of his being apprehended. It was intriguing for me to find that in the very same year another Chelmsford man named Fryer, Walter Fryer, was convicted along with two others of poultry-stealing, a felony for which he suffered the seizure of all his goods.

A pointer to the Clovile family's affluence in personal belongings at this time is afforded by an inventory of household goods stolen from the Hall on 16 August 1593, when the house was occupied by Jane Clovile, then a widow. The theft, one of larceny, was carried out by two West Hanningfield 'gentlemen'. They took a gold chain worth £60; a gold chain with a sweet pomander, £5; two jewels valued at £5; a damask tablecloth, £2; two towels worth £1; three cambric sheets, £10; three lawn sheets, £10; six pillow beers (pillow cases), £1; a square damask wrought with bone lace of gold and four tassels of pearl and gold, £5; some parcels of linen coming to £20; a bed valance (a hanging border of drapery) of orange tawny velvet and damask fringed with silk and gold, £3; two books worth 4s and a horse estimated at £2. This was quite a haul; hence, perhaps, the need for a horse. Most of these items were presumably stored in a great chest, the equivalent of a modern safe, and the evaluations suggest that the family kept accounts to refer to.

With the stunning, untimely death of Percival, his brother Henry, later to become Sir Henry, inherited at the age of twenty-one. He was to prove the last prestigious head of the family.

So much about the man is tantalizingly obscure. We know he married Anne, daughter of Thomas Ryvett of Woodhall in Rattlesdon, Suffolk. We know, too, from several sources, that he had by his wife a prodigious total of sixteen children. Sometime after the death of his mother, in 1604, he vacated the Hall – perhaps because of overcrowding. The most likely date is 1614–15, for in the latter year the Skinner arms appeared there. Where he went to live in the parish is unclear as well. He owned 'Pinners', now beneath the reservoir, and held the aboriginal land of Twenty Acres. But more probably he took a lease on New Peverel Hall, the manor of which had once been Clovile property but had gone to the Tanfield family through marriage.

Even the place and date of his death lie hidden. He was alive in 1634 and was then fifty-seven. Of a will there is equally no trace. The parish registers show that by 1610 he was a knight and his wife styled Dame or Lady Anne. Perhaps he was one of those knighted at Theobalds when James came south to become Elizabeth's successor. Why he received a knighthood is not known, although the distinction of his family, especially that of his father's record of public service, must have played a part.

But if he remains somewhat out of focus, much could be written of his offspring and their connections.

Taking just a few in some order, there was his namesake, Henry, 'living in 1614', and Jane, 'that died without issue'. Lucretia, who married when she was twenty-three, made an important match, her husband, John Eylmer or Aylmer, being closely related to the Bishop of London with the same name. Young Thomas, born in 1608, was 'baptised the twelfth day of January in the great chamber of Haulk Hall because there was one buried the week before that was thought to die of the plague'.

Elizabeth Clovile, who arrived in 1611, was to eventually become Mrs Elizabeth Kempson and reached the great age of eighty-nine, joining her ancestors in the church in 1700, two years before the coronation of Queen Anne. She married twice, her first husband being William Goldingham, who died when she was thirty-seven. He was a man to be reckoned with in these parts, a Puritan and the Elder of West Hanningfield church when a Presbyterian was put in by Parliament to replace the Royalist parson, Edward Aylmer, 'forced from his station' to flee to Oxford after the outbreak of the Civil War. Mr Goldingham was zealous in the politics of religion, his influence spreading to the parish of Stock.

Another link with Stock can be traced through Katherine, born in 1617 and the sixth girl in a row. She married Thomas Adler. In his will he left his home in Stock, 'Lyllystones', to his son and heir John. Almost certainly this was on the site or close by the present Lilystone Hall, a Victorian mansion built by an ironmaster and now converted into luxury apartments.

Petre, of 1621, was the last of Henry's sons and may have been named in honour of William, second Lord Petre. The very last of the children, Susan, came in 1622. The following year the Lady Anne Clovile died.

The long saga of the Coviles was now drawing to its end. Edward, who had been born in 1605, seems to have been the last but one of the line in the parish.

The last of the three surviving wills of the Hanningfield Coviles is that of Carmard or Carmarden Clovile, one of Edward's sons. In his testament, drawn up in 1672, 'being very sick and weak but blest be to God sound in memory', he leaves bequests to his parents, his sister and three brothers. One of these, Henry, was to move to Stisted. Thomas at the time was out of England. The third brother was Rivet, an unusual name which recalls that of Lady Anne's father.

And it is Rivet who takes the final bow. As Sir John Bramston threw light on the Clovile's origins, so he does on their demise: ' ...Rivet, the son of Edward Clovile, sold the reversion of the seate Hanningfield Hall (given to their familie by William the Second) after his father's life unto Mr Thomas Whitbread (there being only at this day in that name 100 pound per annum) ...'

So in selling off the Hall Rivet Clovile brought down the curtain on the family's history here. There is one other reference to Rivet to be found at the tail-end of that century. It can be seen in the Essex Quarter Sessions Records under 1673–4 and reads: 'John Heath cordwainer [shoemaker], 'Wignol' Bigg gent, both of Felsted, and Thomas Balls of Gt Dunmow currier [one who curries or dresses leather]; Heath to answer, having threatened to kick and cut the legs of Mary, wife of "Rivet" Clovell of WH and abused her in other bad language.'

Morant concluded his summary of the Coviles with the words, 'This estate now belongs to Mr Richard Finch.' This was in 1768. 'Little Barns', an attractive, very small cottage with white clapboards standing near Wantz Corner on the Ship Road, has a plaster inscription over its front door, 'REF 1747'. These are the initials of Richard Edward Finch.

The Coviles are important in our social history for their forgotten typicality. There are scores of 'halls' around the county, now under the guise of pub or farmhouse, which could yield a comparable story of more distinguished days, each with its own unique profile of the past.

Of the fall of the House of Clovile, the questions we can pose are legion. What was their experience of the Reformation and the early Puritan movement in the Established Church? What was their response to the severe financial pressures exerted by the Stuart Kings: to the 'Benevolences, to the so-called Free Gift of 1626 and the Forced Loan? Did taxation and the frequent failure of the harvest grimly combine to impoverish their estates at a time when they had shrunk? And were they for Crown or Parliament, or, as seems likely, divided by allegiances to both? And how did they fare in the traumatic Civil War and under the Commonwealth and Protectorate?

If one day we are to have even partial answers to such questions, they will probably be found elsewhere than in the margins of the county archives. Of the old Coviles we must say with Lamb: 'Be satisfied that something answering to them has had a being. Their importance is from the past.'

7

Crondon Park

As you will by now have gathered, I have a particular fondness for the little places in the countryside. One of these, old Crondon, is but a winding mile or so away from where I live. For a thousand years it was a spot cherished by noblemen of Church and State.

Until very recently Crondon in the fair parish of Stock was marked on the Ordnance Survey map as Crondon Park. One of the two main dwellings in the locality has retained the older name. Crondon is situated on the western side of the B1007 between the village and Galleywood Common. For centuries it was one of those ecclesiastical oddities, a 'detached portion' of the far-off Thameside parish of Orsett. Such portions existed elsewhere in the county, notably on Canvey, which was divided up between eight mainland parishes, and are probably best explained as remnants of the manorial system in which a lord's holdings were often scattered miles apart.

In origin the name Crondon refers to the lie of the land. Its earliest recorded form in documents of the thirteenth century is as 'Crumden'. This literally means a 'winding valley'. The element 'den' signifies 'valley' but in course of time it came to be pronounced and written 'don', which means the exact opposite, a hill. The winding valley here is that of the River Wid, a stream, in fact, like most other Essex rivers.

Today Crondon is almost totally arable farmland. A survey taken of the manor in 1556 shows it to have extended to over a thousand acres. Before the Reformation it had belonged for centuries to the bishops of London whose estates were very numerous in Essex, the county lying within their diocese. Many of these medieval prelates came to Crondon to relax and hunt. From a document of 1275 we know there was at least one deer-leap here at that time. In particular the park was much frequented by Bishop Stephen de Gravesend, who stayed close on forty occasions between 1300 and 1346.

If only the soil could speak, for Crondon was one of those places which witnessed the stirring of the Peasants' Revolt in the convulsive summer of 1381.

One of the Essex ringleaders came here, but the details are stark and brief. At the Chelmsford assize on 3 July it was reported that 'John Geoffrey, Bailif of Easthanyngfeld, caused all the men of the vills of Easthanyngfeld, Westhanyngfeld and Southanyngfeld to go against their wills to the Temple of the Prior of St John of Jerusalem in England.' The records go on to tell us that he also 'summoned certain persons to meet him at the church of Great Bedewe to go against the Earl of Buckingham and others'. The web of incitement was spread still further. 'He also went to the Bishop of London's park at Crondon.' Here, in addition to haranguing his followers from the Hanningfields, Woodham Ferrers and Rettendon, he caused the men 'to swear that they would ride against the King whenever he (Geoffrey) summoned them'.

As anyone versed in the history of Essex will know, the final defeat of the rebels took place near Billericay, by tradition in Norsey Wood, on 28 June 1381. Five hundred 'rustics' were slain and eight hundred horses captured. Some of the insurgents fled demoralized to Colchester but were finally dispersed at Sudbury. John Geoffrey was among those tried and hanged at Chelmsford in the presence of Richard II. All those found guilty were betrayed by compatriots 'seeking grace and mercy'.

When Henry VIII granted the manor of Crondon to Sir William Petre, this royal favourite turned it exclusively into a park for venison and timber, one of the five he had in the county. Forest Wood and Forest Lodge, the latter now the site of the turkey farm opposite the Ship public house, are names which are reminders of that time. Perhaps the hunting lodge was where the bishops' residence had been.

Then, in 1551, the eastern half of the estate, styled Crondon Old Park, ceased to be parkland and was leased out as five lots with a rent fixed at 1s. 8d an acre. A crudely drawn plan of about 1575 depicts the changes. Among the houses indicated is an 'Orsett Lodge'.

The Petre family's ownership of Crondon ended with the sale of the land in 1923. Formerly, as one of their properties, many more people had lived and worked here than now. A number were Roman Catholics employed by the Petres, notable for their adherence to the Old Faith, and their spiritual needs were met by the Ingatestone Mission from 1759 to 1831.

Records from Elizabethan days show that Crondon Park was inevitably a target for poachers. On one occasion in 1578 a small party including two 'gentlemen' of Stock, James Hanchett and the somewhat notorious Antony Errington, made off with two stags.

Among the names of tenants which have come down to us from the sixteenth century is that of Alice Humfrey or Humphrey. She was the wet-nurse to the infant John Petre who later became the first Lord Petre, Baron Writtle. Her husband was the 'acater', caterer cum butler, in Sir William Petre's household at Ingatestone Hall. Alice's cottage is shown on the map of 1575, where it is marked 'widow Humfrey'. It was on the edge of Crondon Park adjoining Stock Common. From the position, if accurately placed, it looks as though it might be the house now the Ship. The oldest part of the pub dates from the latter half of Alice's century. The tiny strip of grass in front, looking as though it might once have been part of a green, still belongs to Lord Petre.

The fields of Crondon go gently down in folds to the Wid and Molehill Common at Margaretting Tye. It is likely that 'Molehill' here does not refer to moles but to 'Mollmani'. These were 'molemen', a feudal term for a category of peasants bound by certain well-defined services to their lord. This is undoubtedly the explanation for the Molehill Common at Felsted.

There is no road today which takes you right through Crondon. At the Stock village end, Crondon Park Lane leads down into the broad valley from just by Greenwoods. This name is yet another pointer to what the area was once like. Now the County Centre of the West Ham Central Mission,

Crondon Park

it is an interesting house and still aptly named. It marks the
site of Little and Great Greenwoods mentioned in a will of
1537.

Crondon Park Lane is one of those little roads to nowhere
found in so many parts of Essex. From the corner there is a
length of warm red-brick wall, solidly buttressed and
bulging under the weight of years. In a few yards the back of
Greenwoods, architecturally so different from the front,
comes into sight, and the lane then curves away downhill.
To the left the land is at first richly wooded on steep slopes
descending to a brook, a tributary of the Wid. Somewhere
on here may have stood the 'great tree' felled by John
Mudge, one of John Petre's carpenters and woodmen.
Beyond the trees lies Tye Green, 'Tiger Island', on the road
to Margaretting. Its windmill is no more, but the tumulus on
which it stood remains.

From the margin of the wood as one walks down to the
farmhouse, some of the most splendid scenes in the county
begin to open up, with remarkably distant views. Such a
panorama is barely hinted at from the busy main road you
have left behind. On a clear day Galleywood, Chelmsford,
Writtle and the tree-lined heights of Fryerning can be seen.
It will come as a revelation to anyone who still thinks of
Essex as uniformly flat and, by some amazing inference,
uninteresting.

8

At the Sign of the Cock in Stock Village

The very position of this ancient pub at the hub of the village is of historic interest. It stands right on the old boundary between the parishes of Buttsbury and Stock. Buttsbury, no longer a parish and regrettably not even marked now on the Ordnance Survey map, took in much of the High Street from the Cock to Greenwoods. In fact the road on some old documents and photographs is called Buttsbury High Street.

An odd little story has been handed down of how once there was a dispute over a corpse in one of the houses on the dividing line. The friends of the dead man could not afford to bury him, so the funeral became a charge on the parish. But the question arose, which of the two was responsible? The decision arrived at was comically simple. The parish in which the head of the deceased was lying had to bear the cost!

At an oblique angle on the corner of Back Lane, the pub faces what was once the village square. The square as such has gone, although keeping the name, being filled in long ago with houses, but its outline remains and the little shop calling itself 'The Shop in the Square' keeps alive the memory of its existence. In the Middle Ages there was a market here, established by charter in 1239.

Being on the boundary of the two parishes, it is fitting that it was from the Cock that the ancient custom of 'beating the bounds' commenced each year. A detailed account of the walk written in 1817 shows that it began 'at the middle of the Tap Room Window'. And it was at this precise point, too, after such thirsty work, that the long perambulation to mark the boundary ended up. Today the pub has a Buttsbury Bar. The original house would have been smaller

than that to be seen now. By repute it is a little over five
hundred years old, which is quite likely. In the absence of
deeds from those far-off times, its exact age is difficult to
determine. Although very much changed, parts must date
from the sixteenth century at least. But there is no doubt that
as a pub the Cock has been in business for well over four
hundred years. This makes it in probability the oldest of the
four licensed houses now in the village.

The Bear, a few yards across the way, is a close runner-up,
being mentioned as 'Le Bear' in 1557. Both pubs may have
acquired their names from those cruel pastimes of our
forefathers, cock-fighting and bear-baiting, although the
sign of the Bear today is of a polar one.

It seems that the very earliest reference to the Cock is to be
found in the will of a John Ponder of Buttsbury made in
1527: 'y bequeth to Johan [Joan] Croxton my daughter, a
fetherbed that is at the syne of cokk ... y will that the gret
lede with a curbyll that standeth at the sine of the cokk be
not removed thence.' The great 'lede' or lead was the
cauldron used to hold the wort in the brewhouse, while
'curbyll' looks like a variant of 'curb', the frame around the
top of the brewing pan. John Ponder also left the alehouse to
his daughter and her husband, William Croxton 'the elder',
but with the proviso it was to be sold to pay his debts and his
funeral expenses. The pub's tradition is that the original
tenant gave it to his daughter as a wedding present.

The next mention of the Cock comes in one of Lord Petre's
documents dated 3 February 1529, the twentieth year of the
reign of Henry VIII. This is a charter granting 'le Cok' to
Ralph Rowlat, 'merchant of the Staple of the vill of Calais',
which means he was a merchant trading with the Continent,
probably in wool.

Another early reference to the pub comes from 1556,
when it was ordered that 'the tenant of the land of the Cocke
should make up a ditch to a length of 12 perches below the
Cockying Stole.' The expression 'make' means here 'to
repair, to make good'. (Twelve perches are sixty-six yards.)
Again, in 1581 repairs to the ditch had to be carried out.
Robert Newman of the Cock was required to 'make twenty
perches of ditch so that the water flow easily from the pond
called Cucking Stole Weyer towards the common called Tye

The Cock in Stock Village

Common'. From this it looks as though the pond in question
was that just off the square opposite and which can still be
seen from the garden of the Bear. The 'Cucking Stole' was,
of course, the stool or chair used for ducking scolds and
others in the village pond. Much of the disgrace in
undergoing this punishment must have come from the name
of the object itself, for 'cucking' is from the old verb 'cuck',
to void excrement, and the stool used was often a privy stool.

The pub is mentioned again by name in a will of 1586, two
years before the Armada. Among the provisions in his will
Matthew Dale, a yeoman of East Hanningfield, left to his son
Richard 'Great Greenwoods and three other tenements called

Potters, Legges and Wymans and a meadow lying behind the Cockhouse in Buttsbury'. Potters probably took its name from the occupation followed there. Stock and Buttsbury ranked with Harlow as the outstanding centres of the craft in Essex.

The laws on the keeping of alehouses were very severe in the sixteenth and seventeenth centuries, but it could have been in the Cock in 1558 that, 'A common victualler permitted 12 persons to play at cards after midday about the time of vespers on a feast day, on his own confession.' He was fined 3s 4d and warned that any recurrence of the offence would mean 'being placed in the stocks for 6 hours on some feast day, openly in the market place, and exiled', i.e. banished from the parish.

In the same century there occurred what could be styled 'The Curious Case of the Stock Cuckolds'. In 1585 Stock was set about the ears by a scandal, not without humour, in which the Cock figured with some prominence. F.G. Emmison in the first volume of his *Elizabethan Life* (1970) gives at length the colourful details, but in brief this is what happened.

A letter purporting to come from the curate of Fryerning spoke of thirteen men in the village as 'cuckolds', victims of unfaithful wives. It was addressed in the first instance to the miller Charles Whiskarde, who had bought a windmill in Stock several years earlier for the sum of £180. Among those branded as cuckolds was Robert Newman of the Cock, doubly insulted as 'cuckold and cuckold-maker'. No doubt the others, including Whiskarde himself and the 'crocklegged smith' William Lynes, were alehouse cronies, although there was then another inn in the village, the Swan, which they may have also frequented.

The most important target of the libel was Master William Pinder, the rector of Stock from 1580 to 1626, although, as he held another living elsewhere, he was absent for much of the time. He was noted, it seems, as a brawling and argumentative parson. Disputes between him and Whiskarde, along with a William Newman, had led to these two parishioners being allowed to attend another church in the district.

Among the other 'cuckolds' there were three at least who had been in trouble with the law. There was a John James who with his quarrelsome wife had been ordered out of Stock under threat of a whipping. She had 'brawled and scolded' with the Crondon Park bailiff of Sir John Petre, the lord of the manor. She had also confronted the man with firebrands. Her punishment was to be dipped in the pond on the cucking stool. James and the bailiff, Roger Veale, had adjoining cottages up the road at Crondon and must have been uneasy neighbours.

It was the bailiff's son Christopher who was said to have come under the spell of the Stock witch, Agnes Sawen, also of Crondon. She was accused at Quarter Sessions in Chelmsford. Robert Newman of the Cock was involved in that as well. He was described in the proceedings as a 'husbandman'. No doubt he was one of the woman's accusers, for he was bound over to keep the peace 'especially towards Agnes Sawen'. In the Session Rolls for October 1576 she is called 'a common enchantress of both men and beasts'. It was alleged that on 20 September 1574 she did 'bewitch and enchant' Christopher Veale. He had become lame in both feet, and one was wasting away. The widow Sawen pleaded 'not guilty'. During the hearings she was probably kept locked up in Colchester Castle. As there is no record of her execution, it is likely she had to endure the pillory.

The case of the cuckold libel was heard by three magistrates: Sir John Petre, John Butler and Eustace Clovile. It looks as though the real culprit, the sender of the letter, could have been a Thomas Petchey. He was apparently an innkeeper. Another member of the family, William Petchey, was the bailiff of Lord Petre's manor at Ingatestone. His house can still be seen in the High Street there and is now the Bell.

It certainly seems that the whole affair masked a paying-off of old scores.

In 1628 there was a petition, signed by, among others, the rector, for the closure of the tippling houses in what they called 'our little street'. The petitioners were prepared to tolerate the two inns, the Cock and the Swan, but not the other five or six dens of iniquity. William Newman's name again turns up as one of the 'disordered tipplers'. As a result, all, with the exception of the Cock and probably the Swan, were suppressed.

Several years later, in 1634, a peculiar entry was made in the parish registers on the seemingly strange circumstances surrounding a birth at the Cock: 'John ye sonne of John Fisher (as was sayed) & of Margaret a stranger brought to bed some four days before, was baptised ye same time, being ye 15th of March pact; on which day in ye night ye said Margaret, as they called her, and her sayed sonne were together with one they called her sister secretly conveyed away – ye host and hostess not knowing therof.

The Cock in the mid-eighteenth century was on the route of the Maldon coach. This came through Stock via Great Baddow on its way to Billericay. (The doctor's surgery by the war memorial was formerly a coach house.) Perhaps this explains the positioning of the six pubs on the Stock section of the route: namely, the Ship and the King's Head at either end, and the Baker's Arms (formerly the Jolly Millers), the Hoop, the Bear and the Cock strung out through the village itself. Only the latter two and the King's Head are mentioned by White in his *History of Essex* of 1848, but he does give two beershops as well. The Jolly Millers was well named, for it stood close by the impressive trio of windmills once to be seen against the skyline on Stock Common. All these pubs were certainly placed to advantage for the passing trade to and from Chelmsford and remain so today. The population of Stock alone (six hundred souls in the middle of the last century) could never have justified so many taverns over the short distances.

For some years the Cock was a tied house of the Lambirth family. Henry Lambirth, who died in 1834, was one of the county's most successful brewers. He had an impressive works at Writtle, and the inventory compiled on his death makes interesting reading to the enthusiast for industrial archaeology. The family stayed in the business until 1902. In addition to the Cock they owned nineteen other outlets for their beer. Among these were the Crown at Ingatestone and the Compasses in West Hanningfield. The Account Book of the Lambirth estate, covering the years 1861 to 1867, gives details of expenses at the Cock and at the other pubs. The book is now kept at the Essex Record Office.

The Cock has come a long, long way from its earliest days as a primitive village alehouse brewing its own beer.

Recently it has gone 'up market' with a small restaurant and a wine bar, following a trend which is everywhere becoming apparent.

The clientele of the new-look pubs have little in common with the tipplers of yesterday, least of all with those good old boys who trudged from field and cottage to sit and stare and gossip 'dipping great thoughts in beer'. However, a few are left, and not everything of the jerry house has been lost. Many a refurbished house like the Cock keeps a precarious hold upon the past, if only with a few authentic beams, a tradition or two, and a character in the corner. Despite all the current tastes and fashions, often more of the brewers than the public, it is antiquity and local colour which remain the lasting attraction.

9

The Galleywood Races

It is now close on fifty years since the last of the once-celebrated Chelmsford Races were held at Galleywood.

Today, traffic speeds across the open Common where horses thundered on the turf to a stern uphill finish. But apart from some old white railings there is little left to remind us of Galleywood's great equestrian past. A small compound of former stables, painted a racecourse green, marks the site of the enclosure. Here, too, the jockeys' changing-rooms have been nicely converted into modest homes. Nearby, on the main road, 'The Paddock' is a name now assumed by a new suburban estate. Two of the locals also have reminiscent names, the Running Mare and an older house, the Horse and Groom, hidden away behind shrubbery and gorse.

Not so far to the south of this latter pub and standing right by the old course is the house which was the Admiral Rous. Named in the last century after a well-known patron of the sport, it was a small tavern with a tea garden right up to the 1930s. It is now called Rous Cottage. Tastefully modernized the house has kept its period character.

The pub was used as a grandstand until one was erected by the newly formed Chelmsford Race Stand Company in 1863. Yet there had been a stand on the track long before that, for on 1 January 1779 the *Chelmsford Chronicle* angrily reported its deliberate destruction by fire. Much later, by the present century, two grandstands had been provided. The main one, still there in the 1950s, was a copy of the members' stand at Windsor and had cost £6,500 to put up.

The great common of over five hundred acres fortunately escaped the last of the Enclosure Acts. It not only came to be

The old Galleywood racecourse

a fit setting for a racecourse but was also the location of a military camp in Napoleonic times and for long after. In our own day it could well be scarred at the lower end by the new road, under construction as I write, which will sweep around Chelmsford to the south. Galleywood Common is not all grassland. There is a picturesque landscape of copses and hedgerows, and within the northern perimeter of the course a wooded hollow which I suspect may be the remains of a star-shaped redoubt.

There are other earthworks hereabouts. In his *People's History of Essex* of 1861 D.W. Coller wrote: 'In August, 1803, the fortifications and ramparts from Widford to Galleywood Common were commenced; about 1000 of the guards and the Lancaster militia were employed upon them; the Star Battery, where the windmill stands, being mounted with 48 pounders to protect the road to London. With the camps at Galleywood and Mole-hill Commons the number of troops in the neighbourhood amounted to eight or ten thousand.' With just a few houses, and these mainly screened by trees, the whole area is a rambler's delight. Virtually the entire length of the racetrack can be walked.

Although it has been said that Charles II patronized the course, racing really began here at the very end of George II's reign, in 1759 to be precise. For over a hundred years two flat-race meetings were held annually. And for most of that time they had royal support. In 1770 the Master of the Horse announced in the *London Gazette*: 'His Majesty is graciously pleased to give the sum of 100 guineas to be run for at Chelmsford, by four-year old mares, carrying eight stones & a half, the best of three heats, two miles to a heat; and orders, as Her Majesty landed in Essex, that this shall be called the Queen's Plate.' 'Her Majesty' was Queen Charlotte, the wife of George III. She had landed in England at Harwich on 6 September 1761 and married the King three days later. The Royal Plate, until its abolition in 1887, came out of the Privy Purse.

In the programme for 1798 there were three events held on consecutive days for the Guineas. The meeting must have been one of the most disappointing on record. The field on the first day consisted of four horses, one of which broke down. Then on the second day only two ran, while on the third there was the climax of a walkover!

There are several old maps held at Chelmsford which show the course as it was in the late eighteenth and early nineteenth century. On Chapman's county map of 1777 the original loop on the common is clearly indicated. (Later it was to bisect the main road twice, the junctions being covered with oak-bark tan.) The church within the racecourse is not shown. The impressive St Michael and All Angels, with its spire rising 127 feet, which makes it such a landmark for miles around, did not come until a century later. It has often been said that the Galleywood course is the only one in the country to encircle a church. This may be so, but it is doubtful if any racing took place around the church after it was built in 1873. A map of 1810 marks a post-mill inside the course. This has long since gone, but Mill Hill and a house called Mill View near the Eagle public house perpetuate its memory.

Another map, or rather plan, seems to date from shortly after 1817. This covers 'Part of the New Mile Course at

Galleywood Common belonging to the Rt. Hon Lord Petre'. It shows the starting post, by the side of the Stock Road south of Bakers Lane, and the quarter- and half-mile points. A spinney now covers the southernmost part of this course.

I have heard it alleged that this Lord Petre, the eleventh Baron, acquired Napoleon's celebrated white stallion 'Marengo' which had been ridden at Waterloo. Many of the Petre family documents were destroyed in the fire at Thorndon Hall in 1878, but should this story ever be substantiated, we should have the fascinating possibility that the Emperor's horse may have appeared on the turf here.

Hunt-race meetings were a feature of the racing on the common early last century. They were arranged by Colonel Cook, Master of the Essex Hounds from 1808 to 1813. The prizes included a 50 guineas cup. Only horses which had been 'in' at the death of at least four foxes were allowed to enter.

In 1862 the Galleywood Race Stand Company was inaugurated with a nominal capital of £2,000, there being two hundred shares of £5 each. The Chelmsford Race Committee, a separate concern, had to rent the facilities provided by the Race Stand Company in order to stage events. The Committee's minutes for the years 1867 to 1922 are lodged at the Essex Record Office. They fill two sturdy volumes. As one would expect, much of the routine business of managing the course is recorded. This includes inspections of the track, the appointment of stewards, tenders for refreshments and arrangements with the local constabulary. Accounts and the state of the bank balance also figure among the entries, especially in the earlier years. However, the books yield a wide variety of items of far more absorbing interest.

Although the races in the 1860s were very popular, the minutes for those years and into the next decade show debts being frequently discussed. There was a continuous loss at the three meetings being held each year. It looks as though they were subsidized from the pockets of gentlemen who put sporting pleasures before gain. The programme planned for the summer meet of 1869 listed a number of locally named handicaps along with their prize moneys. So we can read of the Galleywood Handicap (£30), the Hylands (£40), the Marks Hall Stakes (£25), founded by Squire Honeywood, the Witham (£30), and the Great Baddow Handicap (£40).

In 1871, no doubt as an attempt to bolster falling receipts, it was resolved 'that the Course be let to any Gentleman desirous of trying or galloping horses any day'. Fridays and Sundays were excepted. It does not appear to have caught on, for several months later the idea was dropped.

Runners and riders were not entered in the minutes, but a notable event of 1879 was the winning of the Royal Plate by Prince Soltykoff on 'Thurio'. The following year the autumn meeting was abandoned, there being only sixteen entries.

In February 1881 the Committee decided to approach the Master of the Horse 'that Chelmsford may retain the Queen's Guineas'. This strongly suggests that royal patronage was about to be terminated. In fact, six years later the Royal Plate was discontinued.

By the April of '81 a real financial crisis was reached. A letter, no doubt gratefully received, from the Golden Lion Hotel in Rayleigh, requested the use of the course for a one-day pony event.

In March 1885 a water jump was agreed at Galleywood. It was sited near the road with a regulation six-foot ditch and a fence. 1887 saw a resolution to have a race styled 'The Galleywood Open Hunt Steeple Chase Plate'. There were to be twenty-five entries and the charge of £6.5.0 each, included a weighing-in fee. Three years later it was decided that, 'The Roothing Steeple Chase Plate be 3 miles according to the new rule of the Grand National Hunt.' In the same year it was also resolved to have '5 Races one to be a Military Race provided the officers of Colchester and elsewhere find the Stakes'.

Then, on 4 February 1892, the idea of going over to steeplechasing was discussed. At first the members turned it down, but five days later, following an offer of fields for that purpose, a resolution was passed for a steeplechase and hunt meeting to be held 'under Grand National Rules' on 28 March. This seems to have marked a decisive turn in their fortunes.

It was in this year that Sir Claude de Crespigny won the Baddow Steeplechase on 'Twelfth Cake'. Sir Claude, 'the

Mad Rider', was a colourful character in the locality and a legend in his own lifetime. He could have been a prototype for Allen Quartermain. An all-round sportsman, his exploits make stunning reading. He was no mean fox-hunter and ventured abroad to pursue big game in Africa. He had been in the King's Royal Rifles and in 1889 was a war correspondent up the Nile, where he swam the rapids. Yachtsman and cricketer, he was also a prodigious walker almost to the end, walking to the Grand Hotel in London for a token wager of half a crown, a distance of forty-five miles. An event of particular distinction was his crossing of the North Sea in a balloon, 'The Colonel', with Joseph Simmons. They were the first two to do so, travelling from Maldon to Flushing. Sir Claude held two decorations for his aerial exploits: the Gold Medal of the Balloon Society and the International Medal of the Royal Aero Club. He lived at Champion Lodge, Great Totham, where he built his own racecourse. He did not give up the hurdles until he was sixty-nine. As a grand old man he lived on to eighty-eight, dying in 1935.

A flamboyant, fairground atmosphere surrounded the events later in the nineteenth century, with booths, clowns, prizefighters and cock fighting. The scene was more raucous than in the late 1700s, when, according to the local paper, 'The company at the assemblies was numerous and gentile', and 'elegance of the entertainments' was a notable feature. But there were the inevitable gypsies. In 1885 they appear to have become a major irritant. In March that year the Secretary of the Race Committee was instructed to prosecute all gypsies camping on the common and for damage caused. Three were summonsed and fined 10 shillings each.

In 1893 a letter was received by the Committee proposing a nine-hole golf course on the common. Despite an encouraging reply, no more seems to have been heard of this.

Another resolution of this time is of topographical interest. It was for 'a post and rails to be placed across the course by the Horse and Groom to prevent traffic along the Course towards the church'. Perhaps this was in response to an ecclesiastical complaint. Railings near the pub today could well mark the very spot.

It was agreed in 1896 to have one combined ticket for both

the stand and the paddock. The price was 7s 6d, going up to 10 shillings in 1901.

The modern age began to make itself felt when in 1897 the grandstand was wired for 'telegraphic communication', as the minutes put it. The next year it was arranged to make a steeplechase course a little over two miles.

The placing of bets, if not actively discouraged, was required to be unobtrusive, for the benefit of the gentry. As the new century got under way, the Committee firmly resolved 'that no betting men were allowed to place themselves where the carriages are charged for and that printed notices be placed to notify the same'. They followed the golden rule of Victorian society: 'Out of sight, out of mind.'

At the commencement of the Edwardian era, 'The Chairman proposed the health of the King, and also the health of the Queen and the Royal Family.' At this meeting, held at the White Hart Hotel in Chelmsford, the toast 'was drunk with musical honours'.

In July 1914, only days away from the outbreak of war, the minutes gave yet another sign of the changing times. The carriage trade was giving way to the motor car. The charge for parking cars at the races was fixed at 10 shillings. But there was to be little racing at Galleywood during the next four years. The only minutes are for February 1915 and July 1917. There was some unspecified damage to the grandstand by the army in 1917 and the Committee negotiated compensation to the value of £230.

The great days of the Chelmsford Races had long been over. In 1922 the Race Stand Company put itself on the market at the Corn Exchange. The Committee made a forlorn bid of close on £1,300. Their end came on 11 August of that year, when they held a final session to wind up their affairs and dispose of the assets. Some items of furniture went into private hands, as did the weighing-in scales and a portrait of Admiral Rous, which must have become collectors' pieces.

Intriguingly, while I mention this, I'm wondering what became of the Chelmsford Cup found in the Nazi loot in 1945. Equally puzzling is how it got there. The *Illustrated London News* reporting it at the time described it as 'a magnificent silver-gilt cup, 18 in high, inscribed with the arms of the third Baron Foley. Under the rim of the base are inscribed the words "Chelmsford Races", from the hallmark, the date is 1816.'

Some sporadic racing continued at Galleywood under a new but short-lived company which included two National winners, F.B. Rees, who had won on 'Shaun Spodah', and W.B. Rees, on 'Music Hall'. 'Golden Miller' won his first two races here over the hurdles. This remarkable horse went on to become one of the greatest chasers in the Sport of Kings. In the thirties he won five Cheltenham Gold Cups consecutively. In 1934 he became the only horse ever to achieve the double of the Cheltenham Cup and the National. In the latter he set up a record time only once to be broken later by 'Red Rum's' 9 minutes 1.9 seconds, 18½ seconds faster than the 'Miller's'.

The last of the Chelmsford Steeplechases was held on Monday 29 April 1935. Pony Turf Club races took their place the following month. At the inauguration meeting on the 20th there were ninety-three entries for the six events.

However, the final closure of the ancient course for organized racing was in sight, its fate sealed by the Second World War and the purchase of the land by Chelmsford Council.

Part II

In the Rural Heartlands

The Viper at Mill Green

1

The Forest Retreat of Bedemans Berg

There are tiny corners of our land which have a fascination though all but gone from the landscape. Often they hang on to the past solely by virtue of a magic name. Such is old Bedesmans Berg. But first let me tell you of its wider setting.

The site lies deep within the groves of Highwood. On the leafy heights about Fryerning, it is in the very extensive parish of Writtle, formerly a royal manor and liberty but granted to Sir William Petre in 1554 by Queen Mary. Writtle Park has stayed to this day in his descendants' hands.

The name Writtle derives from the River Wid, poetically meaning 'the bubbling or purling stream', and it has the distinction of being one of those few Essex place-names which can be followed back as far as the seventh century, when it was recorded as 'Writola burna'.

Highwood in the south-west of the parish is one of the four surviving tracts of the ancient Forest of Essex, the others being at Hatfield Broad Oak, Hainault and, of course, Epping, the most impressive. 'Highwood' is more correctly 'Highwoods', for here on the elevated ground there are a number of lovely woods and copses. Here, too, there are names which reflect the character of the landscape and its links with local history. King John may well have hunted hereabouts in the glades. A strong tradition connects him with a large moated site.

The Viper pub, its name recalling that adders were once prevalent in the district, is an excellent point from which the rambler can head out along the paths into the woods. The Viper can claim a small prestige: it appears to be the only pub with this name in the whole of Britain. A curiosity mounted outside its door is a gnarled fragment of a branch suggesting a face, a grotesque image tricked out with paint to enhance the resemblance, the work of an Austrian woodcarver. Originally two cottages and well over three centuries old the house has retained its character, thanks to the publican Mr Fred Beard who has been here since a boy. It looks particularly delightful in high summer when the front windows are screened with everlasting sweet peas.

In former times deer came to drink in Deerslade Wood. The 'slade' is from the old language for 'dell', a word often used for moist, low-lying land and, by extension, for a watercourse. Further to the west across farmland Birch Spring was 'Birch Hatch' in the thirteenth century. A hatch was a woodland gate, and the one at this spot stood on the boundary of the forest. Kelvedon Hatch and Iford's Aldborough Hatch acquired their names in the same way.

A further indication of the antiquity of the forest land here lies in the name 'Redindike'. In the parish of Fryerning in the thirteenth century it was 'Writtledich', so called from its nearness to the Forest of Writtle, the 'dich' being the forest boundary composed of a ditch and a bank. 'Ridden' or 'redden' is a common Essex name for a field or clearing in a wooded area. There is one quite near my home, Riddens Croft, but it is the new name for what was 'Morwena', a house taking its name from a Cornish saint.

Mapletree, Coppice Wood and Ivybarns require no explanation, but College Wood gets its name through being given to New College, Oxford, by that great English prelate William of Wykeham. Writtle was a 'peculiar', which means it was not under the jurisdiction of the diocese. Instead, it was a possession of the Warden and Fellows of New College.

In the very heart of these woodlands is Monks and Barrow Farm. Early in the fifteenth century it was recorded as 'Monkes at Barrow'. The barrow was a berg or hill, and the combined name gives us the clue to what must have been the most solemn nook among the trees. For it was here that once could have been seen the monastic cell of Bedemans Berg.

This small, austere hermitage was founded by one Robert, a Benedictine, in 1135, the year that Stephen, the last of the Norman monarchs, was crowned. Later, during the reign of Henry II, the King granted it to the Abbey of St John the Baptist at Colchester, and it became the lonely dwelling place of two monks or beadsmen. No structural details are known, nor is its dedication.

Professor Reaney gave Bedemans Berg as 'the hill of the man of prayer'. The expression 'bead' is a now obsolete term for a prayer. Thus, a beadsman was one endowed to pray for others, and his spiritual function was akin to that of a chantry priest. The name also came to be used for the inhabitants of an almshouse, hence 'bead-house'. They were expected to pray for the founder. Because of the connection which developed between saying prayers and keeping a count by 'telling beads', a beadsman also later came to be a man who used prayer-beads. Thus the forerunner of the rosary, with its paternosters, aves and set meditations, was in use as early as around 1100.

The charter of Henry II required the two anchorites in their 'elected silence' in the woods to pray for his salvation and for the repose of the souls of past kings. In return they were privileged to gather nuts from the forest, and they received 4d a day from the manor. Theirs must have seemed an heroically ascetic life even by the standards of their day, objects of awe to lord and peasant alike. In their remote vigil such men lacked the relief afforded to other contemplatives who in their cloisters could enjoy the pleasures of community.

Of their house not a vestige remains. Another monastic hermitage in the area, just a couple of miles away to the south, has also gone into oblivion. This was on the other side of the Wid, in the old parish of Buttsbury. Even the site is uncertain. Possibly it stood in or near the field called 'Chapel Pieces' off Swan Lane (long since in Stock). It was mentioned in manorial documents of the sixteenth century as 'le Ermitage' but by 1571 it had vanished, leaving a piece of waste ground half a rood in extent. Prior to the closure of the monasteries it was held by St Leonard's Nunnery at Stratford Bow. No doubt, like Bedemans Berg, this cell stood in a secluded, wooded place.

It is not surprising that we should know so little about these outposts of the spirit. Their inmates drew their cloaks about them in a life of self-effacement. They were obscure from the world even then, and time has done the rest. Their values are not of our age. Indeed, they are totally alien to all that most of us hold dear. Yet, as we walk in the hermits' footsteps, we can enjoy what they no doubt delighted in as well, the peace and rustled silence and what S.L. Bensusan so beautifully called 'the litany of green things growing'.

2

Norton Mandeville

As elsewhere throughout England, there are villages in Essex which proudly carry the names of feudal noblemen who gave their lustre to the old estates. Stanstead *Mountfichet*, Stapleford *Tawney*, Tolleshunt *d'Arcy*, North Weald *Bassett*, Woodham *Ferrers*, Thurrock *Grays*, *Sir Hughes* ... they read like a roll-call of the landed gentry, greater and lesser lights still signalling from the horizon of our medieval past. And little Mandeville shines among them.

You can reach it with ease from High Ongar for it is only a mile or so away. Here in the centre of Essex both the Ongars, especially Chipping, provide an excellent starting point for excursions into the depths of the Essex countryside.

The place is one of the merest of hamlets. Despite its minute size, however, it is no disappointment to lovers of rural seclusion. Its population in the eleventh century was barely a hundred, and there cannot be many more in the parish today. Before the Conquest it was simply 'Norton' or 'north tun', a homestead or village tucked away in the north of the Ongar Hundred. In the reign of Edward the Confessor the manor belonged to St Paul's. According to Morant, by the year 1190 it had been leased to the Dammartin family and it was then it acquired the more impressive name.

Galiena Dammartin's second husband was a Ralph Mandeville, by whom she had a son, Robert. Later on, in 1251, Ernulf de Mandeville was the lord of the manor. The family name, sometimes given in ancient records as 'Magnaville', derives from Mandeville in Normandy. They were related to the Geoffrey de Mandeville who landed with Duke William at Hastings and whose grandson, also Geoffrey, became the mighty first Earl of Essex. Other places which have taken the name are Hardington Mandeville in

Cottage at Norton Mandeville

Somerset and Stoke Mandeville, Berkshire.

The Manor House, timbered and with many gables, is very picturesque. One of its three chimneystacks bears the date 1610. It stands a mile from the church, which is approached down a very long, narrow and winding lane leading off from the road between Norton Heath and the Willingales. At first there are a few council houses set back on the left. Then on through open country you meet a house or two and a farm, Dodds Farm, about a third of the way along. Finally, at a dead end, there is that typical Essex combination of a church and a hall in close proximity. With its church, its striking Victorian farm buildings of red brick, a pond and two fine agricultural cottages, there can hardly be another spot in mid-Essex to give such a pronounced feeling of remoteness.

The first time I came here, drawn by the signpost, was on a lovely cloud-flecked August day. There was not a soul about and the fields were rich in standing corn. I made my way to the little church past numerous exotic ducks and geese.

All Saints is a church of total simplicity. Inside, it is very musty and in places much in need of new plaster. Serviced from High Ongar across the fields to the west, it can be little used and looks almost certain for eventual redundancy. However, it is in good structural condition, having been substantially restored in the last century. It is all of a piece, being solely one of nave and chancel with no transepts or aisles. It is mainly of the fourteenth century, although there are signs of an earlier, Norman building, the church of the first Mandevilles here. There is a little wooden bell turret which was added to the fabric in the fifteenth century. The church lacks monuments and any adornments of particular note, although there are crudely carved bench-ends.

Standing in this modest place of worship so devoid of the usual attractions, I had that sense of Eliot's 'earth feet, loam feet' which one gets in churches of this kind – the awareness of generations of slow-moving peasants toiling and praying down the years.

Although unmarked, there are local gentry beneath the paving stones. One such is an Elizabethan rector, William Pawne, a layman of High Ongar. In his will of 1578 he asked to be entombed on the right side of the chancel for which he left 100 marks. Perhaps he had carried out those repairs to the church which had constantly been urged upon him. Perhaps, too, Thomas Bainbrick, a curate in the 1540s, is buried here. He has secured his little place in the margin of the parish's history through refusing to read the burial service by a graveside because of 'a great wind'. He was afraid of catching cold!

The churchyard has an appealing feature in its fir trees which match those in the grounds of the Hall across the way. From the unused south porch a short avenue of twisted and sprawling yews slopes to a surprisingly abrupt end at a ditch. It certainly looks as though there was once an approach to the church here but today all that can be seen beyond the fence are fields.

Norton Hall now has a farm of some two hundred acres. In the eighteenth and nineteenth centuries it was part of the vast Forest Hall Estate which reached to over a thousand in its heyday. The building of an aerodrome during the last war resulted in its final spoliation.

The present owner, Mr H.W. Chumbley, has done much in recent years to improve the look of the farm and the immediate surroundings of the Hall. It is good to find in these days a farmer intent on replacing dead trees, especially the ill-fated elm, with a whole variety of other species which will look at home in the Essex scene. Happily, he is not of that number who regard a tree as 'only a green thing standing in the way'. This personal commitment to the appearance of the land would have pleased old Cowley, the seventeenth-century poet, who protested at those of his day,

> That can the fair and living trees neglect,
> Yet the dead timber prize.

And there is more than a touch of class to the farming here which would have impressed him. 'We may talk what we please of lilies', he wrote in his essay, *Of Agriculture*, 'and lions rampant, and spread-eagles, in fields d'or or d'argent; but, if heraldry were guided by reason, a plough in a field arable would be the most noble and antient arms.'

Although there are no deeds for the Hall, it stands on the site of at least one other. Maps of 1740 and 1777 show this clearly. There was also once a local called the White Horse with a sign which was mounted in the road.

For anyone who wants to get close to rural Essex as it was, a visit to Norton Mandeville should prove a rewarding experience.

3

'Delicious Leez'

Leighs Priory, or Leez to give it the old-world spelling, is one of the loveliest of secluded places to be discovered in Essex. Between the villages of Little Leighs and Felsted and close by the once deer-haunted Hartford End, it is set in a little valley by the River Ter, a gentle tributary stream of the Chelmer which winds across country from its source above Stebbing. The rare charm of this wooded spot lies in its tranquil marriage of art and nature, for here are the stately red-brick ruins of a once great house which in turn stood where a monastery had been. The remains are inhabited still. The family who own it today share the old walks and retreats with the shades of those here long ago, with hooded monks and gilded lords and ladies and iron-willed emissaries of a reformed religion. All have gone into the quiet night of history, 'all passion spent'.

The priory was founded around 1220 by Sir Ralph Gernon for the Augustinian canons. It had a dual dedication to St Mary and St John the Evangelist. A wealthy house, one half of its estate was in Suffolk. When its doors were finally closed in 1536 and the community transferred to Waltham Abbey, the net annual rent was assessed at £114.12s.4d. Virtually nothing of the medieval priory remains above ground, but excavation has revealed much of the foundations which have been left exposed and are now marked out to give the wandering visitor some idea of the building's shape and extent.

With the Dissolution, the monastery passed into the grasp of Sir Richard Rich. The first Lord Rich was aptly named, for his was a career marked with an avarice and opportunism hardly equalled in the England of the sixteenth century. In the key position at the Court of Augmentations, he handled the spoils of the monastic estates seized by Henry VIII. From being Speaker of the House of Commons, Rich rose to be Lord Chancellor for a short time. He supported Lady Jane Grey but, quickly sensing the change in the wind, switched his allegiance to Mary Tudor. On resigning the Great Seal he retired to Leez. In the course of his public life Lord Rich acquired over a hundred estates, and his will is one long recital of manors and other properties. The superb tomb monument in Felsted church shows him reclining in his Chancellor's gown. To my eyes the face is mean and with a trace of arrogant cunning. His one enduring act of generosity was to found the celebrated grammar school at Felsted. Among his successors, the second Baron married Penelope Devereux, the 'Stella' of Sir Philip Sidney's sonnets, and he purchased at great expense from James I the title of Earl of Warwick.

Richard Rich dismantled the greater part of the old priory at Leez and used some of the material in the construction of

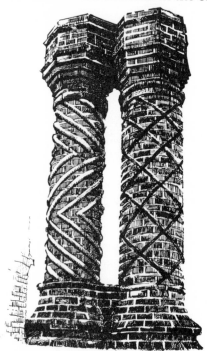

Elizabethan chimney at Leez Priory

his ambitious mansion on the site. It is the substantial fragments of the house which draw people to the spot today.

Although exceeded in stature by Layer Marney, the boundary walls and towers had few other rivals in Essex. On bright, sunny days the deep redness of what remains glows with warmth. Two ranges of the outer courtyard have survived along with two magnificent gatehouses. Their walls are patterned with dark blue vitrified bricks in diapers and other designs. Of the gatehouses it is the inner one which is the more ornamental. The original decorated chimneystacks are particularly eye-catching.

This is how the eastern tower was seen by the historian Miss Fell Smith in 1901: 'Cows and horses are stabled between its massive oaken outer doors, where the Tudor rose, the fleur-de-lys, and other badges are carved upon the pale and worm-eaten timber. An ancient pony stumbles through the little postern under the carved stonework of the Rich arms, with their motto *Garde ta Foy*. Through the broken casements overhead white doves flutter in and out. To these and to the owls and bats, the once magnificent, but now floorless and windowless, upper chamber has long been entirely devoted.'

From the roof there is a wide view of what is left of the parkland, with its lake and the ponds reflecting in their still waters the walled kitchen garden. These were the 'stews', the old fishponds of the monks. The two superb brick barns of Tudor date can also be seen from here to full advantage.

In the Civil War the family allied itself with Parliament against the Crown, and from the walls and embattled roofs of Leez in 1648 a Royalist force of around two thousand men was seen advancing to 'borrow' the armoury from the second Earl. A graphic account of what followed still survives, written by his lordship's steward, Arthur Wilson. Although some of the weapons were seized by the King's men, much had been successfully concealed in time. The defenders, hopelessly outnumbered, were led by Lady Warwick and the steward, the Earl being absent at the time. (There seems to be no documentary support for the tradition that some of his weapons were thrown in the lake to prevent their capture.) The Royalist officers were 'correct' in their behaviour, but the soldiers at large were very unruly.

Among them were hundreds of boy apprentices from the
City. The army withdrew upon the approach of Parliament-
ary troops and made its way to Colchester, where the
Royalists were to endure the terrible siege, the last major
event of the war.

Among the depredations at Leez, deer were slain in the
parks around the house. These were very extensive,
remnants of the medieval 'Forest of Felsted'. Of the three,
Litley Park was four miles round, Pond Park was over four
hundred acres and the third, unnamed, was nearly of the
same size. Arthur Wilson concluded his account: 'So we lost
some horses, two brass guns, a great part (though not half)
of our arms, barrels of powder, some match and bullet, and,
after drinking some twenty hogsheads of beer, one hogshead
of sack, and eating up all our meat and killing at least one
hundred deer in the three parks we were rid of our ill guests.'

The area has many connections with Oliver Cromwell and
his family, for Robert Rich married the Protector's daughter
Frances. Their wedding feast was held in great style at
Whitehall, followed by seven days of celebrations at
Warwick House in Holborn. Three months later he was dead
of consumption and lying draped in purple where the echoes
of the festivities had barely faded. Frances re-married. She
lived on till 1721, over sixty years after her father and nine
after the death of her brother, poor 'Tumbledown Dick'.

Robert Rich was the grandson of the great second Earl.
But Robert predeceased him and left no heir. The third Earl,
another Robert, followed at Leez for only a year. The fourth
Earl, Charles Rich, was the last of the family to hold the title.
He married Mary Boyle when she was fifteen, the youngest
of Sir Richard Boyle's seven daughters. Sir Richard, the
great first Earl of Cork, had an equal number of sons, one of
whom was Robert Boyle, a founder of the Royal Society and
the chemist and physicist who formulated the famous 'Law'.
Like his sister Mary, he was deeply committed to religion. He
did much for the propagation of his Faith, especially in New
England and the East, and founded the Boyle Lectures for its
defence.

The most remarkable woman ever to grace Lees, Mary,
Countess of Warwick, deserves to be rescued from the
footnotes of history. Virtually unknown today, she would

have made a fitting addition to Virginia Woolf's *Lives of the Obscure*. There are passing references to her in that fine collector's piece Miss Eliza Vaughan's *Stephen Marshall: a Forgotten Essex Puritan*, published in 1907, but the definitive life of the Countess was researched by the Essex historian Charlotte Fell Smith. Written in 1901, this volume, too, has become a rarity.

To her father's grave displeasure, Mary Boyle rejected her first suitor, and he was equally annoyed when she responded to the advances of the young Charles Rich, who had not the wealth to go with his station. It was in a little house at Hampton Court, where Mary was recovering from a sickness, that she finally said 'yes' to her suitor. Shunning a public wedding, they were privately married at Shepperton. Lord Boyle relented his anger with a handsome dowry, though not paid out all at once. In later years Mary was to become obsessed with her act of disobedience.

So it was that in 1641 as a very young bride she first saw and fell in love with Lees, 'delicious Leez' as her brother Robert was to call it. And here she met her father-in-law, the thrice-married Robert, the second Earl. Among the august offices he held in his lifetime, he was Speaker of the House of Commons, Lord Lieutenant of Essex and Lord High Admiral of the Fleet. Miss Fell Smith wrote of his appearance, as painted by van Dyck: 'His dark, lean face looks out with all the sincerity of a Puritan, all the spirit of adventure of a great Elizabethan, and all the humour and jollity of an English sailor.' His first wife, Frances, lay buried at Felsted in the family vault. The spectacle of her funeral in 1623 must have remained long in the minds of the villagers. A contemporary wrote: 'On Wednesday night the Countess of Warwick was carried out of Holborn to be buried in Essex, by more than two hundred horse, all with torches, and above three-score coaches, among whom were both the Duchesses ...'

At the time of Mary's arrival at Lees, Sarah was the Countess. She was followed in 1646 by Eleanor, Countess of Sussex. Married four times, she was to be called 'the old men's wife'. Warwick was her third husband, and they wed when he was sixty.

Mary's first child was a girl, Elizabeth, but she died when only one year old. A son quickly followed and was christened

Charles. When he fell ill at the age of five, Mary vowed to become 'a new creature' if he recovered. He did so and she embraced the Puritan cause she had so vigorously opposed. After her conversion she was to censure herself for her conduct in the earlier years. Looking back, she accused herself of being vain, for 'curious dressing' and reading romances and for being a lover of the Court and London society.

In the first years of her marriage, while her father-in-law was still alive, she lived at Lincoln's Inn, although she was frequently at Leez, at Warwick House and sometimes at Beddington House in Surrey where the gardens were always a special joy. It was at Beddington that the first orange trees were planted in England, and pomegranates were grown there too. In London, Chelsea Gardens, those of Sir Hans Sloane, were also a favourite haunt. But it was Leez which held first place in her affections. When in 1659 the old earl died and Charles, then twenty-three succeeded to the title, she realized her strong desire to retire to the seclusion of what her chaplain, Antony Walker, extravagantly called 'a secular Elysium, a worldly paradise'. But although Mary and her coterie sang its praises, there was another side to the idyllic picture, for it was then and long remained a damp, malarial place and very conducive to fever. It tried the body while it nourished the soul.

The Admiral had been to the New World, and for Mary Leez was to prove hers. The heart of it was the Wilderness. This sanctuary lay beyond the purling stream in a wooded dell. Here she came to the walks nearly every morning to spend two hours in prayer and meditation. The monastic spirit must have risen with the mist. The spot was her spiritual magnet.

With its wilderness and densely wooded parks, she turned the priory into a retreat for eminent preachers and divines, many of whom had been ejected from their livings. The list is long and impressive, and to give a profile of each would fill a small book. But among those I find of particular interest is one who had a link with my own home parish. This was Nathaniel Ranew, one of Mary Rich's most frequent and favoured of guests. He was a Cambridge man, of Emmanuel College. The Classes, an approved list of ministers drawn up in 1648 by the Presbyterians then in the ascendant in Parliament, shows him to be then at West Hanningfield. His stay was brief, as was his next living at Little Eastcheap, both very brief in fact, for other records show him as the vicar of Felsted from 1647 to 1662, in which year he went to Billericay as a licensed Presbyterian minister. The third Edmund Calamy noted for his *Account of Ejected Ministers* printed in 1701, wrote in his book of Ranew: 'He was a judicious divine and a good historian which made his conversation very pleasing. He was well beloved by the late Earl, Charles and the Countess of Warwick, who allowed him twenty pounds per annum during his life.' His lengthy work *Solitude Improved by Divine Meditation* was doubtless among the devotional books read by the Countess. Its very title was in full accord with her interests. When published in London in 1670, it carried the words, 'first intended for á person of honour, and now printed for general use'. Although it is dedicated to Charles Rich and to several others, the 'person of honour' must have been primarily Mary herself, for the book has a prefatory epistle addressed to her.

Ever since the Restoration the expression 'Puritan' has been one of reproach, an epithet synonymous with bigotry, self-righteousness, the denial of the 'innocent' pleasures of the flesh, and a contention and wrangling which turn spiritual molehills into mountains. Over and against this stark image we have been pleased to counterpoint the sweeter sounds of old Walton or the kindly wit and wisdom of Dr Fuller. Yet a closer reading of that theological age shows this to be a caricature. Though at the extremes we find different breeds of men (at one end the strongly disputatious, knife-edge keen, at the other the staunch conservatives in the Anglican tradition), all shared a moral earnestness. The central pivot of their thought was that sin, as Chesterton remarked, was a fact as practical as potatoes.

It would be so easy, and erroneous, to visualize Mary Rich closed in a circle of fanatics. Her thought was narrow, yet if challenged on this, were she with us in this more indifferent era, she could reply with the Gospel: 'Strait is the gate and narrow is the way, and few there are that find it.' She was, in our jargon, a 'militant', yet a most gentle one. In fact, her sympathies in the church were wide. George Herbert stood among her books, as did St Bernard and Augustine, Baxter and Jeremy Taylor, and she knew Dr Gaudon of Bocking well. And when the news came of King Charles' death as she lay recovering from a nervous illness, she was later to write: 'News of that barbarous and wicked action of beheading King Charles the First was of a sudden told me, which did again endanger me, for I had a great abhorrence of that bloody act, and was much disordered at it.' All her life she kept the date of his death as a solemn fast.

More than all else it is her preoccupation with the Last Things which divides her and her age from ours. Death for her was not the Gorgon's Head it is for most of us. The terror lay rather in the shadow of the Judgement. The thought of death was her daily *idée fixe*. Once at least she enacted her end in a macabre act of imagination. In her diary on 4 March 1671 she wrote: 'In the morning as soon as up, I had, while my lord slept, very large meditations of death.' It was the day her brother Hatton was to be buried in the family vault in the church at Felsted. 'I had very moving thoughts of my lying down in the bed of darkness ... of my lying in my cold bed, and of the worms feeding upon me, and of my turning to dust.' This thought she says was 'a little frightful and amazing to me, but it pleased God to let me of a sudden find an extraordinary and reviving joy to think that nothing died finally and totally in a child of God but sin, and that my vile body should be raised and made a glorious one.' This then led her to 'rejoice with joy unspeakable'. Not to modern taste, but I do not find this 'unedifying' as did Miss Fell Smith. The contemplation of our end is surely only morbid when it is not seen as a gateway but as a blank wall. On immortality Mary Rich would have been at one with Richard Jefferies, who on the downs could cry, 'I have had the glory of the thought.'

This is from the secret life of Mary Rich, known then only to her God and confided perhaps to her chaplain. But, no anchorite, she spread grace and light all around her. John Aubrey, no friend of sectarianism, paid her a glowing tribute in his *Brief Lives*. He wrote of her: 'She needed neither borrowed Shades nor reflexive Lights to set her off ... Great by being the greatest Mistress and Promotress, not to say the

Founderess and Inventress, of a new Science – the Art of obliging, in which she attained that Sovereign Perfection, that she reigned over all their hearts with whom she did converse.'

Her circle of friends and acquaintances was very wide in town and country. One of these was Lady Maynard, not far away at Easton Lodge. In the fullness of time the Maynards would be invested with the title of Warwick and produce a countess as intriguing and enigmatic as Mary Rich and like her a lover of nature and princely gardens.

Our inside knowledge of the Lady of Leez derives from her private writings: her autobiography, diary and 'Occasional Meditations'. From the diary we know she wrote the account of her life in just two days in February 1672. She was then forty-seven and had six years to go in her vale of tears. She styled it 'Some specialities in the Life of M. Warrick'. The diary spans her last eleven years. It runs to twenty-nine books, four of which are missing. Both autobiography and diary are of historical importance, for events, public and domestic, are precisely dated. For large stretches the diary makes tedious reading. Mary Rich was no stylist. Moreover, church visits and sermons written from memory abound. Phrasing is repetitive and all went down on paper without re-working. Her trials and tribulations with her husband, for years afflicted with gout and 'the stone', are a constant theme. Intensely introspective, her endless self-criticism and abasement also fill these pages. Yet here and there a line shines from the page, like, 'Let me spread my sails for heaven.'

It is in her 'Meditations' that she is at her most appealing. There are 182 of these in all, full of charming, concise observations and quaintly turned moral lessons suggested by the life about her. Many are taken from her country walks and have, as it were, the dew still fresh upon them. Spontaneously written, they exhibit a holy simplicity which even the caustic Horace Walpole looked upon not unkindly. Each meditation begins with a prelude, at times akin to a mystical 'opening' or epiphany. These are drawn with immediacy from her surroundings. In her 'elected silence' she read nature and people as a coded book, a Book of Revelations. A few will convey the flavour of the whole, and in giving her initial 'snapshots', I will leave the reader to speculate upon the lessons they evoked.

The first looks 'resurrectional' in character' 'Upon walking and being much delighted with doing so in a very glorious morning in which the birds sing very sweetly.' This was written in the spring of 1671 after 'my long restraint from walking by the ill weather'.

'Upon observing a snail creep constantly forward in the walk without turning back.'

'Upon observing in the Courtyard many several paths towards the house.'

'Upon a dam that was made to stop water, but after a little time the water found its way through.'

'Upon a flower that opened itself towards the sun.'

'Upon the opinion that moles never have their eyes opened till just before their deaths.'

'Upon observing my coach-horses, when I was near home, went much faster than they did in all their journey.'

Her meditation 'Upon the cutting down of the Wilderness' reflects a double sadness. Her husband had ordered his woodman to cut back her beloved trees, a ruthless act which opened the wounds in her mind of her son's death. Her only boy, Charles Rich, had died of smallpox in 1664, two years after his marriage.

> This sweet place that I have seen the first sprouting growth and flourishing of for above twenty years together, and almost daily taken delight in, I have also now to my trouble seen, by my lord's command, the cutting down of, in order to its after growing again thicker and better, though I often interceded with him to have it longer spared.
>
> This brought to my sad remembrance afresh the death of my only son, whom I had also seen the first growth of in his childhood, and the flourishing of, to my unspeakable satisfaction, for almost twenty-one years; and, in a short space of time, to my unexpressible grief, by my Great Lord's command, cut down by death, that he might rise again in a better and more flourishing condition, though I often implored, if it was agreeable with the divine will, he might be longer continued to me.

In 1673 to her great distress the fourth Earl of Warwick died. For years his life had been blighted and soured by suffering.

Frequently Mary had been lashed by his tongue, sometimes in the presence of others. Although she broke at times, she bore his disparagements with unnatural patience and fortitude, constantly seeking its rationale in herself and the inscrutable designs of Providence. As her *via dolorosa* drew to its end, her husband's temper softened. His religion seems to have been only nominal. He must have been intimidated by her piety at times, yet he respected it as well as finding it curious. He left her his entire estate as there was no heir.

Mary's last years were very busy, often drawing her away from Leez. When her end came, in 1678, it was an easy passage and mercifully swift. Only a few months before, she had remarked: 'Now I have done my drudgery I will set to the renewing of my preparations for eternity.'

Walker, her old chaplain, left a moving account of her final hours, and he preached her funeral sermon – 'A Virtuous Woman Found' – when she was lowered to 'the bed of darkness' at Felsted. It was magnificently inflated and extravagant, and totally sincere: 'Oh, for a Chrysostom's mouth, for an angel's tongue to describe this terrestrial seraphine; or a ray of light condensed into a pencil, and made tactile, to give you this glorious child of light in *viva effigie.*'

So passed the devout and spirited Lady of 'delicious Leez', having spent her serenest days in the little valley 'with dying thoughts to die with living hopes'. She was fifty-three.

When I first began to read about her life, I did so because I saw in her a fascinating oddity, a stranger to our time. But slowly she emerged as a woman so much more than that. Beneath the verbiage of her pen there lies a very human being and complex saint. All saintliness, whether in the wider world or in the cloister, is of heroic proportions and unlike 'natural' goodness pushes to extremes. Climbing the Himalayas of the spirit, it breeds its very own species of eccentricity.

In some of her writing Mary Rich has been mildly likened to Madame de Guyon. Certainly she shares with many a Mother Superior the fruitful if tense union of the contemplative and active life. Dogma apart, she stands close in her lifestyle to such as St Teresa of Avila. Had she been a Roman Catholic, she might by now have been enrolled in the

calendar of the saints. I like to think as well that, in her love
of garden retreats and in her oft-thwarted desire to abandon
the encroachments of the world, she would have had much
in common with Vita Sackville-West in her tower at
Sissinghurst.

There being no direct descendant, the great Essex estate
was divided among six co-heirs. The priory with its land
went to the Earl of Manchester. From his family it was
purchased by the trustees of the young Duke of
Buckingham. On his death in 1753 it passed to his
half-brother, Charles Herbert, and shortly after it was
acquired by the Governors of Guys' Hospital along with
other properties in the county. It was to save money that
around 1753 they committed the deplorable folly of reducing
the fine mansion to the remnants we see it in today.

But the spirit of the place endures.

> '... here
> Lies peace beyond uneasy truancy.

And here we may think of Mary as we read these other
lines from Vita's *The Land*'

> My life was rich; I took a swarm of bees
> And found a crumpled snake-skin on the road,
> All in one day, and was increased by these.
>
> I have not understood humanity.
> But these plain things, that gospel of each year,
> Made me the scholar of simplicity.

4

Through the Rodings

A small book alone could be written on the Rodings, even though from a car window they may seem to have little to offer in the passing. Of the eight, only one or two have villages in any picture-book sense. And yet they form a region which is quite distinctive, having an undefinable, organic unity of hamlets and arable land, and a rich corn-bearing countryside, dotted with little churches, thatched cottages and aged farmhouse halls, many of them moated. Here small is beautiful, and it is doubtful if any of the Rodings exceeds five hundred souls.

One writer at the turn of the century called it 'Windmill Land', for he noted that every village had one to show. There are but two left standing now. He was also struck by the remoteness of these parts. At no great distance from the spreading metropolis as the crow flies, it is still incredibly peaceful and unspoilt and demonstrates well that 'nearness to London is not to be measured by miles'.

Defoe remarked of the Rodings that they were 'famous for good Land, good Malt, and dirty Roads'. The lanes are excellent now and have the merit of being largely unfrequented by through traffic. Another author, Hope-Moncrieffe, wrote in his travel book on Essex in 1901, 'We are now bisecting a circle of a dozen miles in diameter, within which no railway rattle is heard, a green, sleepy hollow, little changed, but for better roads over its heavy clays, from what it was in Georgian or Carolean days.' Much has altered since then, but of its unhurried air there is no doubt. If I was forced to an invidious choice, I think I should say that for me this is quintessential Essex.

The same writer also picked this up: 'A scandal goes that this group of secluded villages and hamlets looks on itself as

Aythorpe Roding windmill

the hub of creation.' I understand such pride. Anyone who
has lived here long must feel it. And, as we shall see, this
land has not been without prestige.

The Rodings are also the Roothings and appear thus on
several signposts. The name testifies to their origins as 'the
settlement of the people of Hroda or Hrotha', the latter form
giving us the alternative name. Yet in the year 1050 these
were, apparently, only 'duae Rodinges'.

The eight parishes lie between Fyfield and Dunmow. If
you approach them from the south, out of Ongar, the first to
be reached is Beauchamps Roding. I'm not going to tell you
at length about them all, but something must be said about
their names.

Beauchamp has been linked with two personal names, that
of a John de Bello Campo of 1233 and William Beauchamp
of Bedford.

Leaden Roding, pronounced of old as 'Leedon', is thought
to have taken its name from having at one time a church

with a lead roof, probably the first of its kind in the area. The parish church has for a rarity a pre-Reformation pulpit. Particularly striking outside is a superb short avenue of yews to the south door. Unlike most of the Roding churches, this one stands by the main highway.

Abbess Roding was held as a dependency of Barking Abbey. Barwick or Berwick Roding was a manor in this parish and was also known as Bernes or Barns. This is literally a 'corn farm' and here signifies a grange belonging to the nuns.

Aythorpe was the holding of William, son of Aitrop or Eutropius, of around 1200. Friars Grange belonged to the Cistercians of Tilty Abbey, and Monks Farm to the community of Colne.

Margaret Roding derives from the dedication of the church here. Regarded as the finest of the Roding churches, it has much Norman work, including a splendid doorway. There were two ancient manors here. One was Merks or Marks. The other had the manor house called Garnish Hall, otherwise Garnets. A property of the de Veres, earls of Oxford, it was also held by the Olive family. They were here when the house was styled Shingle Hall. Later it was known, too, as 'Olives'.

White Roding was formerly also 'Great'. This gets its name from the church as well. The walls of St Martin's are mainly of rubble and were probably whitened. A ninth and now lost hamlet of Morrell Roding was eventually incorporated into this parish. There is a Ralph Morel on record for 1205. The name endured to the mid-nineteenth century, and an old chapel, long used as a pigeon house, went around 1870.

White Roding had two manors. White Roding Bury alias Monks is still on the map. It was held from the Crown in lieu of keeping hawks and a greyhound for royal heron-hunting. The other, Mascallsbury, also kept greyhounds for the king. It was surveyed by the Walkers of West Hanningfield, and their map shows a kennel.

Berners or 'Barnish' Roding was entered by the scribes in Domesday as held by Hugo de Berneris. The family came over from Bernières in Normandy. It used to be accepted without question that the famous if shadowy nun Dame

Juliana Berners was the daughter of Sir James Berners, a lord of this manor. She became the Prioress of Sopwell Nunnery at St Albans, and the *Boke of St Albans*, first printed in the 1480s, is attributed to her, or at least the verse treatise on hunting contained in it. Sir James was executed for his support of Richard II in 1388. The exact date of Juliana's birth is unknown. A rival explanation for her name as Berners is that she was the Dame or Lady of Julian's Barns near St Albans.

The plain little church at Barnish, its dedication unknown, stands well back to the left of the Hall, a modest farmhouse. At the height of summer it is almost totally screened by trees, so it is easy to miss. Yews are abundant in the churchyard. Each time I have been I have found the door locked. The bell-turret is weatherboarded, while at the east end of the church the two windows are of sixteenth-century brick. If you peer through the windows of the nave, you will glimpse little by way of embellishment in the dim interior. It seems little used. The atmosphere is one of sad dilapidation.

Hall and church are near the beginning of a long, unhedged lane which winds through several lone farms and finally peters out. Here, a year ago, I came to a decaying house tucked away to the rear of impressive Torrells. I looked; a curtain trembled; a hand came round a half-opened door to pull it to. I promptly made off, feeling very much an intruder. It remains a haunting moment.

But to return to Beauchamp Roding. St Botolph's, 'the church in the fields', is a familiar landmark from the main highway. The road sweeps round the land in the middle of which it stands conspicuously by itself.

I re-visited the church last year. The November day was cloudless and clear, everything to the far horizon sharply etched in frost light. In this spectral season the churchyard can look a little eerie. It is bounded by a ditch, and some aged tombstones lean at intervals in the bushes along its course. In the shadow of the church, on the north side, there is a large, mysterious, triangular flat stone, roughly shaped and reddish in colour. Nearby, half-hidden in the grass, is what I take to be the fragment of a grave, a sculptured head of Christ, the worn face looking upward to the sky. Another object detached from time can be found here, a huge and rotting beam lying by the path.

The church itself, however, can allay such residual feelings of disquiet. It is a simple one of nave, chancel and tower. An aperture in the wall on the south side of the chancel arch indicates the former presence of rood-stairs. A nice little feature in this church, not mentioned in any guidebooks I have seen, is at the western end. The pew-benches here are raised, and in their base are what seem at first to be tiny, narrow drawers, each with a small, ringed handle. Pulled out, they give a surprise: they are steps up to the pews.

A rector here was the troublesome William Lynche. In 1564 he was accused of being a drunkard. 'He hath not walked', said the judge, 'so wisely as he should have done' and he was warned to stay away from the alehouse. He had to give 20 shillings to the poor and to confess 'on Friday next in the market of Chelmsford with a white sheet and a white rod'. There was a second fine 'for missing four sermons'. Only the year before this, the aged parson had been in front of the archdeacon's court for allowing his wife to dance in a common tavern. Sir William Addison in his book *The English Country Parson* (Dent, 1947) quotes at length from the records the confessions of both. I doubt the poor man could keep up with his lively, recalcitrant lady.

Two old taverns in the parish at Birds Green have been private houses now for some years. Attractive cottages, they stand only a few yards from each other and both are sited on a corner. They keep their former names: Three Hurdles and Two Swans.

But for a really infamous cleric in Elizabethan times we must turn to Leaden Roding. Matthew Levett held the living as its rector from 1571 for twenty years. His parochial career reads as one long misdemeanour. He was branded as a disturber of the peace and 'a notorious swearer, a dicer, a carder, a hawker and hunter'. He was once in gaol and had fought with another argumentative parson, the rector of Stock, Mr William Pinder, at a Chelmsford inn. When he died, he was awaiting trial for counterfeiting. He had made an 'angel' of gilded tin.

Abbess Roding is the next on the route beyond Beauchamp. To see the church you must turn off at

Longbarns. St Edmund's stands above the road. Although much changed in the last century, there are fine antiquities inside. These include a carved wooden rood-screen of the 1400s and a wrought-iron hourglass stand. There are two early Stuart monuments as well. That on the north wall is the gilded alabaster and marble memorial to Gamaliel Capel, who was interred here in 1613. He was one of the eleven children of Sir Henry Capel and he became a JP. The monument shows him kneeling at a *prie-dieu* opposite his wife. The small effigies below are of his nine offspring. The principal home of the Capel family was at Rayne near Braintree. The other monument, facing on the south wall, is to another local worthy, Lady Lucklyn, who made her exit in 1633. The work of Epiphanius Evesham, she is represented by a demi-figure with cherubs holding open a curtain behind. The inscription on the stone beneath is greatly engaging for both its words and its hourglass shape:

> We bragge noe vertues and we begge no teares:
> O reader if thou hast but eyes and ears,
> It is enough but tell me why
> Thou comst to gaze is it to pry
> Into our cost or borrowe
> A copie of our sorrow.
> Or dost thou come
> To learne to dye
> Not knowing whom
> To practise by?
> If this be thy desire,
> Remove thee one step nigher,
> Here lies a president, a rarer,
> Earth never showd; nor heaven, a fayrer
> She was – but room denyes to tel thee what
> Summe all perfection up, and she was that.'

Another wall memorial is an inscribed brass tablet, a separate brass coat of arms above, to Edward Humberstone of 'Cockerells' who died in 1622, aged eighty. The war memorial plaque (1914–18) is unusual: the last name is that of a woman, Helen I. Capel-Cure. She was one of a prestigious Essex family who are recalled in other tablets here.

To the west of the village is Rookwood Hall. It marks the site, a moated one, where stood the mansion of Antony Browne. In his will he left 20 shillings 'To the church of Abbess Roothing where I was born'. In the will of Sir Wiston (Weston) Browne of 1580, the great-nephew and heir of Sir Antony, there are items relating to the family holdings in the Rodings, with several on Rookwood and its deer park. Like his uncle, Wiston was buried at South Weald, the principal family seat, although he remembered 'the poor people of White Roothing where I was born and christened'.

Through Leaden Roding, turning at the King William IV, a Benskins house, you reach that of Aythorpe. Its white post-mill can be clearly seen ahead as you approach along the main thoroughfare. It stands by Gunners Green. 'Gunners' is thatched, restored in the 1960s, and in 1610 was written 'Gonners'. The mill, renovated and preserved by Essex County Council, dates from around 1760. It went out of use in 1935 but is now back in almost full working order.

Around the back of the village is St Mary's. This is another humble sanctuary of nave and chancel; its north and south doorways are barely five feet high. The belfry is modern but holds three ancient bells.

Towards High Roding there is a tiny and solitary wayside pub, the Axe and Compasses. Weatherboarded, it stands by a crossroads. Late in 1983 it looked very sad, its sign gone, closed and windows masked, awaiting a new owner. However, it has now been refurbished. I have happy memories of this spot, a favourite halt back in the days I whirred along the Essex lanes, a member of the Cyclists' Touring Club.

I highly recommend a detour down the lane opposite to Keeres Green. Starting with 'The White House' on the right, this little semicircular route is pleasing for its old-world dwellings.

High Roding's church lies down a no-through road at the very end. All Saints and a farmhouse with a pond stand side by side.

As you will read in the porch, the church is kept closed because of vandals and is therefore open only when services are held. There was a time when the only vandals we read of were the barbarian tribesmen of that name. Now, of course, it is the current term for spoilers, and churches get fewer by the year which can be found by the traveller unlocked. I suppose one of the most distressing losses of our age is the sense of reverence. From all directions we are instructed in secular things but there is precious little education of the spirit. But this is a pessimism I will not pursue.

I am faint-hearted when I think I might be disturbing other people's privacy. But on my visit to All Saints I had with me a forthright good companion whose enquiries in the village soon elicited a key.

The church is seven centuries old, and in its windows are fragments of stained fourteenth-century glass, two angels swinging censers. It was small, intriguing things here which made the day for me. First, two pictures, framed prints of the church. One depicts it as it was in July 1803. Below is a coloured view of thirty years later, after the spire had been struck by lightning, dated 13 May 1832. The present bell-cote dates from the restoration which followed. Two bells hang in it now; the old ones were sold in aid of funds. Then there are the Joceline brasses, the two of them on the floor, unfigured but with armorial bearings and epitaphs.

When Morant wrote in 1768, the Jocelyns were still in the parish. He noted they were 'of very great antiquity, there being 24 successive generations in their Pedigree'. For longevity the family tree held pride of place in Essex, rivalled only by the Cloviles and by the Barringtons of Hatfield Broad Oak. The common ancestor was a Breton nobleman, Egidius Jocelyn, who came to England before the Conquest. The last in direct line died in 1770. In the sixteenth century one of the family built New Hall, which stood across the fields south-west of the church. This was destroyed by a German bomb in the last war, but its grand old barn of seven bays escaped.

The wills of Sir Henry Jocelyn, who died in 1587, and of his wife are extant. Among the clauses in that of Dame Dorothy's, she left 'To the poor people of High Roothing 20s at the day of my burial, and within one month after my decease I quarter of wheat to be baked and given in bread to the poor of High and Aythorpe Roding'. She was also concerned about the highways and their bridges, bequeathing

20 shillings to the parochial surveyors.

The brass to John Jocelyn merits a full quotation:

John J Esquire, interred here doth lye
S Thomas Jocelines third son of worthy memory
Thrice noble was this gentleman by birth, by learning
great,
By single chast and godly life, hee won in heaven a seate
Hee the yeare one thousand and five hundred twenty nine
was borne
Not twenty yeare old him Cambridge did with two degrees
adorne
Kinges Colledge him a Fellow choose in Anno Forty nine
In learning Tride: whereto hee did his mind alwaies
incline
But others tooke the praise and fame of his deserving witt
And his inventions, as their owne, to printing did
committ.
One thousand six hundred and three, it greevies all to
remember
Hee left this life (poores dayly freind) ye twenty eight
Decab.

A monument or memorial brass is first and foremost a celebration of rank and worth, a declaration to the living of Importance. It establishes a hierarchy of the dead. In total contrast, the lives of common folk have usually gone without a trace. Yet some can be uncovered from the past, especially if they transgressed the law. One such is Elizabeth Petticrew, late of this parish. When wrested from the formal language of the old court records, hers is a poignant little tale and typical of many.

She had been a covenanted servant of Robert Jocelyn. In 1652 she was brought before the Justices and her master, 'beinge then lately come into the parish of High Easter greate with childe and unmarried, endeavouringe there to settle herselfe contrary to Lawe'. We have to assume that she had either been turned out of Jocelyn's service or departed in shame. The churchwardens and overseers of the poor for High Roding were ordered to take her back and provide for her. We hear of her again the following year. Despite the court order, the parish had refused to take her back in her pregnancy. No doubt they saw her as a further burden on the rates. Having returned to High Easter, she had been 'delivered of a Bastard female child'. Her home parish was now admonished 'to be obedient'.

Elizabeth's case came up later, in 1653. From this hearing we learn that the child had been born 'about the XVjth of February last past' and that a John Billings of Dunmow Priory had been declared 'to bee the reputed father of the said base female child'. He was given the option of either taking and providing for the girl or paying to High Roding a weekly maintenance cost of 4 shillings backed by a bond of £50. As for Elizabeth, she was ordered to be sent to the house of correction for one year!

But this case was by no means over. The wrangle between the two parishes continued. At a third hearing in 1653 we find that Elizabeth Petticrew had been removed to High Roding but had then quietly absconded to the house 'of one Crowe' in High Easter. The court now had to decide if she was there as an inmate or a housekeeper. Of the 'father' and the child we hear no more. It looks as though the unfortunate Elizabeth avoided the dreaded penalty of correction, and it is at this indecisive point that her ordeal vanishes into silence. Hopefully, she was finally left in peace.

High Roding probably took its name from being the principal village, perhaps the first to be settled. It is certainly the most conspicuous, being mainly two long rows of houses along a Roman road. Scarfe calls it 'a medieval ribbon-development'. Virtually every property repays close study.

If you head out of the village street in the direction of Dunmow, you will come to a finger-post which points to a hamlet with a strikingly unusual name, Pharisee Green.

Place-names in Essex with 'Green' in them are legion. They frequently denote clearings in the forest which once covered much of the county. 'Pharisee Green' may be thought to have a biblical ring, an odd, satirical comment, perhaps, on its inhabitants of long ago. But this is not, of course, the explanation. On their map of 1777 Chapman and André marked it as 'Fairs Green', which brings us closer to the original if ambiguous meaning. But there is no evidence to my knowledge that a fair was ever held here. There would be no necessity, with the thriving market once held close by in Great Dunmow. However, an obsolete Essex word may give us a clue. In the revised edition of Gepp's *Essex Dialect Dictionary*, (1969), 'Pharisees' is given as meaning 'fairies', an expression which lingered on into recent times in the Brightlingsea district. In Pharisee Green, then, we could have one of those rare names which derive from local folklore. Unfortunately, I have not been able to trace the name here back beyond the late eighteenth century. Morant does not mention it, nor is it shown on the map of the Dunmow Hundred in his great work. So just how old the name is remains a puzzle. But there is a further complication, as so often occurs in elucidating place-names. It is quite possible that 'Pharisee' is a corruption of 'Fairs', pronounced as 'Fairsee'. Moreover, this could ultimately come from an Old English word for pig, 'fearth'. Unlikely as this may seem, there is a parallel at Felsted across country, for there 'Fairy Hall' is certainly derived this way.

The hamlet is down a no-through road, the first lane on the left past that to Bacon End. In open, level country it has at least four or five interesting houses worth the diversion.

The very first to be seen is Pharisee House on the left, isolated at the end of a lengthy drive. It is a long, impressive house, with a dominant central section which has two prominent white gables. Above the dormer windows an attractive miniature turret stands out against the sky. Its age is difficult to make out from a distance. Despite a Tudor-like appearance, this house, unlike the others, is not shown on Chapman's map.

Further along the way is Bedfords, a family name which has been traced back to 1341. The old gatehouse has a pond in front and a small thatched dwelling by the gate.

A few yards further on the lane comes to a T-junction. To the left is a private road leading to a farmhouse called Tanners. Like Pharisee House, it stands alone against an open skyline. This is certainly of the sixteenth or seventeenth century at least. One side of its roof slopes almost to ground level, a catslide. By the house is a tall and gaunt black barn, and just beyond that a pond. A 'Tanners' stood here in 1476 and has been associated with a Richard

Tannere living in this place a century before that.

Going back to the junction, the road leads through the fields to another ancient farmhouse. This is 'Minchins'. This obscure name comes from the ancient 'myncen', meaning a nun. The name at this spot is explained by the fact that the Augustinian nuns of Clerkenwell Priory in London held hereabouts a virgate of land, about thirty acres. Their male counterparts had the priory in Little Dunmow just $2\frac{1}{2}$ miles away. The original holding of the nuns here, which they acquired as free alms in the twelfth century and which was added to later, had been previously held by a layman who obtained it through trial by battle at Oxford. The nuns were granted properties in fifteen other places in Essex.

In the sixteenth century, after the seizure of all monastic lands, Minchins came into the possession of the Glascock family, who had it until late next century. William Glascock left £20 to employ poor people of Dunmow in spinning. The house was formerly moated and the interior has been much altered down the years. Not so far to the west, near Puttocks Green, another house is styled 'Minchams'.

Pharisee Green has neither church nor pub. For these you have to return to High Roding, where, for refreshment, you have the choice between the highly picturesque, timbered Black Lion or the simpler, more intimate Old Lamb. But while in the area a visit to Bacon End, or Beacon End as it formerly was, should not be missed.

Turning off from the B184, you will meet one delightful house after another. You should take the road from Bacon End itself to the point where Highcross Lane East finally comes to the A120 which runs between Bishops Stortford and Great Dunmow. Watch out on your left for such houses as Stomps, Fairhaven, Cranberry Cottage, The Elms and Hobbs, which is superbly thatched. On the right, Woodlands deserves a special mention. All have been cared for with deep pride. The wayside is particularly appealing by Bacon End Green, for here is a stretch lined with decorative trees including fine cedars and Scots pines. Almost at the end of this journey is yet another lovely house which comes into view. Newlands is set well back from the lane. Like some other country places with this name, it may go back to when the land was newly taken in from the forest and laid beneath the plough.

When you get to the main road, the spell of this route is likely to be broken. But across the way is the southern perimeter of what was a great estate, the ancient seat of the Maynard family. To discover that portion of the past you must travel round through Dunmow.

5

Easton Lodge and the Maynards

In the heart of the Essex countryside near Dunmow, the village of Little Easton is one of those places which looks and feels more isolated than it really is. In fact it is just off the main highway but it gets relatively few visitors for much of the year. Yet those who elect to follow the signpost cannot fail to be delighted.

This is very clearly an estate village. The road which leads towards the church, or rather the more direct road of the two, has charming 'agricultural' houses along the way, some of which are marked with a plate bearing a leaping stag and the bold letter 'M', a badge denoting they were once inhabited by tenants of the ancient Maynard family.

The church, a mile from the village, is a very fine one, mainly Perpendicular in style and with some remnants of its Norman origins. It is full of absorbing interest, a church to linger in and go back to time and again. Among its treasures are fading wall-paintings of the twelfth and fifteenth centuries, tomb chests, brasses and a remarkably tiny effigy of a medieval knight, a curiosity indeed.

Close by beyond the churchyard wall is a lovely group of buildings dated 1624. This is Little Easton Manor, recreated in the 1920s by the stage and film producer the late Basil Dean. They form an enticing setting looked at through the ornamental gates. With stately trees and topiary work, the gardens are opened to the public once or twice a year.

But, above all, it is what cannot now be easily seen which gives to this tranquil place of Little Easton an extra dimension of meaning. To take the road to the edge of the grounds of Easton Lodge is to follow a memory lane. For here in a once splendid landscape stood one of the most important houses in the county, the home of a family of more than local significance.

Little Easton Manor

The history of the Essex branch of the Maynard family began in 1590, when Elizabeth granted the manor of Estaines Parva to Henry Maynard Esquire. He was private secretary to Lord Burleigh and for many years the MP for St Albans. Sir Henry decided to build his residence on the site of an old hunting lodge. It was in this way that Easton Lodge became the family seat rather than the medieval manor home then in a ruinous condition. Sir Henry Maynard died in 1610 and was interred in the south chancel chapel of the church. His alabaster tomb has effigies of himself, his wife and their ten children.

His heir, William, was the first Lord Maynard, being made the Baron of Estaines Parva in 1628 by James I. His second wife was the only daughter and heiress of Sir Antony Everard, who lived at Langleys in Great Waltham. Among the many offices Sir William held was that of Lord Lieutenant of the county. He died in 1640 from a sudden fever. His wife lamented that the times had 'curdled all the

summer in his blood'. Like his father, he is remembered by a
fine monument in the church, on which he is portrayed as a
Roman commander with his wife as matron. Part of the Latin
inscription reads, 'when the madness of the fanatics daily
increased, when even religion itself was banished, then he
bid adieu to a restless, rebellious and ungrateful country'.
An inventory of the Lodge made in his lifetime has survived.

The second Baron Maynard, also a William, was
impeached and twice imprisoned by Cromwell. However, he
fared well at the Restoration. He was married twice, his
second wife being a close friend of Thomas Ken, rector of
the parish. Ken later became the Bishop of Bath and Wells
and is celebrated for his contributions to hymnology.

Moving quickly down the years, the last of the Maynards
to hold the title of Baron was the fifth Charles. He became,
however, the first of the Viscounts of the family. Unmarried,
his life ended in 1775 at the age of eighty-five.

Two eighteenth-century diaries have interesting entries on
Easton Lodge. The first of the two, very short, dates from
June 1759 and was written by the Rev. William Cooper,
curate of Thaxted. He gives a short sketch of the then Lord
Maynard and this description of the estate:

> Easton Lodge is situated in a very large and extensive park
> containing upward of three hundred head of deer. From the
> dining room windows you have a most noble and delightful
> prospect. The romantic Tilty (for so it properly may be called)
> adds not a little to the grandeur of the scene. Although Easton
> Lodge is very judiciously laid out, yet the chapel, which
> contains some paintings wonderfully well executed upon glass
> and the library, which contains a very fine collection of books,
> are best deserving the notice of the curious.

The reference to 'romantic Tilty' is to the ruins of the
Cistercian abbey which could be seen across country;
perhaps there was more to be seen than now.

The chapel which the curate so admired dated from 1621.
Its six panels of painted glass in the east window were to
survive the disastrous fire of 1847, rescued along with the
choice wines stored 'in groined cellars under the library'. Six
ancient benches were also saved and placed in Thaxted

church; the Maynards were its patrons. The rare glass is now in the windows of the Maynard Chapel in the parish church, donated by the last Viscount Maynard in memory of his wife. (The beautiful eighteenth-century wrought-iron screen to the chapel was formerly a gate at the Lodge.) The panels of glass are of the early 1600s. South German in style, they depict scenes from the life of Christ.

The Rev. Cooper was well acquainted with Lord Charles Maynard, and his enthusiastic, even fulsome, account of the estate is perhaps explained by his candid remark, 'I agreeably spent my time with those whose integrity and good sense might be of service to me in my further progress through the world.' That would make a suitable epitaph for a snob.

He is cutting in his observations on lesser fry. After styling Maynard's two chaplains 'my particular friends', he proceeds to put them down as follows: 'Mr Pinsent lives in the house and is a constant companion to Lord Maynard; he talks little but eats much; the fat of his Lordship's venison has fed him to a very considerable size. Mr. Forester is a very good-natured well-bred man, not over-stocked with polite literature, yet serves properly enough for the office of a country rector.' The diarist goes on to note that the rector's house is in the park, where he has in his garden 'a very pleasant arbour in which he sometimes reads a piece of divinity, sometimes a newspaper; also a fish pond well supplied with Tench, which however he is not remarkably expert in catching'.

The Maldon miller, John Crozier, entered a short account in his diary of a visit he made with some others to Easton Lodge in May 1786: 'The house is very ancient, of no form of elegance; the views from it are fine and the gardens and park modern and pretty, except in one part of the garden; there is a large kind of rotunda, first formed by making a frame of wood, and then planted outside with hardbeam or some such trees which have entirely grown over this model and forms arches within the alcoves and altogether is one of the sweetest bowers I ever saw.' Crozier, whose diary I refer to several times again in these pages, much appreciated his reception at the Lodge. The family were obviously away at the time, leaving their stately home open to visitors. 'I cannot but mention the gentility of the steward and housekeeper who, after showing us every part of the house, treated us in their own apartment with cake and wine.'

The third and last Viscount was Sir Henry Maynard. He was the son of the Rev. Henry Maynard, rector of Radwinter and vicar of Thaxted, and nephew of the second Viscount. Like his forebears he was Lord Lieutenant of Essex, an office he held for forty years.

In 1847 Easton Lodge was rebuilt to the designs of the architect Thomas Hopper after the fire which had destroyed the greater part of the old house. Among the rarities lost were the majority of the grave goods which had been excavated from the Bartlow Hills at Ashdon.

When Sir Henry died in 1865, there was no male heir, for his son had died four months before him. So he left the Easton estate to his granddaughter, Frances Evelyn Maynard. She was just under four years old when she inherited, and until she came of age the estate was of course managed by trustees.

One of the most intriguing women of her generation, Frances in her earlier years was a noted Edwardian beauty, as photographs and her memorial bust in the village church clearly show. She quickly established herself as a bewitching hostess. She was also to achieve the dubious fame of becoming an intimate of Edward VII. Later she earned more public notoriety as a convert to Socialism.

She was born in 1861. Her father was the Hon. Charles Maynard, son of the third Viscount, while her mother, a Fitzroy, was descended on both sides from Charles II. Upon the death of Charles Maynard, her mother re-married. Frances' stepfather was Lord Rosslyn, who turned the Lodge into a glittering centre of Victorian society. At fifteen Frances was earmarked by the ageing Disraeli for marriage to the Duke of Albany, Prince Leopold, the youngest son of Queen Victoria. Eventually a formal offer of betrothal came from the Palace, but it was declined by the Maynards, to the relief it seems of both Frances and the Prince. Instead she met and later married an equerry, Lord Brooke. The wedding took place in 1881 in the Henry VII Chapel at Westminster Abbey. It was one of the great social events of the year: ten members of the royal family were present, including Edward and his wife Alexandra. Three years later Frances' husband became the fifth Earl of Warwick, and in 1885 they took up residence in the great castle. Their marriage was to last until 1924, when the Earl died.

Frances became a regular member of the celebrated Marlborough House Set. Before her liaison with the Prince of Wales developed, she was involved with Lord Charles Beresford, an affair which narrowly missed becoming an open scandal. It was after the relationship between Edward and 'Jersey' Lillie Langtry began to cool that Frances took priority in the affections of the heir to the throne. They remained close for around nine years. (Her 'successor' was the Hon. Mrs Kepple, whose daughter Violet was to have a tempestuous affair with Vita Sackville-West.) Edward was a frequent guest at Easton Lodge and often walked with Frances across the park to attend Sunday worship in the parish church.

The Countess wrote two volumes of memoirs, more in the nature of rambling reminiscences and meditations than closely thought-out autobiographies. Most of the archives at the Lodge were destroyed in a fire in 1918, and she claimed that the loss of her more personal documents had made precise narrative impossible. The first of her memoirs, *Life's Ebb and Flow*, was published in 1929. This was followed in 1931 by *Afterthoughts*, which has passing references to the Easton estate.

Her love for the place amounted to a passion. The house then stood in a square mile of parkland. For much of the time after leaving Warwick she lived in one wing of the house. As early as 1914 her extravagant mode of life had plunged her into crippling debts but later her finances recovered, although she had to be careful. She was to claim, too, that she had been the victim of a massive swindle. Her difficulties were such that she was forced to part with the collection of pictures at Easton. There were sixty-two offered for sale by auction at Sotheby's in November 1934. Many were family portraits. The others included two of Charles I and paintings of notabilities of the seventeenth and eighteenth centuries. Only £1,147 was realized, each painting going on average for £18. A picture of a white horse fetched the highest price, outdoing works by Lely and Kneller.

In the 1920s and thirties Lady Warwick regarded the Lodge as the Chequers of the Labour Party, politicians and Trade Unionists frequently gathering there. She had a vision of the house becoming a 'People's University' but the General Strike aborted the plans.

The grounds were noted for peacocks and deer. In her younger days she had enjoyed hunting, but she later rejected its 'aristocratic' image. She preferred to ride through the woods, in which no snares were allowed.

In a remote corner of the Park were the remains of a house, Stone Hall, thought to be of medieval date. It is marked on Chapman's map of 1777. A house still bearing the name exists on the same spot to the north of Canfield End. Around it Frances created a 'Garden of Friendship'. Here, by its lawn with a yew-tree sundial, she encouraged her friends to plant trees, shrubs and flowers, each staked with the name of the giver. Some of the trees were planted by Edward when he was Prince of Wales. Stone Hall itself, a 'little Elizabethan pleasure house', was decorated and furnished by Frances as a discreet place of assignations for her guests.

The Countess also kept a bird sanctuary and a monkey house. When she died in 1938, she left thirteen dogs and five hundred assorted birds to her housekeeper, who, in her turn, gave over two hundred budgerigars and canaries to the RSPCA. The rest she kept with her at her cottage on the estate.

Few traces of these things remain. The Park was virtually obliterated by the construction of an American bomber base in the last war. Twelve thousand trees were uprooted from the deer park! The great airfield has thankfully gone, the concrete of its runways now lying under the Brentwood bypass. Today the estate is farmland owned by Mrs Felice Spurrier, the daughter of the Hon. Greville Maynard, the only son of Frances. The Lodge itself, which had been requisitioned and ill used in the war, went in 1948 after yet another fire two years before. The way to the former parkland is now barred, and notices leave one in no doubt that entry is forbidden. However, there is a footpath from the south on the Dunmow-Bishops Stortford road. Here a gatehouse can be seen and by its side a small memorial to the American Air Force.

It was also nearby, at Little Canfield, that Lady Warwick had her own railway station built in the spacious days. The branch line, 'the Dunmow Flyer', is now disused.

In Frances' time Little Easton was a haven for celebrities. They put the little village on the map. On at least one occasion W.G. Grace played cricket at the Lodge. Ellen Terry was a frequent guest, reciting and acting in the lovely Barn Theatre which stands in the grounds of the Manor. A portrait of her, unnamed, hangs just inside the barn door, and another reminder of her love for the place is the memorial plaque in the church. Elinor Glyn also visited Frances. A red-haired, exotic beauty, she is chiefly remembered for her then sensational *Three Weeks* (1907) and other 'tiger-skin' novels. The character of Lady Tilchester in *The Reflections of Ambrosine* (1902) was modelled upon Frances.

In 1913 the Barn was hired from Lady Warwick by the Dunmow Progressive Club, who put on two plays in the summer of that year. From 1928 performances were staged by the Barn Theatre Committee with Frances as its President. Many local people were involved in these productions. Basil Dean took over the Barn as a repertory theatre in 1932, and its use as a place of occasional entertainment has continued to today.

'There were giants in the earth in those days.' There were those of the mighty initials GBS and GKC. When *St Joan* was first produced, Shaw dined with H.G. Wells at the Lodge. It was in 1912 that Wells came to the estate to live at the Old Rectory, the Glebe, the Georgian house near the two ponds. Here he wrote a number of his books, including the novel *Mr Britling Sees It Through* and his huge *Outline of History*. He remained for over seventeen years until shortly after the death of his second wife, Catherine, in the autumn of 1927, a tragedy made all the more poignant by their son's wedding in Dunmow the very day after.

G.K. Chesterton was frequently at the Glebe. He and Wells designed a toy theatre, a passion they had in common, and they used it to perform rumbustious satires on the Poor Law Commission. When Charlie Chaplin came to dinner at the big house, he also went across to the Glebe, where, with Wells, Catherine and Lady Frances, he played charades.

Other literary guests included Arnold Bennett, Dorothy Richardson, noted for her *Pilgrimage* and *The Tunnel*, Philip Guedalla, the historian and biographer, who leased 'The Laundry' on the estate, and H. de Vere Stacpoole, author of *The Blue Lagoon*. He lived at Stebbing, where he wrote *The Story of My Village* in 1946.

The countryside writer S.L. Bensusan was often at the Lodge. He ghosted much of the Countess's writing. The notorious Frank Harris briefly appeared on the scene, *en route*, and on the run, from Paris to the USA. Oscar Wilde had said of him, 'Frank Harris has been received in all the great houses – once!' Mercifully, Frances' name does not appear in his *Life and Loves*, although she could be the 'lady with a title' in the chapter on Prince Edward. Harris does not figure in her *Afterthoughts* either.

Gustav Holst was also known at Easton Lodge, travelling over from his home in Thaxted. And Kingsley Martin, the renowned editor of the *New Statesman* and *Nation*, lived close by the village pub, the Stag. Its friendly publican, Ken French, has been here over thirty years. His house of call has seen many a famous face, Michael Dennison and Dulcie Gray among them. Wells he never saw, but his chauffeur was often in for a pint. The Stag is modest indeed but marvellously rural with its uncarpeted taproom and a chocolate box for a martin's nest above the door.

Another occasional visitor to the mansion in the 1930s was Geoffrey Barber, who in his little book *Country Doctor* remembers the declining Lady Warwick with affection.

The Countess endures in local memory above all as a kindly landowner and benefactress. In her last years she was tireless in the cause of improving the lot of the agricultural worker. One of her most conspicuous acts was to open a short-lived but memorable school for the children in the villages around Dunmow.

Yet unknown to her tenants and the public at large was her attempt back in the summer of 1914 to sell to the Palace her correspondence from Edward, intimate letters full of royal confidences if not state secrets. In effect it was her silence she was selling. The inside story of this remarkable piece of intrigue, in which Frank Harris was her accomplice, has been bitingly told by Theo Lang in his book *My Darling*

Daisy. The whereabouts of these letters remains something of a mystery. They may have gone up in flames in 1918. More likely they were destroyed by Court order.

Despite this shadow over her, or perhaps partly because of it, the last of the titled Maynards, Edward's 'my own adored Daisy wife', remains a very colourful and complex character. In her final years she lived between two worlds and had no place in either. But in the words of her memorial in the church she continues to make 'a sunshine in the Shady Place'.

6

The Bell at Castle Hedingham

The inn sign of 'The Bell' was sometimes used to represent the racing trophy of a silver bell awarded up to the reign of Charles II, but in the vast majority of instances it denotes a hostelry in close proximity to the parish church. Essex examples are legion, and the ecclesiastical connection can be readily seen at such places as Purleigh, Woodham Walter and Willingale, and this is also the case at Castle Hedingham.

The Royal Commission on Historical Monuments dates the major part of this L-shaped home from the latter half of the sixteenth century. The earliest reference to it as the Bell is on a plan of 1592, where it is marked by name. Behind the plain façade there are many old beams, although the interior has been much changed down the years. Outside, the sign is displayed in an ornamental iron frame, of sufficient merit to have been noted by Miller Christy in his *Trade Signs of Essex* of 1887. But perhaps the chief attraction, a totally unexpected feature, is the old Assembly Room upstairs at the back. As a result of the enthusiasm of the licensee, Sandra Ferguson, this has been beautifully restored and given a Georgian elegance. Beneath the barrel-vault ceiling, it is once again the setting for entertainment as it was late in the eighteenth century.

The Bell was formerly very much a focal point for the commercial and social life of the district. In the 1700s it was customary for the Trustees of Yeldham Grammar School to meet here. It served, too, as a political centre for the local Tories, notably the Hinckford Hundred Conservative Club, often the subject of leaders in *The Times*. In 1849 Disraeli, then joint leader of the Tory opposition in the Commons, addressed a rally in the Assembly Room before attending a banquet in his honour in the great hall of the Castle.

The Bell, Castle Hedingham

The inn was the appropriate meeting place each year for the hop-dealers who also gathered annually on Crouch Green, the site of the ancient market place and fair. A Press advertisement dated 31 July 1787 reads:

> This is to give Notice, that the annual HOP-MEETING will be as usual, at Joseph Tomlinson's, at the BELL INN, on Monday the 6th of August next. All gentlemen that favour him with their company will much oblige their humble servant.
>
> Joseph Tomlinson
>
> Dinner at Two o'clock.

Joseph Tomlinson was the publican for thirty-two years, from 1772 to 1804, the year before Trafalgar.

The licensees of those far-off days are now solely names. In the mid-nineteenth century one landlord, a James Knight, was also a wine and spirit merchant. A few years later a woman with the uncommon name of Frances Bangs Newdick ran the hostelry. Auctions were also frequently held on the premises (to as late as the 1920s), when the house was styled 'The Bell Hotel'. Much more intriguingly, at the turn of the century the widow of the publican requested the exhumation of his body, but neither her reason nor the outcome is known.

The growing of hops in the two Hedinghams can be traced back to the sixteenth century. Both parishes provided the finest crops in Essex, rivalled only by the hops produced in the nearby Maplesteads. By 1790 some two hundred acres were devoted to the cultivation of hops in Castle and Sible Hedingham. Four hundred poles per acre were needed each year, so many spinneys of ash and chestnut were planted. There were forty acres of these in Castle Hedingham. Lewis Majendie at the Castle, noted as a botanist and a member of the Society of Arts, reclaimed the Marsh, using it for hops as well as creating a fine promenade there. For a while hop production at Hedingham was a very lucrative if mainly part-time occupation, profits sometimes soaring to four hundred per cent a year.

In the eighteenth century the Bell was possibly the scene for theatrical performances. A notice in the *Chelmsford Chronicle* for April 1777 told its readers: 'At the Theatre in Castle Hedingham on Sat April 12 will be presented a new Comedy called The Maid of the Oaks, with all the music, scenery, dresses and decorations incidental to the piece as performed thirty nights successively at the Theatre Royal, Drury Lane. To which will be added a Farce call'd The Deuce in Him – Boxes 3s, Pit 2s, Gallery 1s. To begin at exactly 7 o'clock. On Monday Romeo and Juliet.' These plays may have been performed by the circuit players of the Norwich Company who are known to have visited other Essex towns. As no building or site has been identified as such at Castle Hedingham, perhaps 'the Theatre' was an *ad hoc* arrangement in the Bell yard, for the modest dimensions of the Assembly Room cannot be visualized with boxes, a pit and a gallery.

As well as for club meetings and the like, the Room was used for balls and concerts. A notice of 1794 gives these details:

MUSIC

To be performed at the Assembly Room, Castle Hedingham

Consisting of

Overtures, Concertoes, Songs, etc.

Several selected airs will be performed on the Musical Glasses.
The concert will begin at 7 o'clock, after which there will be a ball.
N.B. The moon will be favourable to those who come from a distance, being then at the full.
Tickets 5s each.

In the 1760s Arthur Young, 'the father of modern agriculture' and a keen observer of the rural scene, found the Bell to be 'clean and reasonable', although he deplored the deterioration in the local roads. The inn was a stopping place for the 'old Bury coach'. A coloured print of around 1800 depicted that of John Wood's Sudbury, Hedingham and Braintree 'machine'.

It was in the second half of the eighteenth century that the publican of the Bell began to operate a post-chaise service. This facility became widespread in the remoter parts of the county as the regular coach services dropped many of the smaller staging posts from their routes.

Although today the Bell is no longer a hostelry in the strict sense, it continues as a Grays house its long tradition of excellent hospitality to the traveller.

7

Dynes Hall

The first time I came upon Dynes Hall, I had been on a visit to Castle Hedingham and then on to Halstead to sample its architectural delights, for I had only driven straight through before. Having 'done' the more obvious sights in the town along the climbing High Street, far too quickly I'm afraid to do them justice, I then acted on an impulse on my way out. I chose at random a road I had never followed before. I have long since found this to be the most rewarding way of making discoveries in the countryside, 'for where all before you is unknown, all things are possible', obeying the sudden thought, 'What lies down there?' These casual, on the spur of the moment excursions can yield surprises, rather like those we have on dipping into books.

Dynes Hall at Great Maplestead is a country house of great charm and has had a long and distinguished past.

It stands in the corner of a quiet parish. Among the more minor attractions to be savoured here is the teasing name of Toddishall Cottages. More grandly this was Tolldish Hall in the 1700s. Tradition has it the house was so named because of a miller who took toll of the sacks of wheat he received, but I suspect this could be a nice piece of imaginative etymology.

The name 'Dynes' comes from the medieval lords of the manor. The house as it is today dates mainly from the late seventeenth century. It lies a mile south of the parish church, set back off the winding lane which links with the A604 at Doe's Corner near Halstead. In undulating country the position is a commanding one, for the Hall looks over park and farmland sloping to the valley of the Colne. Privately owned, the estate is not accessible to the public but there are fine views from the entrance to the drive and from the

Dynes Hall, Great Maplestead

roadside when the leaves fall. I did walk right up to the house without being shot. The owner came out to meet me, or more correctly I should say to confront me. At first he was suspicious, perhaps rightly so. We were seemingly the only two souls in that wide landscape, though the sound of a tractor came from afar. However, we were soon chatting freely.

The mansion has all the distinctive features and elegance we associate with the Queen Anne style. Its façade is beautifully framed by lawns and there is an ornamental garden beneath a walled terrace.

A previous house on the site was bought in 1575 by William Deane. A man of substance, he came from the north to be the steward of Lady Malltravers at Gosfield Hall. They later married, an unusual if not totally uneven match. By the time of his death in 1585, he had rebuilt Dynes Hall. Married twice, he was succeeded by his son John, who was knighted in 1603, the year of James I's accession. Among his civic offices Sir John served as Lord Lieutenant of the county. When he died, a fine wall monument was erected to his memory in the parish church, St Giles. Dating from 1625, his effigy reclines in an arched recess. The figure is shown in plate armour. His head rests on his hand, the 'tooth-ache' position, and his feet are on the family crest, a muzzled bear's head. On a shelf above, his family are represented with small figures: his widow, two sons and four daughters.

Even more notable in the mortuary chapel is the

monument there to his wife. Its central feature is her effigy,
thought to be a true likeness, standing in the gloom of the
family chapel 'impressive and ghostly' in a shroud or
widows weeds. A long inscription reads as a litany of her
virtues:

> Her shape was rare, her beauty exquisite
> Her wytt acurate, her judgment singular
> Her entertaynment hearty, her conversation lovely
> Her heart merciful, her hand helpful
> Her courses modest, her discourses wise
> Her charity heavenly, her amity constant
> Her practice holy, her religion pure
> Her vows lawful, her meditations divine
> Her faith unfaynged, her hope stable
> Her prayers devout, her devotions diurnal
> Her days short, her life everlasting.

How one wants to learn more of this lady after that. Her
passing must have dimmed the life of the parish. The
monument was erected by her son in 1634. The work of
William Wright of Charing Cross, it is one of a number of
superb funereal pieces he made. Both the Deane memorials
were restored to their original colours in 1961 by the then
owner of the Hall, Mr J.A. Hart.

In 1667 the Elizabethan manor house was purchased by
Mark Guyon, who came from a very wealthy family of
Coggeshall clothiers. He was knighted by Charles II and in
1689 he started to reconstruct most of the house, giving it
the look it has now.

Sir Mark died in 1690 and his only son the following year.
Through marriage the estate passed to the Bullock family.
Then, around 1765, it was acquired by the Sperlings. Like
the Guyons they were merchants, fur traders, who bought
their way like many another into the ranks of lesser gentry.
Swedish in origin, they had lived at Chigwell to be near the
London centre of their business before moving to Great
Maplestead. They were to remain here for some 150 years.
Along with the Hall, its five hundred acres and its wooded
park, they also held the lordship of the manor. Like the
Deanes they have left their mark on the church with

numerous wall tablets and stained glass. Of the former one is to the memory of the Rev. James Sperling who died in 1850 after being the vicar for fifty-three years. Another is to Lieutenant Charles Auriol Sperling, who was killed at the Battle of Jutland.

One of the Sperling girls, Diana, suddenly became of some note in 1981 with the publication of two of her three surviving sketchbooks. These contain seventy watercolours, impressions of family life at Dynes Hall and elsewhere, and have been reproduced under the title of *Mrs Hurst Dancing and other Sketches of Regency Life 1812-1823*. Diana, a daughter of John Sperling, spent over forty years of her life at the Hall before her marriage in 1834. She lived to the age of seventy. Her miniatures are a delight. Many look as though a curtain has just been raised to catch a moment in a play or pantomime. Full of gaiety and verve, much of the appeal comes from the eccentricity of the figure drawing. As pictorial comment, along with her own concise and often satirical captions, such as 'Mrs Van murdering a spider', they give us a peepshow into an order of life akin to that in the novels of Jane Austen. One of the paintings shows a little boathouse of thatch and reeds by the lake made in the time of the family. Another shows a stone kiosk in the grounds, grandly and perhaps ironically styled 'The Temple'.

She must have known the truth about a local tradition, that under a plain stone without any inscription lying in the church nave a King of the Gypsies is buried. It is said that, for many years after, his daughters came to visit his grave.

Dynes Hall is no more an ancestral home. The Sperlings have long gone but the house has not survived as an empty shell. With all the prestige conferred by its looks, its location and its past, it remains a home, a living place, which happily in the years to come may add yet more engaging figures to the landscape.

8

Berden and the Crump

I first went to Berden in search of the Crump, having come across this very peculiar name in a guidebook to the county. It was apparently the title of a pair of cottages. It turned out to be even more curious than that.

Berden is away in the north-west corner of Essex very close to the border with Hertfordshire. The land here rises to over four hundred feet, and the tiny village is in a steep, narrow valley, one which you almost plunge into. In the census of 1971 the population of the parish came to no more than 289. Up to the time of enclosures in the eighteenth century the village stood among vast fields with many scattered strips, a late survival of the distinctively medieval type of farming. Now in our time the removal of hedgerows is again giving the land a very open and rolling look.

The parish church has a thirteenth-century chancel and a fourteenth-century tower. It was brutally 'restored' in 1868. But I find its chief interest in its dedication to St Nicholas, the original Santa Claus. The church is one of the twelve in Essex which bears his name. He was a very popular saint in western Christendom from the eleventh century, the patron of such diverse groups as children, sailors, merchants and pawnbrokers.

St Nicholas was a fourth-century bishop of Myra in Asia Minor but his relics were stolen from there by Italian merchants in 1087 and transferred to Bari on the Adriatic. The mystic number 'three' dominates the legends around him. He is said to have saved three girls from prostitution by throwing three bags of gold through their window one night. These bags or purses became the emblematic gold balls of the money-lenders. One of the saint's many miracles, worked even from the cradle, was to restore to life three children

'The Crump' at Berden

murdered and concealed in a brine tub. In 1969 Pope Paul VI removed his name from the Roman calendar of the saints. Other dubious figures to go included two of immense popularity, St George and St Christopher.

The church at Berden is one of that rare number to have perpetuated in our century the trappings of an ancient custom, the ceremony of 'the Boy Bishop'. (It is also kept at Par in Cornwall.) This was one of those colourful and venerable traditions suppressed at the Reformation. As originally kept on the feast day of St Nicholas, 6 December, a chorister was elected by his fellows as a mock bishop. He held the office for three weeks, with two others who acted as deacons, yet another variation on the archetypal 'three'. The mitred 'bishop' went in solemn procession to the church and presided over the service. Afterwards with his aides he went from door to door in the village singing and collecting the diocesan subsidy. Here at Berden the ceremony was introduced at the turn of the century as an innovation and was enacted each year until 1936. The cross and the staff were specially made and can still be seen in the church. In more recent years the custom has been revived several times, but it has been in abeyance since 1966.

The manor house by the church, Berden Hall, has a seventeenth-century date on a rainwater head. However, this impressive brick-built house is mainly Elizabethan. It is particularly noted for a very fine staircase.

But the chief visual attraction, on the north of the village, is a superb timber-framed farmhouse, also Elizabethan. This is the priory, and it stands on the land of a monastery founded around 1214 for the Augustinian friars. Before that there had been a hospice here.

Of all the old monastic houses of Essex, the Austin canons held the most of any Order. They were very active in going out and about among the people and were particularly involved in areas where there was not at first a church. Their centre at Berden was a small and poor establishment. It was dedicated to St John the Evangelist. Little is known of its history, but a major and traumatic event occurred in 1300 with the almost total destruction of its buildings by fire. Yet although small it must have been highly regarded, for twenty-one bishops appealed for the restoration of the priory. And as an inducement they granted a forty-day indulgence or remission of sins to all who helped in the work. Apart from that, about all we know is that a few years later the abbot of Walden became the monastery's patron. A post-Reformation map of 1600 shows a dovehouse at the priory and the layout of the gardens there at that time. On a yet later map there is a hornbeam grove behind the house. An antiquity which remains is a wellhouse with a treadmill once used to draw the water from a depth of 150 feet.

It was while admiring the house, a photographer's delight, that I was approached by the farmer. Had it not been for this genial man, I doubt if I should have found the elusive Crump, for at that time it was not marked as such on the map. From the farmer, too, I learned what it really was. Local people, especially those with roots in the district, are so often that much more informative than outsiders. Above all they know the minute things which make up the soul of a place.

The Crump lies well away from the village on the lane to Brick House End. (On the way a signpost points to Little

London, one of several in the county which seemed to have been named in ironic jest.) The two white cottages styled 'The Crump' are a sheer delight. Side by side at right angles, they stand alone in the countryside surrounded by lovely gardens. Both are thatched and with exposed beams. They form a single home and are straight out of that dream of an England which perhaps never was. They bear no name upon their doors or on the gate, but the place can readily be found by looking out for the small red Victorian postbox which stands opposite. Yet the cottages are not the Crump itself. That lies well hidden and inaccessible to the rear, an enigma in the garden.

The old English word crump means 'crooked'. It was used in the eighteenth century for a crooked person, a hunchback. It is perhaps more familiar to us from the line 'the cow with the crumpled horn' in 'The House that Jack Built'.

Here at Berden the Crump is a concealed and overgrown mound, a small circular earthwork some ten feet in height and with a diameter of 123 feet. There is a depression within, and it is surrounded by a ditch probably of a defensive nature. The origin and date of this odd 'hump' remain unknown but it is possibly prehistoric. According to the farmer at the priory, there was another of a similar type on farmland in the parish some years ago but it was levelled by bulldozers.

The mound mentioned in Methuen's *Little Guide to Essex* (7th ed. 1952) as being at Stocks Farm is in fact the Crump. A map of the whole parish dated 1783 'Taken by Order of the Worshipful the Governors of Christs' Hospital London' shows two fields marked 'Thos. Stock' in one of which is the moated mound. It indicates as well a little road along the southern side of the cottages and leading to a block of fields made up of strips. This has become a footpath with vestiges of a green lane. The map also shows a moated copse in the immediate area, directly across the fields in line with the lane which turns off to Little London. This is probably the one which was removed from the landscape. Another map from the same century gives Brickhouse Farm as part of Christ's Hospital estate.

Since the Crump is now protected in a garden, its future seems assured. It is now also marked by name and not just by a symbol on the latest Ordnance Survey map. Those who decide to visit this charming spot should, however, keep in mind that its teasing antiquity is very much on private land, where, undisturbed, it keeps its ancient secret still.

9

Greensted juxta Ongar

For Greensted I return to where most of these 'heartland' discoveries began, in the vicinity of Ongar. No writer on Essex worth his salt has left out the Saxon church of Greensted. It is and hopefully will ever stay a rural treasure without equal, a 'green place' which its name still testifies.

It would seem that after all the tributes there could be few indeed in the county now who know nothing of the little nave of wooden walls, unique, the sole one of its kind in England. Indeed, its fame has gone out far abroad, as the visitors' book will eloquently show. But the times, I fear, they are a changing, for I continue to meet many, especially among the urban young in southern Essex, who have not heard it stands here, let alone seen and savoured this ancient place. Moreover, although the main facts have been well written up in popular guides, there are odd corners in its story which seldom get a telling. So I make no apology in including in these pages this celebrity of our landscape. Writing about the past and its alliance with the present is an act of constant renewal and recovery.

It is Greensted juxta Ongar to avoid confusion with the other, Greenstead by Colchester. There is also, you will note, a slight difference in the spelling.

Greensted is about a mile from Chipping Ongar, along the lane which branches from the lower end of Ongar's high street. Because of its proximity to the town, Greensted in the Middle Ages was styled 'By Aungre atte Castell' – 'Ongar at the Castle', the castle of Richard de Lucy, the mound of which remains.

I find the name 'Greensted' of interest in itself. 'Gernesteda' in the Domesday Book, it reached its present form by 1236 (Greenstead near Colchester appears earlier in

St Andrew's, Greensted juxta Ongar

the records, in the tenth century). This is surely an odd name
to give a place when just about everywhere else would have
been green with woods and fields. Almost certainly the 'sted'
was not just 'place' but had a precise application which is
lost to us. Perhaps then it was a wooded spot, a remnant of
primeval forest surrounded by farmland. Another possibility is a green, a clearing, for there is a Greensted Green
here to the west.

Greensted is barely a hamlet. Apart from several lone
houses, its heart is that customary Essex grouping of church,
hall and farm, standing here upon the Essex Way, the
long-distance 'footpath' running from Epping to Dedham.
Here, too, we are on the route followed by medieval pilgrims
from London to the shrine at Bury St Edmunds.

The first sight of the church is through the little gate into
the churchyard. Most of our old parish churches bear the
tell-tale marks of their changing growth and fortunes. Here

the varying styles of the years are clearly set before our eyes at once. At first the walls we have travelled far to see look small and rather insignificant. They are dwarfed by the large expanse of roof and its dormer windows. The little tower, white weatherboards with a shingled spire, is in sharp contrast to the dark colours of the nave. At the east end is a tiny red-brick chancel. Each period stands out, so dissimilar from each other, yet holding together in a strange and peaceful harmony. All goes together, although it is beyond me to analyse why. The churchyard with its ancient trees frames it well.

It is when we walk forward for a closer view, and when we go inside, that the 'time-stained' wonder of this church becomes fully apparent. The nave, the central section, is none other than the *lignea capella*, the wooden chapel, mentioned in the old monastic records of the abbey at Bury. It marks the spot where the body of King Edmund rested overnight in 1013 on its way from London to the shrine awaiting it in Suffolk. Slain by the Danes at Hoxne, by tradition tied to a tree, done to death by arrows and then decapitated, he had been taken to London for safety. There, in the church of St Gregory, the revered body rested for three years. I say 'marks the spot' for there is a shadow of doubt these are the very walls in which the East Anglian saint lay. That the building existed before the event has become much more likely since dendro-magnetic tests in the 1960s revealed that at least some of the logs date from around 850, but whether the structure was a church in 1013 or became so later remains an open question. That it was a forest cabin which was later consecrated by virtue of St Edmund's presence strikes me as highly probable.

We know from Dugdale's *Monasticon* (ed. 1655) and other ancient sources that, 'A certain sick person at Stapleford gave houseroom to the body of the saint on the return from London, and for the cure he received (in consequence of his pious hospitality) he gave to St Edmund his manor of Stapleford.' Stapleford is some way off from Greensted, but this could mean the anonymous donor had a property there or that the body was rested at Stapleford Abbots as well.

What may be in error is to suppose that Greensted's tree-trunk church is typical of Saxon wooden churches in general. This is to infer too much from the lone survivor.

The ancient nave was competently reconstructed in 1848 by Messrs Wyatt & Brandon and the roof renewed in 1892. Two of the dormer windows are original Tudor. The Saxon roof was presumably thatched. The one here now is of open timber and in three bays. In P.H. Reaney's little book *Essex*, published in 1928, there is reproduced a drawing showing the church from the south in 1748. With just one dormer window, it has a much more rugged, even dilapidated, appearance than now.

The walls of the primitive church amaze with their look and their construction. They are made of split oak logs, not Spanish chestnut as once thought, and were doubtless hewn in the area. Sixteen line the southern wall and twenty-one the north, with three more added in the last century, filling a space where there had been a door. On the outer side each is rounded. They rise six feet from oaken sills which needed to be replaced at the general restoration. A brick plinth was also then provided. Tongued and grooved, the tree trunks were fixed by the Saxon carpenters above and below with wooden pins, and here and there the marks of the adze they used can still be seen.

The church looks even smaller once you are inside. Even on sunny days the light is dim and there is a distinct feeling in the box-like interior of being in a forest sanctuary. The dimensions, excluding the chancel, are minute: a little under thirty feet long and seventeen feet wide. It is easy to share the mood of Reginald Beckett, who, after standing here at the turn of the century, wrote in his *Romantic Essex* of 1901: 'Surely we shall recall with affectionate reverence the honest enduring labour of those old-time craftsmen, as well as the procession of chanting priests and the torches around the dead King's bier.' A carving or two can be made out in spandrels of the beams above: crowns and the head of the king watched over by a friendly wolf. A nice touch this, done when the church was restored, to commemorate the legend. A small arched panel painting of the martyred Edmund, showing a Dane dressed as a Roman soldier, is a far older memorial, dating from around 1500. It may have been part of the rood screen. The surfaces of the wooden walls seen on this side are flat. Formerly covered in plaster, they have been given a panelled look. The chancel is early

Tudor. It replaced two which had been here before, one of which seems to have been Norman. There is a priest's doorway on the south. The east end of the chancel is eighteenth century.

Although Pevsner says of the tower that its date is uncertain, others give it as seventeenth and even fourteenth century, which makes it unsure enough. Sadly, in making an entrance to it from the nave, the restorers took out the Saxon timbers. The tower has a Gothic window and has, or had when Worley wrote in 1915, two bells.

According to Mee, the wooden covers of the Bible and the Prayer Book here are from the traditional tree on which St Edmund was martyred but there is no mention of this in the fine guidebook on sale in the church. The tree fell last century, and it is said a Danish arrowhead was found embedded in it.

The church is dedicated not as one might think to St Edmund but to St Andrew. It is curious that the one at Greenstead is also a St Andrew's. There are thirty-nine churches in the diocese which bear his name, the patron of missionaries, mariners and, of course, fishermen.

The churchyard holds at least one worthy, Craven Ord, an antiquarian especially noted for his brass rubbings who died in 1832. From the churchyard you can get a fine view of the Hall. Outside it is mainly from 1875 but inside there are things much older. Although the Clees family of the 1690s have left their mark, there is some Elizabethan work including a staircase while another dates from the eighteenth century.

It is difficult to leave this spot, where time and scene are in such holy matrimony, but when you do, head for the Drill House on the road to Toot Hill. I knew it when it was a rustic pub, with a country landlord and a fierce, red fox mounted in a case above the counter of the simple bar, very much a parlour. Perhaps it was also like that when the Tolpuddle Martyrs were for a while settled in the parish before going to their final homes in Canada. Two were wed in Greensted's church in 1839. Did they know, I wonder, that the Drill (despite the sign there now, a seed-drill) was a link with the correction and drilling of young offenders? There's a Repentance Field and Cottage in the vicinity.

The old sign of a rifleman has gone but the new Drill House is a good place to call in anyhow. It has a final treat in store before you head for home or venture on along the lanes in these green lovely parts. Look above you as you order. The licensee's 'name' is very prestigious. It reads 'the Baron von Mecklenburg' – but that's another story which you must ask for on the spot.

Part III
On Eastern Byways

New Hall, Boreham

1

New Hall at Boreham

Just to the east on the old road out of Chelmsford lies the parish of Boreham. The ancient heart of the village, its church and a few period houses, is hemmed around by modern properties, and there is ribbon development for much of the way on the route to Hatfield Peverel. But beyond this road and cut off by the arterial A12, there can be seen cloistered in the distance a building stored with memories of a regal past.

Essex is not noted for stately homes, although in Audley End we have the splendid exception. Despite this the county can boast many beautiful houses of more modest proportions. Among these New Hall ranks as one of the finest. It is also very rich in history and was truly stately for so much of its time.

The present house was begun by Henry VIII a little after 1518, having acquired the site the year before. It was built on land owned by Thomas Boleyn (later to become Earl of Wiltshire) and the father of the ill-fated Anne. She was a child of ten at the time Henry acquired the Hall. In 1524 Henry kept the Feast of St George there in great style. Three years later Anne was at New Hall for the summer as one of Catherine of Aragon's ladies-in-waiting. When, in 1533, Anne's daughter Elizabeth was born, she celebrated the event with a magnificent ball in the palace. After she was beheaded in 1536, Henry seized the entire Boleyn estate. The spot was much to his liking, and the King was a frequent visitor even after the tragic end to his second marriage.

Henry called his palace Beaulieu, 'the beautiful place', and it was erected where there had been a house for centuries. 'New Hall' was certainly no new name, for as far back as 1301 a *Nova Aula* had stood there.

The manor had been given by King Harold to his college of secular canons at Waltham. Throughout the Middle Ages it was frequently used by royalty and high-ranking dignitaries, being a convenient stop-over on the route between London and the port of Harwich. Adela, betrothed to Henry I, stayed there on her way to be married. The secular priests were eventually replaced by an abbey of regular canons (monks), and the abbot of Waltham Abbey used the house at Boreham as a summer residence.

King John's bastard son, Henry, was at the hall for a time and earned himself a reputation for dissolute living under its roof. Queen Philippa, the wife of Edward III, entertained there on a grand scale. In 1350 it was in the name of the knight Sir John Shardelow. The house then passed to the Coggeshall family, who held it until 1423. They were followed by Queen Margaret of Anjou, the wife of Henry VI. Later, Edward IV held his court at the hall in 1480, an occasion marked by scandalous revelry. Thomas Butler, Earl of Ormonde, was granted the house by King Henry VII, and he seems to have rebuilt it in the style of an Irish castle. And it is Butler who provides the link with Henry VIII, for it was one of the Earl's daughters who became the mother of Thomas Boleyn.

Hardly anything is left now of Henry VIII's building, which was a large, quadrangular one, but the Tudor house which stands today is still a place of great charm. A few pieces from Henry's time remain in the basement. Much more impressive is the coat of arms, once over the gateway but now in the chapel. With a supporting dragon and a greyhound, its inscription commemorates the royal builder.

It was Henry VIII, of course, who closed the monasteries and lavished much of their wealth on his friends and supporters, creating a 'new rich' with a vested interest in the Reformation. Yet, two and a half centuries later, by one of those ironic twists of fate, New Hall became a convent, a home for refugee nuns fleeing the French Revolution. And it has remained a convent and school to this very day, with the distinction of being the second nunnery since the Reformation to be founded in Britain. The first was Bar Convent, York, 1686.

The house has seen a long procession of the high and the mighty. For two, however, their prestige was short-lived and came to an end on the executioner's block. In addition to Anne Boleyn there was Lady Jane Grey, the 'nine days queen'. She knew the hall as a guest of Mary Tudor.

The house was one of a number left to Mary by her father, Henry VIII, and was her main Essex residence during the short reign of her half-brother, the boy-king Edward VI. She appointed six priests to serve there and when at home she attended Mass every day. Here, as elsewhere, she was under almost constant watch by the Protestant government, for apparently she not only heard Mass herself but had parishioners in for the forbidden service. But despite sustained pressure she held to the practices of the ancient faith. A dramatic plot to get her to safety abroad failed to materialize, getting no further than her going to Woodham Walter Hall, another of her properties, which was closer to the proposed escape route. From there she was to have gone in disguise to a point on the Blackwater near Maldon, where waiting at dawn in a churchyard, the plan was to take her out to a Flemish ship. However, by cruising off the shore for some days, the vessel aroused the suspicion of the coastal guards and the scheme was dropped.

While at Boreham Mary made several visits to the Petres across country at Ingatestone Hall. She was particularly friendly with Lady Petre, another stalwart Catholic. It was at New Hall in 1553 that Mary's ordeal came to an end, for there she received the submission of the Crown's ministers on the fall of Northumberland, his attempt to put Jane Grey on the throne having failed. On becoming queen, Mary leased the house to Sir Thomas Wharton.

Elizabeth, too, knew the house well, both as a young princess and as queen. She stayed there several times on her royal 'progresses' or tours of East Anglia. One of these was in 1561, after a short stay at Ingatestone. Several months before her visit, John de Vere, the sixteenth Earl of Oxford and Lord Lieutenant of Essex, suddenly descended on New Hall from his castle at Hedingham and had the place searched. 'Instruments of superstition' were discovered, objects which included roods (crucifixes) and pictures which had belonged to Queen Mary. Thomas Wharton, who still had the lease, was a known Papist. Several years earlier he had been accused by the Attorney-General of hearing Mass in his house. His was the unenviable distinction of being the first in Elizabeth's reign to be prosecuted for this offence. He had been sent to the Tower as a result but was later set free. Lady Anne Wharton had also been confined to the Tower, but she was not so lucky. She died there and was taken to Boreham for burial. Perhaps the search of Wharton's home before the Queen's arrival was to ensure that no offending religious objects would meet her gaze. It must certainly have proved a deterrent.

It was Elizabeth who later gave the house to the Earls of Sussex. As we see it now, it is very largely the work of the third earl, Thomas Radcliffe, the brother of Lady Wharton and one of the Queen's few real favourites. Before going to Boreham he had lived at Woodham Walter in the hall which had been Mary Tudor's. In 1573, the year he received the gift of New Hall, he began to modernize the north range. This was demolished in the eighteenth century but what is left of his work on the house is outstanding. The southern façade of the building, flanked by two projecting wings, has seven bays with very fine windows. Although badly damaged during an air raid in the last war, it has been well restored. Up on the parapet there is a sundial with an inscription in Italian to Elizabeth. She is hailed as 'wisest queen on earth, brightest star in the sky, a virgin generous, learned, godlike, elegant, just and beautiful'. Few praises to royalty can have been more sycophantic than that!

Thomas Radcliffe's father had been with Henry VIII in France, receiving his earldom at that great diplomatic showpiece the Field of the Cloth of Gold. Thomas himself had much to be grateful for. He held a succession of high appointments. Under Elizabeth he was Lord Lieutenant of Ireland and Lord Chamberlain. A few years before, he had been important in securing the marriage of Mary to King Philip of Spain.

Thomas's will makes fascinating reading, for it tells us much of the interior splendour of New Hall as he lay dying. As his wife Frances had been heard to voice doubts about continuing to live there after his death and as he was also childless, a great deal was left in the care of his brother Henry. Thomas Radcliffe regarded his house as still being a royal household at the disposal of the Queen whenever she cared to visit, so he was at pains to make sure that much of its contents should remain *in situ*. The house was lavishly furnished. Among the many items in the will are the 'hangings', costly pieces of wall tapestry used for decoration and also to keep out the draughts. Of the many hangings one displayed the Sussex family coat of arms while another depicted scenes from Greek mythology. There were 'seven pieces of forest work with fountains' and 'eight of white lions'. One tapestry sounds particularly intriguing, a 'Dance of Death' in Her Majesty's Presence Chamber. Numerous beds with their curtains and bedclothes are also itemized, as well as carpets, some from Turkey.

Among his more personal effects the third earl left many jewels, a great abundance of gilt plate and the sword presented to him by Philip of Spain. Where are all these good things now, if indeed any still exist?

With all this in the house it is no surprise to find that it was broken into at least once. In 1579 a local man took £11 worth of goods, mainly articles of silver. He was hanged.

Henry Radcliffe succeeded Thomas. One of his achievements, as the Governor of Portsmouth, was to get the Queen's ships ready to face the Spanish Armada. In all there were six earls of Sussex, the last dying in the seventeenth century. The first three lie beneath splendid tombs in Boreham's parish church.

In Stuart times New Hall went to George Villiers, the Duke of Buckingham, who bought it for £30,000 from the fifth Earl of Sussex. After the Duke's assassination at Portsmouth, it was owned by his son, also George Villiers. Charles I was most likely a visitor in 1638 on the occasion he went to Chelmsford.

Towards the end of the Civil War the house was the scene for a meeting of Royalist leaders *en route* with their forces to Colchester, where they were to endure the celebrated siege. Then after the war and because it was a traitor's estate Oliver Cromwell purchased it for the nominal sum of 5 shillings! But he did not like it, preferring Hampton Court instead. He sold it to three merchants for £18,000.

The next owner and occupier was General Monck, who brought back Charles II from exile. Charles was a frequent visitor, perhaps attracted by the horses which the General bred on his New Hall estate. Monck made full use of the house, living there in great style on the handsome pension which was his reward from the King. In honour of Charles' marriage to Catherine of Braganza in 1661, Monck held a huge firework display in the grounds. Other notable visitors to the house during his residence included Nell Gwynne and the diarist John Evelyn. Nell acted in *The Merry Wives of Windsor* when it was staged in the great hall. The house was much admired by John Evelyn, particularly its setting with the mile-long avenue of lime trees. The avenue was later to be bisected by the railway, and the splendid trees in two double rows have long since gone.

Yet another king, James II, was a guest at the hall in May 1686.

It was Monck who had the painted window resited in the chapel. It had been buried underground during the war to protect it from Puritan vandalism. The window was sold later, by the first Lord Waltham, and was eventually acquired at a price of 400 guineas for St Margaret's, Westminster, where it remains. Made in Holland as a gift from Ferdinand and Isabella of Spain for adorning the Abbey, it was given by Henry VIII to the Abbot of Waltham when relations between the two countries deteriorated. It was the Abbot who installed the window in his chapel at the Hall.

New Hall was General Monck's sole residence for the last ten years of his life and he ended his days there, dying of dropsy. The house passed to his son, Christopher. He died in Jamaica.

Another distinguished owner was Benjamin Hoare of the banking family. But his main residence was Boreham House nearby, which he enriched with material from the hall. (Boreham House is now one of Ford's training centres.) Hoare parted with New Hall in 1737 and it was acquired by Lord Waltham, a deputy governor of the Bank of England. He left it to his son and heir, the second Lord Waltham, MP for Weymouth and later Maldon. He had the remarkable name of Drigue Billers Olmius, the 'Billers' deriving from the family connection with Sir William Billers, a Lord Mayor of London.

The second Lord Waltham married the niece of a Mr Coe, and this brought him £10,000. Coe was an extremely wealthy merchant and a leader of the Whigs in Maldon. Drigue

Olmius, unlike his father and Mr Coe, seems to have been prodigal with his money. John Crozier wrote of him as 'a dupe to his friends and generally kept an elegant house where he maintained almost a set of gentlemen who were of no great consequence in themselves or credit'. At one time he spent a brief period in Chelmsford jail, a victim of 'swindlers'. This was the age of 'rotten boroughs' and he sold his seat for Weymouth on which he made a good profit. In the year he was elected for Maldon, 1784, he held the first ball of the season in the town, and Crozier thought it 'exceedingly brilliant'. He was idolized by his constituents, no doubt for a generosity which amounted to bribery. Lord Waltham died three years later.

A totally new chapter in the long history of New Hall was opened with the arrival of the nuns on 25 January 1799. In November the previous year the brother of one of them had paid £4,500 for the house and its fifty-eight acres of land. The nuns were the Canonesses of the Holy Sepulchre, and they came from Liège. The *Gentleman's Magazine* in 1800 gave these details in reporting the event:

> The venerable mansion of Newhall, the scene of Harry's intrigues and pleasures, is now the retreat of fifty religious nuns exiled from France under a lady abbess, who has added to their number young ladies of the first families as boarders for instruction. Great alterations have been made in the appendages to the house. The patrons of this institution are the noble families of Petre, Clifford, Mr Smith of Roundhill, etc., who purchased the premises of the heirs of the late Lord Waltham, and have levelled the noble avenue, a mile long, of 1,000 lime trees in two rows on a side, 250 in a row, many of them 3 feet diameter. They were sold at 8s a tree to Mr Cotes, coal and timber merchant, of Chelmsford, who, by selling them to turners, and to make bedsteads, etc., for the barracks, is said to have cleared £500.

The wheel of fortune had turned full circle, for in a sense the nuns were the female counterparts of the clergy installed by King Harold seven centuries before. The great house which had witnessed such a glittering social life and which for so long had stood close to the nation's affairs now shut its doors and finally renounced all political ambition.

2

Terling and the Rayleighs

There are villages which sprawl and straggle. There are others with centres of such distinctive shape that once having been seen they can be later visualized like a compact plan in the palm of one's hand. Such is Terling, only rarely these days known as 'Tarling' by that declining species of old-timers.

Scenically, Terling is best discovered from the south: from the old road, the Roman road, between Boreham and Hatfield Peverel. Coming from the west, you should take the second signpost to the left. Make the crossing of the A12 and within seconds the continuous slush of traffic evaporates behind you. The long, winding lane you will follow is notable for much of the way for ancestral trees, and at the end of this pleasing way you will come into the village green, large and broad and rectangular. Spacious and tranquil, this is the heart of Terling.

Here are 'divers faire houses' ranged along two sides. Of these the prince is the cross-gabled manor house in the far corner. With an old-world garden, it faces south to the churchyard. Dating from the 1400s, the house displays many exposed beams and there are fine octagonal chimneyshafts. Inside there is preserved the original king-post truss of the central hall.

On the opposite side of the green stands the red-brick Congregational chapel of 1753, an early witness to Essex Nonconformity. From the century before that it has a twelve-branches candelabra.

On the south side is the parish church, All Saints, not an outstanding church for antiquities but stately nevertheless. The prime attraction is the tower, built in 1732 after the thirteenth-century tower collapsed two years before. It has a decidedly New England, or rather New Amsterdam, appearance, having been designed by an Antony Goud, which suggests a Dutch connection. Inside the much-restored church there are several things of particular interest to see, including brasses and wall tablet memorials. The overall impression is of roominess and light.

The registers have the distinction of commencing from the earliest date that registers had to be kept, 1538. There are also churchwardens' accounts which were begun in the year 1668, the earliest of the series being on loose sheets. Judging from published extracts from those of the seventeenth and early eighteenth centuries, it looks as though bell-ringing was a recurring item of expense. The five bells of All Saints were pealed a number of times to proclaim and celebrate events of stirring national importance. Thus, one week after Monmouth's rebellion was crushed at Sedgemoor in July 1685, we have the following:

July ye 13th For a prayer Booke for thanksgiving over
ye Rebells and A proclamation with it   00 01 04
Given to ye Ringers on thanksgiving day   00 05 00

Three years after this last battle to be fought on English soil, the 'Glorious Revolution' of 1688, confirmed by the coronation of William and Mary, provided these entries:

For two Papers of Prayers for y^e Prince of Orange   00 01 00
Given to y^e Ringers on y^e thanksgiving Day   00 03 06
For a form of Prayer for the King and Queene
    and the rest of y^e Royall family   00 01 00
$Feb^{ry}y^e$ 14th Given to y^e Ringers   00 02 06

Naval victories were also rung out from the old tower:

1704. Given to the Ringers for rejoicing at
    Admiral Rook's beateing the French.   00 06 00

That was for the defeat of the French at Malaga only days after Rook captured Gibraltar, while for Marlborough's victory at Blenheim we can read for the same year:

Sept ye 7th Given to y^{e}e Ringers on the
    Thanksgiving Day   00 06 00

For such great events the bells would have filled the air all over England.

The Terling accounts contain numerous entries for repair and maintenance work on the belfry and the tower which could be read as omens of what was to come. There are seven alone for 1669 including 'timber for ye steeple ... iron work for ye bells ... hoopes for ye bell wheeles' and 'shingling ye steeple'.

But for a glimpse of the darker side of the past there is 'Old Sheepey', clearly the village madman:

1697. June 23rd for an order to take Matt Sheepey
    from the house of correction   00 00 06
1700. For the house where Old Sheepey was chained   00 00 06
1703. October the 2nd For three years quit rent
    for the house where Old Sheepey died ending
    at Michaelmas 1703 ...   00 01 00

If only we could get to the tragic story behind those lines!

Terling is very much an estate village, and beyond the churchyard to the south lie the gardens and house of Terling Place, the home of Lord Rayleigh. It is set in two hundred acres of parkland, through which flows the little River Ter, and surrounded by the celebrated dairy farms which carry the family title. You can steal a glance at the mansion if you encroach a little beyond the gate in the churchyard wall, although the grounds are opened to the public once or twice a year.

The family is justly famed for its contributions to agriculture and to science. The Terling branch takes its rise from the Strutts of the seventeenth century, who originating as millers, with water-mills at Maldon and Springfield, speedily made good. John Strutt, who died in 1816 aged

The Manor House, Terling

eighty-nine, purchased Terling Place, pulling down part of
the Tudor house which had belonged to the bishops of
Norwich before the Reformation and which was well known
to Henry VIII, a lover of other Essex haunts such as 'Jericho'
and New Hall. Later John Strutt built the central block of the
house we see today. An MP for Maldon, he was a wealthy
landowner with close on six thousand acres, mainly in
Terling, by the time of his death.

John Strutt and his family get several mentions in the
diary of John Crozier. Crozier's father had been an
apprentice to old Mr Strutt (father of John the 1st of
Terling) at Beeleigh Mills. 'The old gentleman' went to
Wickham Mills and later 'to Bath for the recovery of his
health and returning home died at Devizes in Wiltshire, was
brought to Terling and buried in the family vault'. Crozier
praised his abilities and business enterprise, for certainly it
was the old man who provided the cornerstone to the
family's fortune.

Writing in 1780, Crozier noted: 'Capt Strutt, son of John
Strutt of Terling Place, brought to England and buried in the
family vault.' He may have been the Strutt who had gone to

Constantinople for the good of his health. In 1784 Crozier wrote: 'Dined at Mr Strutts, Terling Place, 1st January. This is his usual day for his tenants paying their rents; he gives 'em an elegant dinner, plenty of wine, punch; we dined in a fine, large room, 50 in number. Mrs Strutt and one son at one table; Mr Strutt and the other son, at another table. A sight pleas'd me much; we spent a very cheerful day.'

This remarkable family were diverse in their interests and occupations. One became a London physician, another a noted antiquary who lived away from Essex. There is a nice touch of eccentricity as well, for John Strutt was apparently the last of the family to defy fashion by sporting a pigtail.

John's successor was John Holden Strutt. He, too, became MP for Maldon. He married well. His wife, the Lady Charlotte Mary Gertrude, was the daughter of a duke, and she became Baroness Rayleigh in 1821. She died before John Holden, and the title went to his son John James. It was in this manner that the Strutts became Rayleighs.

The most distinguished of the line was the third Baron, John William Strutt (1842-1919), who came of age in 1863. One of the lights of nineteenth-century science, he was for many years the Cavendish Professor of Experimental Physics at Cambridge, and be became the co-discoverer of argon with Sir William Ramsey. The third Lord was an authority on optics and sound, and his scientific papers run to seven volumes. He conducted some of his experimental work in his laboratories at Terling which still occupy the west wing of the house built by himself and his son, the fourth Lord. His life was replete with honours. In addition to being a President of the Royal Society, he became Chancellor of Cambridge University and a Privy Councillor. He was awarded the Nobel Prize for Physics in 1904. By receiving the Order of Merit, he had the added distinction of being one of the original twelve members of the Order. His marriage in 1871 was equally prestigious, for he married the sister of that eminent Edwardian Arthur Balfour. He lies in the churchyard, his grave marked with a slab of red sandstone bearing the words from Corinthians, 'For now we see in a glass darkly but then face to face.'

His son and successor, the fourth Lord Rayleigh (1875–1947) was also an outstanding man of science. Like his father he was a Fellow of the Royal Society, and he was Professor of Physics at Imperial College. His other offices included being President of the British Association in 1938 and of the Royal Institution at the time of his death. The particular field of his research was the age of minerals and rocks.

A third star in this firmament was the Hon. Edward G. Strutt, the brother of the third Lord. He was noted as a foremost agricultural improver, managing and developing Lord Rayleigh's dairies, a magnificent example of applied science, for it was the outcome of Lord Rayleigh's investigations into the milk supply needed for a rapidly expanding population. They built up a herd of nearly fifteen hundred head of cattle at Terling, producing a million gallons of milk a year.

All this is well on record. But a little-known chapter in the history of the Rayleighs is their close interest in the scientific study of the paranormal, an interest which in earlier days was one of active involvement.

In 1919 the third Lord was President for that year of the Society for Psychical Research. Even before the foundation of the SPR in 1882, he had begun to look into the 'glass darkly' of psi-phenomena with other like-minded savants of his generation, putting his reputation at risk in an age when science was far more complacent and orthodox than now. He was to argue cogently against the physical radiation hypothesis for the mysteriously capricious workings of ESP, and as a result of his studies and personal experiences in the field of mediumship he came to accept the case for a life after death. The fourth Lord Rayleigh also held the chair of President for 1937–8. His brother, Admiral the Hon. A.C. Strutt was active as well for much of his life in the affairs of the SPR. He died in 1973 at the great age of ninety-three.

The Society's list of members for 1974 shows that the interest of the family has continued right through to the present time, listing the names of Lord and Lady Rayleigh and two other Strutts. But the bizarre little story I have heard that a piece of ectoplasm remains in storage at Terling Place is surely quite apocryphal, unless it be regurgitated cheesecloth or muslin 'ectoplasm'.

There are other good things to see around Terling if you

saunter away from the green. The White Hart of the eighteenth century is no more, a large house with its own malting and brewery and a stable, but there is the Rayleigh Arms for refreshment. Among fine houses which lie out a bit, you can go to the west and look at Ringers Farm of about 1400, with an original doorway to the screens passage. Certainly you should not miss the windmill which graces the landscape. The mill is a white wooden tower, restored to its original colour and converted to a private house since 1969, making it a most agreeable 'folly'. It first stood at Cressing, where it was built in 1700, but in 1830 it was trundled four miles along the lanes to its present site. It looms above the ford – 'Behold, a giant am I' – with four sails, minus the shutters, and a fantail. Its working life came to an end in 1950, the last of the Essex mills to function, when the miller, Herbert Bonner, was killed in the machinery.

While on these lanes you ought to seek out nearby Fairstead church with its fading murals. Nor can I resist a mention of the pub at tiny Ranks Green, for in my unrepentant scheme of things pubs and churches go together as do body and soul. This one is a truly rural house of call; without the name you would take it for a farmhand's dwelling. When I first found it, three publicans ago, it was a homely one-bar parlour. The mat by the door said, 'Woodbines', and the landlord, one of that glorious breed of yesterday's men, insisted on marking up his ales in pre-decimal prices. The house has been spruced up since but still it keeps its character of 'back of beyond'. Sad to say, its very unusual sign has gone, stolen I've been told. The story goes that a publican had it painted to honour his lovely daughter. And that is how the house derives its name, 'The Pretty Lady'.

3

Secluded Ulting

There can be few places in Essex with a past as obscure as that of Ulting. Although it was entered in the Domesday Book, as Ultingam, its subsequent history is a real puzzle for the historian of minor places, for there is little on record to go by.

Today the parish has a lost feeling to it and has nothing resembling a well-defined village. Even its name is enigmatic. Most probably it comes from a lost river name, the Ult, which takes us back to long before the Saxons came. Perhaps the River Ult was the Chelmer. But Dr P.H. Reaney thought it more likely it was the ancient name for the Ter, which joins the Chelmer here half a mile to the west of the church.

Ulting lies between Hatfield Peverel and Woodham Walter, and it is possible to drive through the parish hardly knowing you are there. Its most conspicuous building is the little church; conspicuous, that is, from the Chelmer and Blackwater Navigation. This lovely waterway should be better known. Many hear of it with surprise; few have sailed along the shallow stream (a mere two foot in draught) or walked its shady banks.

How the river from Chelmsford to the sea was turned to a canal, a 'Navigation', would fill up pages of itself, as would the story of its trading days. Barges no longer gently ply from Heybridge Basin up to Springfield, moving between the banks for nigh on fourteen miles, lifted through a dozen locks. They were loaded with lime and dung, coal and timber, but the coming of the railways and the lorry put an end to that. This is the route *par excellence* to take to Ulting – if you have leisure in plenty. Every gradual mile has its fair prospect: a weatherboard mill, a lock-keeper's house, a distant view of Little Baddow's church and Danbury Hill,

The riverside at Ulting

stables and the 'bothy' where the bargees slept, and original brick bridges. And all the while the towpath, lined mile upon mile with cricket-bat willows: peaceful with the image of a fisherman or lone walker and water-waving weeds.

It was from the pleasure barge *Victoria*, gliding with snail-like serenity on a still summer's evening, that I first saw All Saints in its little setting among the leaves. It proved not so easy to find when I returned on a later occasion by road. A trackway leads to the church by the water's edge. It is usually locked but the key can be requested at the one and only house nearby.

All Saints is of a modest size indeed, measuring just forty-five by eighteen feet. Although mainly of the thirteenth century, it was much restored in 1872–3. Plain and lacking monuments, it is well cared for. Late in the 1400s it had a lady chapel in the churchyard, used by a guild, but in Morant's words, 'There is no footstep remaining.' It probably went with the Reformation. Founded in the reign of Edward IV, the guild was run by two wardens. Unusually, there are two churchyards: the original by the river and a later one much neglected by the lane to the north. The two pieces of church plate, a cup and a paten, are from the sixteenth century. The registers date only from 1723, which suggests that earlier books have been lost.

Chapman's map of 1777 indicates land on the bend in the river as 'The Wick'. Wicks were sheep farms, and we know from a will of 1584 that sheep were kept here then. In his will William Styleman left a flock of thirty-seven sheep along with several other animals and ten hives of bees. One hive was left to the vicar, Mr Francis Sea. His name turns up again five years later when he was accused of 'retaining in his house one Green's wife of Colchester and thereby they live slanderously together'. As part of her defence Margaret Green had to present her husband's will, no doubt to establish he was truly deceased. She claimed she was living in the vicar's house to avoid starvation.

Old records of those far-off times give us several glimpses of scandals which must have been the talk of the parish for many a day.

In 1590 one Barrett of Ulting was charged with having lain with a Kelvedon woman, one of two who seem to have had reputations as ladies of easy virtue. She had the remarkable name of Dionise Crackbone!

In 1597 the then vicar of Ulting, Edward Kynett, ministered to one of his parishioners in a most unacceptable way, 'violently striking William Barker's head with his dagger upon the sabbath day'. It being a sabbath doubtless increased the gravity of the incident. The vicar pleaded self-defence.

Then there was the case, much more alarming to the authorities, of two Hatfield Peverel labourers who in 1594 were accused of seditious speech at Ulting. Complaining of the high price of food at that time, they confessed to saying they would incite others to seize corn. When one was asked, 'What can poor men do against rich men?', he defiantly replied, 'What can rich men do against poor men if poor men rise and hold together?' The spirit of the Peasants' Revolt had obviously long lingered on.

Ulting has had its share of prestigious families, including

the Aylmers. Of the two manors, that of Mugdon Hall was acquired by John Aylmer, Bishop of London from 1576 to 1594. Its land extended into the adjacent parishes of Hatfield Peverel and Little Baddow. Of the bishop's seven sons it was Samuel who inherited this estate. His son John married Lucretia, a daughter of Sir Henry Clovile of West Hanningfield, and they had a son called Brabazon. In Morant's day the Hall was still here, for he noted that over the porch, on a black tablet, there was this inscription in gold letters: 'This house was rebuilt by Brabazon Aylmer 1679.'

In modern times the parish has one 'worthy' to its credit, the Essex historian Robert Copp Fowler (1867–1929). His father was the vicar here.

One does not go to Ulting for old houses, although Tanhouse Farm and Ulting Hall both have Elizabethan work in their chimneystacks, and the latter house is partly Georgian. The Victorian schoolhouse also remains. The population of this secluded parish stays as ever very small. But if there is little 'to see', Ulting delights as a pastoral retreat, a muted witness to times past.

4

The Grandeur of Braxted

Braxted Park estate lies behind a seemingly endless perimeter wall of mellow red-brick. It is very concealed and surprisingly little known despite its size of five hundred acres and its closeness to the A12.

If approaching from this road, you should turn off by the Fox at Rivenhall End and take the lane to Great Braxted. After you cross Appleford Bridge with its weir and delightful Mill House, the wall of the Park comes into sight a little further on. Built between 1825 and 1831, to give employment to local men in the dire times following the Napoleonic Wars, the wall runs its course for $4\frac{1}{2}$ miles. Following part of its length the modest entrance between two gatehouses is soon reached.

Living in the Hanningfields, it was of interest to me to learn from Morant of an ancient link with Braxted. William de Montchensey, who died in 1289, was overlord of both. He is on record as having made a warren on his Braxted land.

A number of eminent Essex families held the manor. They include the Ayloffs, Sir Henry Maynard of Easton Lodge who had it in 1610, the D'Arcys of Maldon and St Osyth, and Peter Whetcombe, 'a Turkey merchant'. But Braxted Park is largely the creation of the Du Canes. Along with the Tollesbury estate, the Lodge was purchased in 1751 by Peter Du Cane of Coggeshall from Henry Cornelisen for just under £19,500. Peter was the elder son of Richard Du Cane, an MP for Colchester and a director of the Bank of England. The family were wealthy merchants of Huguenot descent, having been refugees from the Low Countries in the sixteenth century.

Peter Du Cane was the High Sherriff of Essex in 1745 and like his father on the Board at the Bank of England. Along with his country houses he had a London residence, the site now occupied by the London Library in St James's Square. He died in 1803 at nearly ninety years of age. He was followed at Braxted by his son Peter Du Cane II, who enlarged the estate and whose notable collection of statues in the house seems to have resulted from his tour of the art capitals of Europe. It was around 1848 that the Lodge acquired its name of Braxted Park.

Among the papers of the family held at the Essex Record Office there are fifty-two volumes of cashbooks and ledgers dating from 1694 to 1866. Up to 1751 these accounts are mainly of their market dealings with Italy and Russia. After that date the books principally relate to the running of the Park. They testify to the commercial prestige of the family in its heyday.

One member, Mary Du Cane, married James Houblon, 'the father of the Royal Exchange'. She bore him ten sons. Much later another figure of public importance was Major General Sir Edmund Frederick Du Cane. He assisted in organizing the Great Exhibition of 1851, and much of his career was spent as a prison inspector. Appropriately, he was a Vice-President of the Huguenot Society. He died in 1903, one of the last of the line at Braxted. The estate was sold in 1919, although the family retained a stake in the property to the 1960s. Miss Florence Du Cane kept her connection until her death at eighty-seven in 1956. Others of the family went to America, where they remain.

After the last war the Park was bought by Plesseys but in April 1965 it was purchased by Mr Michael Clark, the son and heir of Sir Alan Clark.

To the first-time visitor it will come as a revelation. The Park is extremely impressive for its landscaping and trees, many of which are of great age, some having been planted in the eighteenth century. It may be unsurpassed in Essex for so many of such vast height and girth. The house although plain stands boldly at the head of a fine, long avenue flanked by eight rows of lime trees, four on either side. This wide drive sweeps down from the gatehouses to a little bridge and then rises to the red-brick mansion on its open site.

The Lodge itself (which is not opened to the public) is of two storeys, and the special feature is the windows with

Braxted Park

white-framed octagonal panes. It has had a complicated building history but as we see it now is mainly of the 1750s, with some alterations made early in the last century. To the right is the old coachyard, a small turret above the entrance, and further on lies an extensive walled garden. Behind, in a setting of majestic trees and flowering shrubs, a wing of the house has been designed to enclose a remarkable swimming pool. Presumably this was once an orangery. It is flooded with light through tall, elegant windows and looking through one can see between them a series of large murals, a panorama depicting a classical coastline. With the white iron furniture at a raised end, this makes it a crystal palace to bathe in in real style.

In the valley below the house there is a fine ornamental lake which covers fifteen acres. To its north is a nine-hole golf course. The walk through the trees along the lower bank leads first to the parish church. This is sited within the Park but can also be reached from outside along a two-hundred-yard avenue of yews.

The church of All Saints has an idyllic setting close to the lakeside. Although much restored, it has a particular interest in its north transept for here above the family vault are the tiered pews of the Du Canes. As in many of our old churches, there are Roman bricks in the walls here. They may have come from the settlement of Rivenhall, but oyster shells have been found at this spot which could point to a Roman site. A great rarity are the traces of a thirteenth-century altar beam near the east wall of the chancel. This was used to display images and relics and is the only one to survive in Essex.

Past the church the walk continues to the end of the lake. An attractive white boathouse, Lake Lodge, serves as a most enviable residence. Here, too, is a Victorian curiosity, an ice-well, formerly covered by a summerhouse. There is a tradition that a hermit occupied it for a year. Perhaps a recluse had been installed as an 'Ornamental Hermit', like those we can read of in Edith Sitwell's *English Eccentrics*. But it seems more likely the Hermitage took the name as a retreat for the family well away from the house and business.

We, too, as fortunate outsiders, can have the brief privilege of withdrawing here from the world awhile,

> Annihilating all that's made
> To a green thought in a green shade.

A mile or so to the west is the tiny parish of Little Braxted. The church is more impressive than its Great neighbour. It is dedicated to St Nicholas and like some others under the protection of this saint is inclined a little to the south-east, in line with the point where the sun rises on his feast day, 6 December. This was the church where, as we shall see, Laurence Washington served quietly as an unofficial curate after his rude ejection from Purleigh.

A small church, forty-five feet long (the length of the one at Ulting), at one time it was even smaller. It was first built in the opening years of the twelfth century, probably by order of a bishop of London. An original Norman window can be seen in the apse. The porch dates from the reign of Henry

VIII and was added to the church from money left by a
member of the Roberts family. They were in the parish from
1480 to 1680, and one, an auditor to Henry VII, is
remembered with a brass on the chancel floor.

Worley, in 1915, remarked on the strangeness of the bells.
As for most of us church bells are antiquities which remain
unseen, this is what he wrote in his *Dictionary of the
County* of those which ring out here: 'There are two bells of
unknown date, but obviously ancient, and of remarkable
shape, each diminishing rapidly towards the crown, where
the diameter is unusually contracted. The clappers are also
peculiar, being made in the form of clubs, but without any
special enlargement at the striking ends.'

Another oddity in this church did not come to light until
1982. During some restoration work on the walls, two holes
were found (since covered up). Expert opinion was sought
and the most likely explanation seems to be that they formed
an aperture for a hermit. By means of a wooden grill he could
have seen into the church from a hut outside and in this way
could also counsel visitors. (It may be, as well, that the hole
was later adapted to hide the church plate.) It is strange
indeed that both the Braxteds may have harboured
anchorites.

Inside, the church is dim but a century back it must have
glowed like a casket in the lamplight. Fading now, the walls
of the nave, chancel and the north aisle are decorated with
murals, biblical and symbolic. These are not medieval but
done by the hand of the rector Ernest Geldart between 1881,
when he arrived, and 1884. An artist and an architect as well,
he was here for just under twenty years. He also designed the
church of St Nicholas at Rawreth. Among his other work he
was responsible for the choir ceiling at Tolleshunt D'Arcy.

Born in 1848, he came from an old Yorkshire family who
had taken root in the West Riding in the fourteenth century.
Ordained in 1873, he came to Little Braxted after holding in
turn two other livings. Then, when in 1900 he retired for
reasons of ill health, he travelled widely, in Europe, Australia
and the Americas. He wrote a *Manual of Church Decoration
and Symbolism*. For relaxation he took up cycling and
photography. 'The Master of Braxted' lived to be
eighty-one, dying in 1929.

In addition to his murals in the church, a luxurious riot of chocolate, crimson and gold, he did the emblematic shields of Christ on the chancel screen and designed the stained glass windows. Of all these idiosyncratic works, Scarfe wrote: 'As a rare monument to the taste of that age it should be carefully recorded if not preserved.' The style, admittedly, is much out of fashion and is eclipsed by the artistry of far earlier times, such as we can see at Copford. Geldart's work is not to my liking; it surprises rather than enthrals. Yet it is a work of individual vision and devotion, as curious as an antique prayer, and I for one hope it is not allowed to go.

5

Purleigh via Cock Clarks

The very name Cock Clarks may lure you here as it did me. If you look on Chapman's map of 1777, you will find it marked 'Cock Lark'.

Scarfe in his *Shell Guide to Essex* (1975) gives it a passing glance and to his credit has been one of the few Essex topographers to have done so. But he was clearly nonplussed by the name for he calls its present form 'meaningless'. Yet it seems to derive from two personal names, John le Clerk of 1319 and a John Coke (Cok) of just a few years later. By the sixteenth century it was recorded as 'Cokeclarkes' and as 'Cocklarkes'.

Cock Clarks is a hamlet in the parish of Purleigh. The nearby villages have equally intriguing names, for to the north lie two of the three Woodhams, namely Woodham Mortimer and Walter, and to the south Stow Maries and Cold Norton. Purleigh itself, on record as such as early as 998, takes its lovely, soft name in part from the Old English for the bittern or snipe. Once a very common bird in the Dengie Hundred, a few were still being caught last century.

In the main the landscape here is very flat, barely a few feet above sea-level, for both the Crouch and the Blackwater with their marshes are only three or four miles away, Purleigh lying midway between the two. But if the land is flat, this is by no means synonymous with dull. Certainly the low levels in this corner of Essex can look desolate indeed on grey, clouded days. Yet given the right weather the skies open up to give an exhilarating sense of vast space and freedom.

One way to approach Cock Clarks is from the north, along Marlpit Road with Hyde Woods away on your right. The houses are few and there is little more to the place than its centre at the crossroads. It has an air of having been only recently discovered by commuters searching for a retreat. Although so far escaping estate development, it is at an ambiguous point in its history. Several older houses have been vamped beyond recognition but there are others which have kept a look of rural authenticity. One of these is 'Whentz Cottage', the name presumably referring to the Wantz or road junction nearby.

The pub, the Fox and Hounds, stands four-square in the centre. CAMRA's booklet *Real Ale in Essex* calls it 'a typical Essex pub'. To see it is to know at once what this means. Of plain red-brick, it is completely without pretension, a homely old-fashioned alehouse, one of the fast-diminishing number to be encountered in rural parts.

The Round Bush, away on the other side of Purleigh close by Mundon, is another humble local. This also merits a visit. If you want to drink good ale in good company, then the Round Bush is a must. It is one of Michael Gray's houses, a

The Round Bush, Purleigh

guarantee of character and hospitality. Here you will meet true locals who welcome the passing stranger into their conversation, which I have never known to fail for kindly wit and sharp observation. With luck you will be introduced to Roy, alias Yogi, celebrated in these parts for his ferrets, his very life, a rare and generous man with no demands upon our age, imbued with the spirit of the land – a character straight from the pages of Richard Jefferies. The pub is run with keen interest and affection by Kevin and Lorraine Harley.

Many years back a publican of this alehouse was an undertaker and is remembered yet for a strange *memento mori*: he kept his own coffin standing in the corner by the kegs.

Getting back to Cock Clarks, a few yards from the Fox there is a tiny white thatched cottage almost hiding from view a plain little church, or rather chapel. Across the road is Hawkins House which serves as the post office. When I went in to buy some stamps, I found myself in a large front room, amply furnished, with a counter in the corner. The name of the house appears to come from the Provost Hawkins noted as a preacher in the parish church last century. A Fellow of Oriel, he was provost of his college and rector of Purleigh from 1828 to 1883. He died at the age of ninety-three.

As you leave Cock Clarks to take the lane to Purleigh village, you may notice that the signpost to Stow Maries reads 'Stow St Mary'. The church there is dedicated to the Virgin but the 'Maries' really comes from an ancient family, the Mareys.

Purleigh's village, 1¾ miles away, straddles a hill. Its great delight is at the top, a perfect visual combination of church, Victorian rectory and pub, added to which is a spectacular view into the far distance.

The hilltop church of All Saints is particularly noted for its tower, which is chequered and banded with flints. There is so much about this medieval church to admire, not least its setting, a dark, romantic churchyard with stately firs and an avenue of yews. It stands on the site of an earlier church which went in the opening years of the fourteenth century, and the incumbents go back to William de London of 1220, when the patron was the prior and convent of Horton in Kent.

A sixteenth-century rector is of particular interest. Edmund Freake officiated here from 1567 to 1575. An Essex man, he was first a friar at Waltham Abbey. At the Dissolution he was one of the community who signed the Act of Surrender. He then went to Cambridge and after graduating went on to hold a number of lucrative positions in the Church: Archdeacon of Canterbury, Canon of Westminster, Chaplain to Queen Elizabeth, Canon of Windsor, Canon of Canterbury and Dean of two other Sees. Clearly an able and ambitious man, he secured the bishopric of Rochester while holding on to Purleigh. He resigned the living when he became Bishop of Norwich.

His wife seems to have much in common with Trollope's Mrs Proudie. She 'directed her husband, spoke reproachfully of learned preachers, and wished to have every honest man out of the Bishop's preserve. It was well known in Norwich that whatsoever Mrs Freake would have done the Bishop must and would accomplish, or she would make him weary of life, as he complained with tears. And if anyone came to the Bishop without a present, she would "Look at him as the divell looks over Lincoln",' this last being an allusion to the Lincoln Imp, the grotesque image in the cathedral there. She outlived the poor man and lies buried here at Purleigh.

But it is the link with America which gives the church its fame. It was here that George Washington's great-great-grandfather, Laurence, was the rector for ten years in the seventeenth century. Deprived of his living as a Royalist in 1643, he went to Little Braxted for a while as its curate, where 'he was suffered quietly to preach'. He is buried at another All Saints, the one at Maldon.

The accusations against him appear in a book of 1643, a Puritan tract with an incredibly long and acrimonious title, beginning, *The First Century of Scandalous and Malignant Priests* ... Laurence Washington was branded as 'a common frequenter of ale-houses, not only himselfe sitting daily tippling there, but also encouraging others in that beastly vice'. A pious, drinking parson, he represents a good clerical tradition that Puritans have cavilled at from his time down to our own. Fortunately, we can learn of his merits from sources other than the hostile indictment of 1643. These are Walker's *Sufferings of the Clergy* and his manuscripts in the Bodleian Library, which include a letter from Henry Ayloffe JP of Great Braxted. Of the sequestered rector Ayloffe wrote: 'I have heard him and took him to be a very worthy, pious man. I have been in his company there (at Little Braxted) and he appeared as a very modest, sober person; and I heard him recommended as such by several gentlemen who knew him before I did. He was a very loyal person and had one of the best benefices in these parts, and this was the only cause of his sequestration, as I verily believe.'

A genealogy presented to the church in 1971 shows George Washington and Sir Winston Churchill, two great champions of national independence and freedom, as having a common descent. The shield of the Washington family with its three stars and two stripes may well be the origin of the American flag.

The diary of John Crozier throws an interesting sidelight on the Washington connection. His entries for 1776, the year of the American Declaration of Independence, include the following: 'Mr Lawrence, coal merchant of Maldon, was drown'd by a sudden squall of wind in the Maldon river [the Blackwater]. He went afishing in his *washington* pleasure boat, to whose name and cause he was particularly attach'd, even to a degree of infatuation; and in opposition purely to the loyal party would make the most unwarranted speeches ....' The merchant's name is a strangely fitting coincidence. The pub, the Bell, which was there in Laurence Washington's day, should not be missed. Cosy and with many old timbers, it serves good food and has a friendly landlord. A small part of the house may well date from the fourteenth century and could have been the priest's dwelling.

The Bell stands with its back on the very edge of the sloping churchyard. Four of the six bells in the church tower only feet away were hung by Lawrence's order. They were cast by Miles Graye of Colchester. His foundry there, at the sign of the Swan with Two Necks, was destroyed during the siege. Born around 1575, he was responsible for some 270 bells, about half of them in Essex. His masterwork is the tenor bell at Lavenham. His son, Myles Graye II, and his grandson were bell-founders. Miles died in 1644, 'crazed with age and weak in body'.

From the windows of the pub you can see for miles across to the estuary of the Blackwater and beyond, where 'plough meets sail'. Bradwell power station, gaunt and unmistakable, can be seen, as can Mersea on a really transparent day.

The pub is on a sharp bend on the road, and if you descend towards Mundon, you will see on the left a derelict brick house which was formerly the village bakery. Further on there is what remains of the little railway bridge which spanned the lane.

Somewhere I've read of how in days long past the dawn in May was greeted with a hymn from All Saints tower. Each time I sit in the Bell, a 'common frequenter' with a pint in hand, I send out a rather wistful hope that such a beautiful tradition may yet be renewed.

6

Battlesbridge to Canewdon

When I began to think about this chapter, I was strongly tempted to head it 'Canute and the Crouch' or even more starkly 'Canute country', for the apparent links with the great Dane in this part of Essex certainly draw a keen response from all who have a lively feel for history. But these links, which are in fact more telling suggestions than proven links, are obstinately tenuous, and therefore, my temperament being what it is, I knew I couldn't walk beyond the evidence. That he was here I have little doubt. As we shall see, the land around Ashingdon has a firmer claim to his presence than the rival site to the north.

And so I opted for 'Battlesbridge to Canewdon' for I wanted to bring in other things as well along the river way, not solely 'old, unhappy, far-off things And battles long ago'.

The actual source of the Crouch is debatable. Three headstreams, we are told, each in the same small area, can be identified. One is a pond at Little Burstead, to the rear of Stockwell Hall (the 'well' in the name is indicative of a stream). Another is between there and Herongate. The third breaks to the surface at Dunton. Its course is fairly unobtrusive until it reaches Battlesbridge, and here, no longer a stream, it swells to a brown and navigable river.

My feelings about Battlesbridge are decidedly ambivalent. My approach via Rettendon Turnpike does not help, despite the coaching-days resonance of its name. Here was a stretch of the turnpike road which ran from Rawreth to Chelmsford. It was short-lived as such, for the trust responsible was disbanded in 1820 after only twenty-six years in business. Recently the junction, a roundabout, has been 'improved' to cope with the increased pressure of traffic, generated largely by the new development of Woodham Ferrers and the new road round Battlesbridge.

Battlesbridge is an untidy and incongruous muddle of the old and the new; the old looks sadly worn, the new thrown-up and temporary. It beckons you in with a railway bridge and a service station with a car lot. The place seems designed only for transportation, as of course it was but never quite like this. Apart from the mills, one tidal, the other a steam-rolling mill, which should be more attractive and interesting than they are, the only antiquity here is imported. You find it in the antique shops grouped together near the Barge, a pub well worth a pause awhile, if only to shut out what is and reflect over your pint on what has been.

The earliest mention of Battlesbridge comes from 1327 and 1351, when it was written 'Batailesbridge'. In all likelihood the medieval bridge was a wooden one. The bridge was rebuilt, again of wood, in 1768 but it is evident from old accounts that the original bridge was thoroughly renovated at least once down the years quite apart from occasional repairs. Thus, in the Essex Quarter Sessions Book for 1656 we have the following: 'It appearing to this Court ... That the Bridge called Battles Bridge standeing over an arme of The Sea goeing into the hundred of Rochford, and a Bridge called Salt Bridge in the parish of Rochford ... are in very great decay and dangerous for Passengers, and time out of mind have beene and still ought to bee repayred att the charge of this County, it is thereupon Ordered by this Court that the summe of Two hundred and Tenn Poundes bee forthwith leavied upon the severall parishes, hambletts and Wardes within this County.'

The eighteenth-century bridge was in turn replaced in the next century but it collapsed under the weight of a new mechanical monster of the day, Messrs Sadds' twelve-ton steam traction engine. A temporary structure served until a new iron bridge, commissioned in 1854, took its place with a span of just under a hundred feet. As of 1983, there is now a bypass which incorporates a crossing of its own.

Although the name Battlesbridge may summon up visionary gleams of 'ruined armour grey', being popularly associated with the Battle of Ashingdon further down river, it is usually traced to a personal name. In his delightfully discursive book *Essex* (1969), Marcus Crouch suggests rather whimsically that it may derive from some local worthy, 'perhaps a Ben Battle'. If the scholars are right, he was on the right tack, for the name has been conjecturally linked with the family of Richard Bataille here in the fourteenth century, the same century the bridge gets its first mention. The association can be demonstrated elsewhere: Battle Wood in the parish of Manuden is probably, and curiously, from a Richard Batayl as well. He turns up in 1248. Perhaps the Battle family got around. And yet, in the absence of more definite evidence for this connection, I'm inclined to suspect the cart may have been put before the horse. It remains possible that the surname of Richard may originate from some ancestral link with a battle or battlefield. If Battlesbridge is standing at the neck of a Canute country, this could account for the name. That bedevilling 'if' must wait until a little further on.

According to Reaney, there is a 'Tryndehayes' hereabouts, which means a 'circular enclosure'. Its age or whether it is an earthworks I haven't been able to trace.

There is no other bridge now below that of Battlesbridge. This must have acted to keep the air of isolation in these parts, a sense of remoteness which grows mile by mile towards the sea, making the country very much an unknown Essex. Probably all will be changed in a very few years. The major development at Woodham Ferrers looks an ominous sign of things to come.

Once over the bridge we turn left into a minor road to follow the course of the Crouch. This is the 'Low Road' which at first is called 'Watery Lane'. This is the route which goes to Canewdon and peters out on the edge of Wallasea Island. The way winds over many a culvert bridge, full of sharp twists and turns. In following this you will find yourself constantly changing direction. Singly placed houses, some old but mainly modern, are dotted along the roadside.

Hullbridge, the first sizeable place to be reached, is a rash on the landscape. The village has been swamped by estate housing. In order to get to the river this growth has to be traversed by taking Ferry Road. Having passed the Ferry Fish Shop and Ferry Pharmacy, the road at length slopes to an abrupt halt at the riverside. Yet, once here, the 'town' has disappeared behind you.

The modern Anchor Inn faces Anchor Cottage, formerly the pub, a piece of the old world all but effaced at Hullbridge. The house is white and timbered – I fancy it has a disenchanted look – and a rounded plaque above the door has the date '1783'. There is a path by the river and a good view from the inn garden. A caravan site of immobile homes, one of the neatest and more attractive I have seen, is right by the water's edge.

The last time I stood here was on an autumn day, blue and clear and with a strong westerly rinsing the land. Watching the moored boats bobbing about, gulls greedily screeching overhead, I fell to thinking about the absence of a bridge. The Crouch is very narrow at this point, and the name 'Hullbridge' certainly suggests that the river was once spanned. I was to learn that it is the name which partially supplies an explanation. The 'Hull' has no reference to boats. Apparently it has two related meanings. Hullbridge is 'the bridge over the Hwolne or Wholve', an old and very odd name for the Crouch. But 'wholves' is also an old Essex word for culverts, many of which took the form of planks over hollowed tree-trunks. The bridge here finally went out of use in the reign of Elizabeth I, when it was described as 'ruinous'. It eventually collapsed. Although no accounts survive as to its type, it was almost certainly of wood, perhaps with arches shaped like 'wholves'.

In 1659 'great complaint' was made about the ferry service being 'totally neglected'. The ferryman, a Richard Baker, had 'from some misdemeanour' run away. Sir Henry Apleton, the owner of the ferry, was therefore ordered to find an able man and a boat, which suggests that Baker had taken his with him.

Back on the main road after leaving Hullbridge you will see opposite 'The Dome' the first of the wooded elevations on the right, truly 'heights' for these flat parts. This is the site of Plumburrow or Plumberrow Mount. It is in the Domesday Book, and Roman and Early Saxon pottery was found in 1914. Despite the Roman finds, Pevsner thinks the mount, seventy-six feet in diameter and fourteen feet high, is of later date. There are fine views to be had from here. No

St Andrew's, Ashingdon

doubt its potential as a look-out has been readily appreciated
by more than one wave of invaders.

And so to even more historic Ashingdon. On your right is
a little church upon a hill. This is St Andrew's, looking in
this direction out across the Crouch, and to the south, but
from this point out of view, the much urbanized village of
Ashingdon, then Rochford and the River Roach.

Although the site of the desperate Battle of Assandun in
1016 was once in dispute, there is little doubt remaining now
that here we stand on the ground where, in Holinshed's
words, 'the Englishmen were beaten down and slaine in
heaps' – even though he placed the action at Ashdon. This
rival claimant is near Saffron Walden. The main argument
advanced in its favour was based on the Bartlow Hills,
originally eight tall barrows but now only four. They were
for long thought to be Danish in origin, but excavations
showed them to be far older, Roman or Romano-British
burial chambers of the first or second century AD. They seem
to form part of an important complex in the area, one which

includes earthworks and traces of a villa. The development
of the name 'Ashdon' also tells against it being the location
of the battle. Reaney observed that its earliest forms bear no
resemblance to 'Assandune'. Ashdon in the Domesday Book
appears as 'Ascenduna', meaning 'hill overgrown with ash
trees', whereas Ashingdon in 1016 was 'Assandune', which
is either 'ass's hill' or 'hill of Assa'. Also, a poem in honour
of Canute or Cnut, 'Knutschapa', gives the name of the
battle as 'Assantun'.

So much for the linguistic evidence. To this we can add
what is admittedly 'the superstition of a name', that of the
historian Freeman. In his great six volume work *The History
of the Norman Conquest* (1867–9) he firmly supports
Ashingdon, making his case to some extent on the nature of
the terrain and capped by the feeling evoked in him by the
place. He wrote: 'As to the site of Assandune I will not enter
into any discussion. I think no one will doubt it who has
been there.' This certainly does not disguise the subjectivity
of his judgement.

'On the down called Assendune' the invading Danes were
confronted by King Edmund with his alliance armies of
Wessex, Mercia and the south. After besieging London and
an indecisive engagement in Kent, Canute had moved into
Essex, raiding for provisions. On 18 October 1016 the
armies met and clashed on the level ground around the hill,
perhaps in the vicinity of lonely Scaldhurst Farm,
'Caldehouse' or 'the cold house' in 1324, lying midway
between Ashingdon and Canewdon. All must have augured
well at first for Edmund encamped above the marshes which
were flooded at high tide. But the day was lost when Eadric,
the cunning Ealdorman of Mercia, deserted his king for the
second time that year and went over to Canute with
treacherous timing. The *Anglo-Saxon Chronicle* was later to
lament the slaughter: 'There was Bishop Eadnoth [of
Dorchester] killed, and Abbot Wulfsige [of Ramsey] and
Ealdorman Aelfric [Hampshire] ... and all the nobility were
destroyed.'

Freeman tells it well: 'There is the hill on which Edmund
Ironside marshalled his army for the last battle, the hill down
whose slopes he rushed with his sword, as the faint echo of
the ballad tells us, like the lightning-flash, leaving in this

charge the royal post between the Standard and the West-Saxon Dragon, and fighting hand in hand in the foremost rank of his warriors. The Raven of Denmark had already fluttered its wings for victory; but it was only through Eadric's treason that Edmund, in the sixth battle of that great year, found himself for the first time defeated.'

Edmund, who for his brave resistance earned for himself the epithet of 'Ironside', was pursued into Mercia. Canute's army, however, was exhausted and at a meeting in Gloucestershire, on an island in the Severn, the kingdom was partitioned. Edmund died in November and was buried at Glastonbury. As for Eadric, he disappears from the red-stained pages of history.

Four years later Canute returned to the scene of his costly victory. He came with 'Archbishop Wulfstan of York, Earl Thorkill and many bishops and also abbots and monks with them and hallowed [consecrated] the mynster of Assandun'. The little church 'of stone and lime' had been built by Canute's order. The loss of life had been heavy on both sides, and the Minster was erected for masses to be perpetually said for the souls of the fallen. Its first priest was the King's chaplain, Stigand. An Anglo-Dane from East Anglia, he rose to become Archbishop of Canterbury only to be ejected by the Normans and to die in prison.

The church, St Andrew's, has no visible workmanship today of the eleventh century. Pevsner tentatively dates the nave and chancel from around 1300. But the dating seems problematic. Worley (1915) surmises a general reconstruction in the twelfth century, while Cox in Methuen's *Little Guide to Essex* (revised 1952) refers to 'evidence of pre-Norman work'. Professor Stenton has argued for a Saxon church before Canute's, giving a date of *circa* 970, although I do not know the basis for this assertion. Pevsner's name would normally carry the greater weight but there is good cause for thinking the foundations at least are those of Canute's church. Everything here at Ashingdon is dimmed through a mist.

The approach to St Andrew's is up a small and inconspicuous lane, Church Road, opposite a service station. The church is partially screened by trees, with a modern house for its rectory by its side.

The hilltop setting should take your breath away. From the churchyard, well endowed with seats, you can see for miles. To the north the Crouch is a coiling ribbon to the sea, and the Danbury Hills lie in the distance. Eastwards Canewdon church stands a sentinel on its hill. Turning southwards you can see Foulness and, when it is really sharp, the Maplin Sands. The prospect is one you are never likely to forget: a place where 'on a clear day you can see forever'.

The church matches the setting, simple and rugged, every inch a testament to its past. Its very smallness is in itself a pointer to great age. More than most it emanates the spirit of its place.

The site is one of great if puzzling antiquity. There is evidence, albeit slender, of earthworks, and I am grateful to an Essex archaeologist, Mr David Buckley in the County Planning Department, for seeking out what few details on this there are.

North of the church there are indications of a possible ridge and furrow. Moreover, the church itself stands in a large rectangular area which on the evidence of photographed crop-marks seems to have been enclosed by a ditch system. Although falling short of proof, this is fully consistent with a fortified space or even battle camp.

Also consistent with the belief that the church stands on the ground of Canute's camp are the excavations of a previous rector, the Rev. F.C. Ewing. In his little guide to the church, *May I show you round?*, he tells us he dug some eight feet out from the eastern end and found lime and stone in line with the walls which could be taken as an extension of the Danish foundations. There is structural evidence, too, that the chancel once went further to the east. A treasure of the church is the silver penny of Canute the Rev. Ewing found in the churchyard in 1928. It was brought to light from a depth of six feet when a grave was being dug. A duplicate is exhibited in the church, the original being held in the Prittlewell Museum, Southend. One face shows the head of the King, while the other portrays Godwin. Apparently this is the only one of its kind to have been found in Britain. Another grave disclosed two coats of chain mail which fell to powder when touched.

The church is full of interest. There are signs of dislocation probably caused by subsidence in the past. A writer, Reginald Beckett, at the turn of the century noted: 'The whole building had been much pulled about.' Through generous donations since, this has been put right, leaving it with a somewhat crooked appearance of great charm. The tower is particularly striking, short and remarkably small in width. The floor is lower than that of the rest of the church. The clock outside is very unusual. There are several modern links with Denmark: the Danish flag; a model of a Viking ship suspended from the beams above the nave; and a small oak diptych on a window sill, a gift from Copenhagen, one panel showing Canute commanding the waves, while in the other carving he is placing his crown on an altar.

The church briefly won another fame around 1300. It was the centre for a cult of a wonder-working image, perhaps of the Virgin. It obviously attracted many, especially childless women, who crawled up the hill on their knees. A diocesan enquiry led to its suspension. For centuries after, an aura of luck led people to be married here, and it is still very popular for weddings.

A mile or two away from the hill there is Fambridge, the two parishes south and north divided by the river. As at Hullbridge there was in the past a bridge here, a lengthy one to judge by the width of the Crouch at this point. Once again the place-name is instructive, the 'Fam' being 'fan' or 'phan', a marsh.

There is little here on the south side of architectural interest; the church was totally rebuilt in 1846, though it keeps a medieval font. There is also a pub, the Anchor, and a lobster farm. But the parish has its stories, moments of excitement in times gone.

In the summer of 1784 Crozier, ever alert for curious news, sat down to write: 'A large balloon descended in a field near Fambridge Ferry with a Major Money and another gentleman, heavy men. They came down there about three o'clock in the afternoon, pack'd it up and convey'd it to Maldon in a cart. The car, in the form of a boat, was superb.'

Several references to Crouch ferrymen can be found in Elizabethan records. Among those named at the two Fambridges were a John Richmond and Nicholas Perrin.

Both were required to account for frequent absences from church on the sabbath, and they pleaded their watery duties. The bridge even then was a thing of the distant past. In a statement made by Richmond, he argued: 'The ferry is the Queen's Majesty's open and common way for all passengers, as well on her Majesty's special affairs as other her Majesty's subjects, to pass to and from the towns in the Rochford hundred ... the benefit of the ferry is not sufficient to maintain a servant, deputy or substitute.' Today you will hail across the water in vain.

The tale of Captain Cammock is too good to be left untold. You can read it as it first appeared in the pages of Morant.

Lord Rich, probably the third Baron of the line, was travelling from his stately home at Leighs, 'delicious Leez', to Rochford Hall. He was accompanied by his daughter Alice and in his retinue one Captain Cammock. The captain was in love with her, and they decided to elope, on horseback. What happened when they reached the river at North Fambridge reads like a happier version of 'Lord Ullin's Daughter'. They found the ferry-boat was on the other side and the current very strong, a 'dark and stormy water'. Pursued, their only choice was to forge across on the horse or to turn back and face an irate father. Despite Cammock's pleas, Alice urged him on, vowing to die with him if need be. So it was they plunged with the horse into the Crouch and headed for the southern bank. They had reached mid-stream when a servant of Lord Rich arrived upon the scene. His horse began loudly neighing, 'upon which the horse that carried the lovers turned round and with much difficulty was brought to keep his course. They rode to Maldon and were wedded and bedded'.

The marriage, I'm happy to add, received the father's blessing. Morant concluded this romantic tale with an 'all's well that ends well' touch. Lord Rich 'seeing she had ventured her life for him said "God blesse 'em" '. Cammock clearly prospered. A widower, his first wife, Ursula, had given him nine children. Alice presented him with thirteen. He died in 1602, and all twenty-five are remembered with a fine monument of marble and alabaster in Maldon's All Saints Church.

Although it requires a detour from the main highway to Canewdon, the village of Paglesham is a decided must if you have not been there before. It is totally isolated and unspoilt. Out from Ashingdon you take the right fork at the Shepherd and Dog. It is here, too, that you can feast your eyes on a solitary house by the corner, timbered and plastered, worn but not decayed and snug in the landscape.

There are, in effect, two Pagleshams, two focal points, but if time is short and you cannot lengthen it out, follow the 'Church End' sign. This will take you to a lovely row of houses, partially bricked and gleaming white with weatherboards, and then at the end St Peter's and the Hall.

The very first is the Punch Bowl. With its storeys, Pevsner says that the house is on 'a somewhat more townish scale' than the others. It does indeed loom up. He gives no date; Mee calls it 'a 17th century inn', but at the bar I was decisively told it has been here for 550 years. The pub has been 'done up', yet not disastrously so. The house is very comfortable and well appointed, lavish in old beams and sporting brass and pewter mugs. The menu is impressive. This pub must be a good refuge when the weather is foul and winds come off the open land outside. The landscape is very flat and open, vast fields beneath an endless sky.

St Peter's has several things about it much to my liking. The embattled tower, rising in three stages, looks very sturdy and weather-worn. Inside, its archway, strikingly tall and elegant for a modest parish church, dwarfs all else. Propped up in the entrance are the inner Great West doors of Westminster Abbey! An odd acquisition, they were given to the church by the Dean and Chapter of the Abbey in memory of a former rector.

Most here is of the fifteenth century but three deep Norman windows remain of the original building. Victorian restoration was fairly drastic yet necessary, for the church had deteriorated badly. The chancel floor is particularly pleasing, having been paved with seventeenth- and eighteenth-century headstones brought in from the church-yard. An exceptional series, their tops are carved with emblems of mortality: cherubs, skulls, cross-bones and the like. One of 1734 has this inscription:

Short was my time the longer is my rest
God took me hence for why he saw it best.

With the church the Georgian hall stands on land at first
held by Croyland Abbey. Just before the Battle of Hastings
the abbot presented it to Westminster, in whose hands it
stayed till 1540. Church Hall is now the property of Caleb
Raynor Farms Ltd. This is an unusual name and is owned by
a son of the Caleb Raynor who around 1930 farmed at
Tanfield Tye in Hanningfield.

At East End, Paglesham, five minutes drive away, you will
be just a short walk from the sea-wall on the River Roach.
The pub in this corner of the parish is the very popular
Plough and Sail. Very old and attractive, it serves an
excellent fare to match the appeal of the place. As at the
Punch Bowl, you can eat oysters here in season.

Of Paglesham and Wallasea oysters Defoe wrote, 'On this
shoar also are taken the best and nicest, tho' not the largest
oysters in England.' Their fame in antiquity spread as far as
Rome, where the Wallasea variety were known as
'Wallfleets'. Late last century thirty oyster smacks worked
on the Roach. The winter of 1963 spelt disaster for this
ancient industry but a recovery now seems well under way.
If you go to the little boatyard, you will see boldly displayed
'Paglesham Oysters' on a riverside hut. Beyond lies Potten
Island.

The parish also had the colourful if dubious reputation of
being the foremost haunt of smugglers along the Essex
shores. The most notorious of these was William Blyth, alias
'Hard Apple'. He was renowned among the village folk not
only for his skirmishes with the Customs men – his cutter
Big Jane made many illicit runs across the Channel – but also
for such winning ways as crushing wine-glasses in his
mouth and consuming whole kegs of brandy. One of his
numerous legendary feats was to wrestle with a bull which
he downed. His contraband he secreted in the church tower
and also in hollow elms standing near East Hall, a spot much
closer to the river.

He was a native, born here in 1756. He ran a grocer's shop
and was not averse, it is said, to wrapping up his sales in
pages torn from the parish registers, although I wonder if

this has ever been checked against the books. They commence late, from 1719. However, a register of marriages kept in his time, covering the years 1754 to 1812, has been lost since 1900. This may have held the answer.

As he lay on his deathbed at the grand age of eighty-four a neighbour read to him from the Good Book. The reading finished, the old rogue turned his face to the wall and said, 'Thank you. Now I'm ready for the launch.'

Arriving at Canewdon revives the question of Canute. If a little doubt still lingers over Battlesbridge, there is now none at all for the meaning of Canewdon. It is not, as the older books used to tell us, 'Canute's hill', though the sound of the name deceptively lends itself to that interpretation, but 'the hill of Cana's people'. This personal name occurs as well in 'Canvey', so perhaps both of these shore places were settled by the very same Saxon chieftain. But the origins of the name Canewdon does not, of course, preclude the presence of King Canute here. He could not have failed to have seen and exploited the advantages of the spot, for the village huddles by Beacon Hill and looks to the west on Ashingdon. Tradition has it, and it is a logical supposition, that he set up camp upon the hill when Edmund assembled on his.

That Danes were familiar with these parts is beyond all question. Canewdon was in the Danelaw, although in Essex generally there was hardly any settlement. This must account for the paucity of Scandinavian place-names. Several of the very few there are remain in question. Danbury is not what it looks so does not count, but the Sokens do, and there are one or two others tucked away in Essex towards the sea.

There are traces of old encampments at Canewdon, rather more prominent than those at Ashingdon. They were found in a field south of the church and originally enclosed about six acres. The Romans were here – try to find a place where they were not – because urns have been turned up, but the dating of earthworks and determining their precise function are often the most baffling tasks in archaeology. Many must have been used again and again down the corridors of time and for a variety of purposes. So those at Canewdon, even if not Danish in origin, could have been adapted by them.

Coming into the parish from the east, you will pass Lambourne Hall. Shielded from the road by a wide green verge and a red-brick wall, the house is timber-framed and plastered. A huddle of gables, it is a lovely blend of different ages and styles from around 1500 to the nineteenth century. The name has been linked with Robert de Lamborne of 1199 and his descendants.

There has been a fair amount of building around the village in recent years but it is the centre and the church you will want to see.

The church of St Nicholas rears up on Beacon Hill, a self-explanatory name and used as such to modern times when in the Second World War the RAF used the tower for signalling and observation. There was a beacon here long before the Nore Light was set up. The tower is most impressive, with the lower walls seven feet in thickness. It rises to a height of eighty-five feet. They will tell you here that from the top you can see seven hundred churches, which is true if you take it as 'Hundred'. I've never been up to the parapet, but all descriptions agree on the wide, commanding view to be had.

Above the west door in the tower, several ancient but badly worn shields are carved. The one in the middle has the arms of Henry V. This may account for the tradition that the church was built or rebuilt to commemorate Agincourt. There is work from the previous century but no sign of the Normans. Roman bricks make their inevitable appearance, in the tower and north wall of the nave. Another coat of arms is that of Mary de Bohun, the mother of the King. So perhaps this church, surprisingly spacious and large, may have had a royal endowment.

The font came from the old, demolished church of Shopland. The beautiful oak pulpit came from elsewhere, from Wren's St Christopher-le-Stocks. (The Bank of England now occupies its site.) Grinling Gibbons may have been responsible for the carving; the pulpit is certainly in his style. The organ, too, is an import, said to have started its life in old St Paul's.

Looking at a list of vicars, my eyes were drawn to Thomas Newman, 1588. People make places and I don't know why but I find a constant pleasure in the lives of our old parish clergy. They produced a goodly proportion of scholars, eccentrics and rogues. Court records of Elizabethan days have a liberal sprinkling of the latter, and Thomas Newman, clerk, is there among them. He appears several times, indulging in behaviour most unseemly for the cloth. In 1602 he carried out an armed assault on a neighbour's house. Accompanied by four labourers, he carried off one Augustine Dawney – bare facts behind which there lies, untold, a little parish drama. Each assailant was bound over and fined £10.

Then, from the previous year, comes this, reported by the wardens: 'He was consenting and privy to the picking of the lock of our parish chest wherein we keep our evidence and writings, out of which chest there was certain evidences taken away at the same time that the lock was picked which concern the lands belonging to the poor; and one Robert Parker now deceased, a smith, did confess before my Lord Riche that Mr Newman and one Mr Kinge did cause him to do the same. Further we say our same vicar is very slack and negligent in going perambulation for these two years past.'

Two years before Mr Newman had the living, there was another nice little scandal to report. This one concerned the curate, George Elmer, complained of as 'a haunter of alehouses, a drinker, and a player at cards and tables'.

It was from this age and that of the early Stuarts that Canewdon acquired its reputation for the black arts. In his unfinished *History of Rochford Hundred*, published between 1867 and 1888, Benton writes of Canewdon producing six witches, which other accounts have increased to nine. One of these was the spinster Rose Pye, who in the summer of 1580 was alleged to have enchanted the one-year-old Joan Snow. The child died one month after. Nearer our own time an awesome figure was George Pickingill; with Murrell of Hadleigh he was one of the last of the 'cunning men', a term of Old Norse derivation meaning fortune tellers or seers. Superstition lingered on and has had a jaded revival or two in our own time.

The village shared in the dark obsessions which were more rampant in the county than anywhere else in England. Parrinder in his book *Witchcraft* (Penguin, 1958) has given some telling figures. In the reign of Elizabeth there were 455 indictments at assizes for witchcraft in the south-east, and almost three hundred of these were in Essex. Then in the shorter reign of James I another seventy Essex cases were heard. The craze faded away after Matthew Hopkins, the infamous Witchfinder General, when a more rationalist spirit began to prevail among the magistrates. Incidentally, it was in the time of Canute that the law against communing with 'evil spirits' became very severe. Banishment or even death was enacted for those who were not repentant.

Among the most feared spells of Canewdon's witches were those for blighting crops and raising storms. Had the floods of 1953 occurred three centuries before, there is no doubt where the village would have laid the blame.

In *The Great Tide* (1959) Hilda Grieve has told in mammoth scope and detail the story of those dark and tragic days in coastal Essex. For much of the route I've taken you on through these pages, the sea broke in with unexpected force and on a devastating scale, covering with corrosive salt some of the richest acres in the country.

The vast campaign to rescue the people and animals marooned and to re-seal the broken river walls was very aptly named as 'Operation King Canute'. That little Danish carving in Ashingdon church, the King on his seashore throne, is not without a local significance. In a sense which could never have been envisaged, this is indeed a Canute country and the Crouch 'the Battle River'.

7

Land's End on the Saxon Shore

There are two places which could well be styled the 'Land's End' of the Essex coast. Foulness is one. I have long wished to visit the forbidden island. As most will know, it is inaccessible to the general public, being zealously guarded by the Ministry of Defence. The closest it can be approached is at the Wakerings.

Once my ambition was almost realized. I got as far as the police post in company with a brewer's rep who had a pass. But the road across was closed that day for repairs. So, turning back, we eased our disappointment in a pub, surrounded by a wealth of curios. The day was, however, redeemed for me when an old and ailing man crouched in a corner was pointed out as the former owner of the Kursaal in Southend. Alas, my boyhood haunt is a pleasure dome no more. Sold off, the site of the Haunted House, the Scenic Railway and the Water Chute has now been usurped by mere houses.

Had my venture been successful, I might have been writing about the never-never land of Foulness here. But although armchair explorations are not to be despised, I never make them until after I have seen a place and stood where I can put out my antenna.

However, I have been many times to that other land's end, to the peninsula where Bradwell and the Blackwater meet the sea.

Bradwell juxta Mare lies in the very north-east corner of the Dengie Hundred. To reach it there are two routes you can follow. The more direct goes out from Latchingdon, which can be reached from Maldon or Woodham Ferrers, to Mayland and then on through Steeple and St Lawrence, and there are one or two beguiling asides to be made along the

St Peter's on the Wall

way. It is a route which provides a succession of names to take the eye.

There is, I regret, no spire at Steeple. The ancient church has gone, replaced in the 1880s with another on a different site. Designed by Frederick Chancellor, it incorporates some of the old material, including a window and a doorway and a long-neglected font from the churchyard. The original church had been ailing for centuries. Morant, writing in 1768, noted, 'The Chancel is in ruins.' But even in 1564 the wardens had reported, 'The chancel is clean down.' The benefice was owned by Richard Rich of Lees, but he does not seem to have effected any repairs.

Morant also speculated on the name of the parish. He wrote that in the remotest times it was called 'Ulfwinefcher-che', which I take to be 'Ulswinschurch', and added, 'which being too long for the inhabitants of the kingdom, that delight in short names and monosyllables, was changed into that of Steple, taken undoubtedly from the Church, which had a steple and the other neighbouring Churches had not'. But there is no warrant for this in Reaney, who gives its earliest form, in Domesday, as virtually the same as now. Moreover, it is a little disappointing, perhaps, to learn that in all probability 'Steeple' does not tell us of a church steeple but of a steep place, even though the land here is barely elevated.

Two farms hereabouts are Gate and Grange Farms. Stansgate, which is Stonegate, standing where the parish meets the Blackwater, gives the clue, for this was the site of a small Cluniac priory founded in the early twelfth century. It must have been lonely for the inmates; when it was closed by Cardinal Wolsey in 1525, there was only a prior and two other monks left. Up to the 1920s the derelict chapel was used as a barn, but today just a single wall remains. Nearby there is Abbey Farm. As a complement to Stonegate there is to the east 'The Stone' at Romsey, while to the west there is Mundon Stone Point. There may at one time have been a stone gate on the shore, an entrance to the monastic estate, or it could be synonymous with a landing stage, similar in function to Traitors' Gate at the Tower (without the sinister associations of course). From the front you will see in mid-river Osea Island, cut off at high tide from Goldhanger opposite. The mudflats between are well called 'The Stumble'.

Looking out on Osea is a good place to reflect on the halcyon days of wildfowling along the creeks and marshes all the way from Maldon to Foulness. Defoe in his *Tour*, after writing dismissively 'There is nothing for many miles remarkable, but a continued level of unhealthy marshes', goes on to say of the Blackwater: 'By our fishermen and seamen, who use it as a port, 'tis called Malden-Water.' He then proceeds;

In this inlet of the sea is Osey or Osyth Island, commonly called Oosy Island, so well known by our London men of pleasure, for the infinite number of wild fowl, that is to say, duck, mallard, teal and widgeon, of which there are such vast flights, that they tell us the island, namely the creek, seems covered with them, at certain times of the year, and they go from London on purpose for the pleasure of shooting; and indeed often come home very well laden with game. But it must be remembered too, that those gentlemen who are such lovers of the sport, and go so far for it, often return with an Essex ague on their backs, which they find a heavier load than the fowls they have shot.

Defoe is sometimes to be suspected of tall tales, or perhaps it is more likely he was simply 'taken in'. An imaginative journalist, he had all the virtues and vices of that breed. But lest we think his 'vast flights' are more of fancy than fact, we have testimony in plenty of their magnitude from a later age.

There is that of Thomas Kemble, a sporting squire of Runwell Hall – he would barely recognize it now – who once saw so many wild geese darkening the sky that he estimated they were spread out a mile long and a quarter wide, sounding like 'fifty packs of hounds in full cry'. Tompkins, giving this in his *Companion Into Essex*, tells also of 288 Dunlin sandpipers felled with a single discharge on a frozen creek. Another instance he gives is of thirty-four punts which put out from Mersea and, reaching the foreshore of St Peter's, our destination, bagged nine hundred geese. They do not come in such numbers in our day. Extermination, drainage and a change of habitat and habit have seen to that. Bird-watching and protection are the keynote now.

By St Lawrence is Beacon Hill Farm, a few feet above sea-level, its name confirming what we should expect, for warning lights are necessary on these shores. Sometimes called St Lawrence Newlands, suggesting land reclaimed from the sea in ages past, this is another tiny place. The church, totally rebuilt in 1877, looks from its crossroads site across a bay. The registers are from 1704, a date which tells us there was a previous church. Three Wedgewood Benns lie here, marked by a floor slab in front of the chancel: one a newly born while the last to be interred was the first, and only, Lord Stansgate. Tony Benn owns the Priory at Stansgate.

Between here and Bradwell on the highway, S.L. Bensusan lived a while at Mote Cottage, one of his several Essex homes. His last was at Langham near Dedham, at 'Godfreys'. Next to the white, weatherboarded Mote House there stands the equally delectable cottage of 'Cobbetts' which, at the invitation of its owners, Mr and Mrs Lawson, I have been fortunate to see inside. Thatched and timber-framed, with small rooms and very low ceilings, it has been beautifully kept. From the spacious garden at the rear there is a panoramic view of the river, and a finer one in these parts can hardly be imagined. This tiny cottage housed in earlier years two families, one of which consisted of six persons!

A framed photograph here is of rare interest, showing an old man in a smock standing outside the house on the lane. This, I am told, is the character drawn from the very life by Bensusan as 'Father William'.

This seems to me to be a point in my narrative to pause and bring to your notice this writer whose name means nothing to our time. He has gone with the way of life he so superbly celebrated as he watched it rapidly going, the distinctive, age-old life of the land. By the few who are now discovering him afresh, his books are eagerly looked for.

Samuel Levy Bensusan (1872–1958) first made his mark in letters as a journalist of no small note. Well read, his sympathies and experience were very wide. In 1897–8 he was the young editor of the *Jewish World*. By the 1920s he was much involved in Theosophy, then still a potent force, acting as adviser to its publishing house in Britain and as editor of the *Theosophical Review*. A formative influence on his life was the remarkable Annie Besant. Among his wide circle of friends were Frances Maynard, Hardy and H.G. Wells. He became a special correspondent, going to many places abroad, and was also a music critic. The diversity of his interests is further shown by his book on Coleridge and co-authorship of a work on the Renaissance.

In 1907 he wrote the first of a long succession of countryside books, but it was with *Village Idylls* in 1926 that he found his real métier in that genre. Among his most memorable books one must place *The Annals of Maychester*, his 'Marshland' volumes, *Fireside Papers* – written in the early forties, the darkest days of the Second World War, *From God's Own County* and *Back of Beyond*, the name he gave to the public for his final home on the Essex-Suffolk border. In many of these he created tales based on the rural folk he knew at first hand. To posterity he has handed on their values and sentiments, their speech rhythms and dialect, their parochial occupations, all seen with a kindly eye and measured with an unerring instinct for the good and true in their little worlds beyond the alien urban understanding.

I have learned from him that, although we cannot turn back the clock, we should beware of those who want to push it forward far too quickly.

On the last page of *Back of Beyond* Bensusan wrote: 'It has been my fortune to witness the passing of the countrymen of Essex and East Anglia, the pace of the builder's progress, the passing of individuals beneath the steam-roller of drab uniformity, driven by men whose virtues are unstained by imagination'.

On reaching Bradwell-on-Sea we find in effect that it lies in three parts. A nice little book to stroll around with is Kevin Bruce's *Dengie, the life and the land*, published by the Essex Record Office in 1981. A photographic record of how it was at the turn of the century, the book has several of Bradwell among its fascinating pictures.

The Waterside was once of importance for maritime traffic. Many sailing barges plied to and from here laden with hay to their mast-tops or with cargoes of manure or Kentish ragstone for the incessant task of re-facing the sea walls. The lights in the windows of the Green Man guided seamen up the river as the beacons do now on Pewit Island. Bradwell Creek was 'Hacflet' or 'Hackfleet' in 1086, a name which seems to refer to its angular bend, 'like a dog's hind leg', it has been said. Incidentally, 'Bradwell' means a broadstream and could well have been the original name for the Blackwater.

Formerly the Quay had a coastguard station. All here is on a small scale and since 1957 has been dwarfed by the nuclear power station which like a grey colossus sits nearby, an intimidating presence. The pleasant village is mainly a huddle of old houses by the church, another restored by Chancellor. The tower is a late addition, brick, from 1706. Among the wall plaques to those late of this parish is one which has a single, stark memorial line, a gaunt testimony to the Protestant work ethic: 'His life was useful.' Opposite the church on a sharply curving bend is the King's Head, the sign being that of Henry VIII. Outside there stands a rarity, a long-disused red box of the Essex County Fire Brigade.

You will surely find the instructions now quite whimsical. Another bygone is a small Georgian lock-up in the churchyard wall, with a third treat only feet away, a mounting-block by the gate.

A worthy among the parsons of St Thomas the Apostle was Thomas Abell. He was chaplain and confidant to Catherine of Aragon. For preaching against the royal divorce he was twice arrested. The Queen gave him the living here but after six years in the Tower he was martyred. His fate was sealed when he published his *Invicta Veritas*.

At the south end of the village there is Bradwell Lodge. This is an architectural joy, a product of the Age of Elegance. It is an unlikely vision in these humble parts. The explanation lies in that remarkable character 'the Fighting Parson' and formidable squire the Rev. Henry Bate or, as he became in his later years, the Rev. Sir Henry Bate-Dudley.

Born in Warwickshire, he is now all but forgotten in Dengie. He was an Essex celebrity and cut a figure on the London scene as well. In town he won passing fame in a variety of ways: as a journalist, editing a paper and founding another; as a would-be dramatist, trying his hand at comic operas; and more notoriously making a name as a duellist and a gallant, a frequenter of Vauxhall Gardens, 'as magnificent a piece of humanity, perhaps, as ever walked arm in arm with a fashionable beauty'. A patron of prize-fighting, he also had a reputation himself for fisticuffs. A libel on the Duke of Richmond landed him in gaol for a twelvemonth, where he entertained his friends. Larger than life, this gentleman of many parts seems to have been determined to leave his mark on his times. Like Chesterton's St Joan, he 'chose a path and went down it like a thunderbolt'.

He appears, although unnamed, in the pages of Boswell's *Johnson*. 'We talked of a certain clergyman of extraordinary character who by exerting his talents in writing on temporary topicks, and displaying uncommon intrepidity, had raised himself to affluence.' Boswell admired his success but the Doctor would not allow the parson such merit, though he recognized his courage 'even when associated with vice'. He likened Bate to a highwayman 'who robs boldly on the highway' which was preferable to 'a fellow who jumps out of a ditch and knocks you down from behind'.

The Reverend was a noted sportsman and being no mean sailor once ventured the sea from Harwich to Ipswich in a hurricane, an escapade he immensely enjoyed. He gets several mentions in Crozier's diary. In 1783, 'Rev. Mr Bates ... gave a cup of ten pounds value, to be sail'd for by 10 Fishing Smacks.' The following year, 'Rev. Bate Dudley gave a cup to be sail'd for off the Bradwell shore under particular sailing orders. The river is very broad there, and a fine day with numbers of boats of various descriptions, with music, etc.'

Bate's vigour as a fox-hunter was legendary. With his pack of hounds he had pursued a fox up the ivy-clad walls of Creeksea church and made the kill on the chancel roof.

He succeeded to the living of North Fambridge after his father, the rector, died in 1775. Later he bought that of Bradwell. But after giving liberally to rebuild the church and improve the lot of the poor in the parish, he was barred from the incumbency by the bishop on grounds of simony. However, he continued to live in at the rectory, acting it seems as the curate. The resentment of his deprivation he was to carry to the grave.

He spent a fortune on drainage, reclaiming over two hundred acres of marshland and improving the roads. And he commissioned the county surveyor John Johnson to refashion the Tudor rectory, later to be called 'The Lodge', with impeccable eighteenth-century taste. Among Johnson's other buildings are the Shire Hall at Chelmsford and Terling Place, designed for John Strutt. The work on the rectory was done between 1781 and 1786 in what Pevsner calls 'a style metropolitan'. The main alteration was to give the house a new south side of two rooms with a circular library between them. A graceful belvedere with Ionic columns was added to the roof. Robert Adam may have had a hand in the interior decoration, to judge from the plasterwork and fireplaces. The ceiling of the drawing-room is by Robert Smirke.

Bate-Dudley held sumptuous and eccentric dinner-parties in this house, often giving an evening the menu and look of a particular foreign country, with his guests dressing accordingly in national costume. Among the close friends who were probably entertained here were Gainsborough, Garrick, Hogarth and Mrs Siddons. A more recent owner of The Lodge was the late Tom Driberg MP, who occasionally opened its doors to the public.

The Reverend was also the local magistrate and in exercising his powers was especially hard on poachers. His sense of his station no doubt saw to that, quite apart from the vicious game laws then in force.

Having been left a fortune by a relative, he added 'Dudley' to his name under the terms of the will. It must have eased his chagrin when he was given a living in Ireland where he went to live for some years. He seems to have had some influence in high places regardless of the black spots in his career, for he was awarded a baronetcy and then, near the end, was installed as a canon in Ely Cathedral. His death came in 1824. He was seventy-nine. One of the last of the roisterous gentry, Bate-Dudley had seen a more sedate and sober age coming in.

Although the attractions of Bradwell Waterside and the village are not to be denied, there is a greater magnet which draws the visitor here, the truly ancient settlement by the Flats. The way runs past the Easts: East End, East Hall and Eastlands Farm, where the road, a Roman one, turns to a track. It leads to the venerable chapel of St Peter-on-the-Wall.

I never fail to be delighted, even moved, when it looms on the left into sight. As at Greensted and Ashingdon, for me the 'still, small voice' of the dim, historic past comes across the ages clear. Made of stone, the gaunt Saxon church stands as a primitive guardian of our ancestral Faith. Small and isolated as it is, it towers against the marshes and the saltings. The setting is most impressive, for the church is all but licked by the sea in a seemingly endless space. When Rider Haggard saw it in 1902, he wrote in his *Rural England*:

The view, looking over the Dengie Flats and St Peter's Sands from the summit of the earthen bank which keeps out the sea, was very desolate and strange. Behind us lay a vast drear expanse of land won from the ocean in days bygone, bordered on the one side by the Blackwater and on the other by the Crouch River, and saved, none too well, from the mastery of the waves by the sloping earthen bank on which we stood. In front, thousands of acres of grey mud where grew dull, unwholesome looking grasses. Far, far away on this waste two tiny moving specks, men engaged in seeking for samphire or some other treasure of the ooze mud. Then, the thin, white lip of the sea, and beyond its sapphire edge in the half-distance, the gaunt skeleton of a long-wrecked ship. To the north, on the horizon, a line of trees; to the west, over the great plain, where stood one or two lonely farms, another line of trees. On the distant deep, some sails, and in the middle marsh, a barge gliding up a hidden creek as though she moved across the solid land. Then, spread like a golden garment over the vast expanses of earth and ocean, the flood of sunshine, and in our ears the rush of the north-west gale and the thrilling song of larks hanging high above the yellow, salt-soaked fields. Such was Dengie Marsh as I saw it in June, 1901. But what must it be like when buried beneath the snows of winter, or when the howling easterly winds of spring sweep across its spaces, and the combers of the North Sea sometimes reach and batter their frail embankment? Then indeed, I should not care to be the tenant of one of those solitary steads.

I have quoted this at length because 'I can always leave off talking when I hear a master play.' The blend of land and seascape stays in all essentials as he described it, though his predominant note of desolation shows he was no connoisseur of marshes. A colleague of mine, who knows and enjoys these flatlands well, once came here with a party which included a Bavarian. This fellow could see no beauty in the place and went on about the mountains and forests they had back home. Having listened to this eulogy on heights, another in the group at last spoke up and quietly said, 'Well, we removed the mountains. We found they were spoiling the view.' The Bavarian might have been given some comfort had he been told that they were looking out on what old maps styled 'the German Sea'.

St Peter's gets its somewhat hypothetical name of 'ad Muram', 'on-the-Wall', because there is excellent reason to believe it stands where there was a gate into the Roman fortress here. Excavations conducted in 1864–5, and some work since, have disclosed the ground plan. The site covered

at least four acres. The fort has been estimated at 520 feet
long but, as the eastern walls and the quay have been
destroyed by the sea, its width remains problematic.
However, the north wall ran for 290 feet. Walls of
twelve-foot thickness have been traced, and these were
horseshoe-shaped bastions at the corners. St Peter's stands
astride the western wall from whence a road went inland.
Vast amounts of broken pottery etc have been unearthed,
and clearly there were settlements here on the shoreline long
before the Romans came.

In all likelihood this imposing fortress was none other
than Othona, built at the close of the third century AD by
Carausius, one of the Counts of the Saxon Shore. Othona
was one of a line of nine defence works running from
Norfolk to the Isle of Wight. There are impressive remains
along the line: Burgh Castle by Great Yarmouth,
Richborough, Pevensey and Portchester. They were designed as bases for scout-ships to patrol the coastal waters,
on the look-out for pirates and sea-roving Saxons.

The *Comes Littoris Saxonici* (Count of the Saxon Shore)
was appointed by Rome to maintain these forts and guard
the seas. Carausius may have been the first. His turbulent
career was brief but remarkable. A coastal pilot from the
Low Countries, he was given the command of the Saxon
shore after showing his prowess at sea. Then, accused of
treachery — turning a blind eye to a pirate fleet and
subsequently helping himself to its booty — he was
condemned to death by the Emperor. Carausius evaded
capture, fleeing to Britain. With the Legions, he ruled the
province in defiance of Rome for seven years. His end came
in 293 at the hand of a fellow officer.

The chapel contains much Roman stone and brick. It is
the oldest church by far, and perhaps the oldest ecclesiastical
site, in all Essex, dating from the middle years of the seventh
century. But its unique age is not its sole claim to distinction.
Anglo-Celtic, it was founded by St Cedd, who came down
the coast from the fabled island monastery of Lindisfarne,
home of the famous illuminated Gospels. He came here
bringing new light where the old had flickered out. His
church here at Bradwell is thus 'the first cathedral of Essex'.
He founded other churches in the land of the East Saxons,

notably at Tilbury, but of that one nothing has survived. Cedd died of the plague, at Lastingham in Yorkshire. Thirty of his Bradwell community journeyed to be with him at the end but all perished there save a boy.

An excellent small guidebook, illustrated, to both fortress and chapel is available here, written by Malcolm Carter, so I will not enumerate the many absorbing details of its structure. Suffice to say that an apse and a little bell-tower are no more, but one has little difficulty in 'seeing' the church as it was. So lost in the mist was its past that in a report to the Bishop of London in 1442 none could say how old it was or who had built it. At that time it was used as a chapel-of-ease to the new church in the village. Later the tower was utilized for a beacon, and the nave became a barn. In 1920 St Peter's was re-consecrated, having been placed by the owner under trustees for the diocese.

No visit here can yield its full potential without a bracing walk along the sea-wall. If you head north of the chapel, you will pass the sheltered Othona Community, and coming to the headland there are views across the gleaming river of Mersea and, around the bend, the grey bulk of Bradwell power station.

Facing St Peter's on the saltings, there are hides. Here, if you are lucky, you may glimpse the protected Little Tern. A few yards from the chapel among shrubs is a lonely bargeboard cottage, formerly the home of Walter Linnett and his family. You can read of this last 'King of the Essex wildfowlers' in the late J. Wentworth Day's *Coastal Adventure* (1949).

Southwards you can walk for miles. The wall goes all the way to Burnham. Inland there is Tillingham, just twenty-two feet above sea-level. The Domesday Book tells us that these marshes supported a thousand sheep. There is also Marshhouse Decoy Pond, one of over thirty decoys in the Dengie Hundred whose sites can still be identified. Further south you will skirt the Dengie Marshes, vast and vacant, barely inches above the water.

On the other side there is nothing but mud-flats and the everlasting pulse of the sea. Looking back along this walk to contemplate Cedd's church and the nuclear power station in your view, it would be easy to hear what Matthew Arnold heard on Dover Beach, the receding tide of Faith, bringing 'the eternal note of sadness in'.

Malcolm Carter has set the contrast very well: 'To reconcile the different kinds of power represented by these two buildings is perhaps the principal problem of the present age.'

You may come here, as I once did, as just a curious tripper; you are likely to return a pilgrim.

Part IV

Countywide Themes and Variations

The old whalebone, Chadwell Heath

1

Unusual Place-names

Essex teems with curious and interesting place-names, as any study of a large-scale map or 'ramble round the shire' will show.

An anonymous 'Essex rhymer' wittily concocted these couplets:

> Willingale Doe and Willingale Spain,
> Bulvan and Bobbingworth, Colne Engaine;
> Wenden Lofts, Beaumont-cum-Moze, Bung Row
> Gestingthorpe, Ugely and Fingring hoe;
> Helion Bumpstead and Mountnessing,
> Bottle End, Tolleshunt D'Arcy, Messing;
> Islands of Canvey, Foulness, Potton,
> Stondon Massey and Belchamp Otton;
> Ingrave and Inworth and Keddington,
> Shellow Bowels, Ulting, Kelvedon;
> Margaret Roothing and Manningtree –
> The bolder you sound 'em the better they be!

Most of these look and sound very odd and could be added to *ad infinitum*.

'Toot Hill' at Stanford Rivers is an unlikely name. It suggests an invitation to motorists to sound their horn. In fact, it means a look-out place. The twin parishes of Totham, Great and Little, derive their name in the same way. Totham was first mentioned in Anglo-Saxon wills of the tenth century, and the earliest settlement there may have been on or near Beacon Hill, a vantage point.

'Nipsells Rayments' is very curious. It can be found at Mayland and East Horndon. The Nipsells was 'Cripps' spur of land' but Rayments is quite obscure. It may be a manorial expression.

209

For total obscurity in meaning 'Billericay' holds pride of place. This is a name which has defied all scholarly attempts at explanation. Only two other places in England have the name: Bellerica Farm in Somerset and Billerica, Kent, a lost name now with its exact location near Court-at-Street also unknown. The one thing the three have in common is their being sited on high ground. Billericay, Essex, makes its first appearance in records of 1291, in Pleas of the Forest. Now a sizeable and ever-growing town, it began as an offshoot of Great Burstead, which today it quite eclipses.

'Wimbish', too, is of uncertain meaning. The first element in the name may be the Old English *winn*, a 'meadow or pasture', and the second a derivative from a word for reeds. It was 'Wimbisc' around 1042.

'The Bumpsteads' have a rustic jollity to the name. Bumpstead seems to come from words meaning 'a hollow stem' and 'reeds', and when Reaney was doing his research on Essex place-names, he noted that reeds still grew in the stream there. Of the two parishes Helions was held in 1086 by a Breton who came from Heleon in France. Steeple Bumpstead once had a steeple or spire to its church, but the village was also formerly called 'Bumpstead *ad Turrum*, 'at the Tower', because one stood nearby.

What are we to make of 'Hobby Binns' at 'Stebbing'? It began as 'Hob of yndes'. William de Inde and Alexander Avynde of the thirteenth century give us the corrupted form 'Bins'. But 'Hob', unless this too is a later form, could be hobgoblin or fairy, the familiar form of Rob or Robin. Hobby Binns is not marked on the usual maps, and if you go to Stebbing, I doubt if you will find it. As Melville remarked of Kokovoko: 'It isn't down in any map; true places never are.'

Another good rustic-sounding name is 'Cumberton Bottom' at Little Chishall. The 'Bottom' can be easily guessed, and the lie of the land confirms it is a valley. 'Cumberton' probably derives from a man called Cumbra who many centuries ago put down his roots here, the 'ton' being his homestead. The personal name is an Old English one, although not recorded for Chishall before the fourteenth century. It also occurs in the name 'Cumberton' in Cambridgeshire.

Chrishall, not to be confused with Chishall, lies in the very north-west corner of the county, just moments away from Cambridgeshire. There are good things here to see: open, rolling countryside, old houses and a lovely church with notable brasses. But its greatest fascination for me is its name, one of the most enigmatic in Essex. 'Chrishall' was written in the Domesday Book as 'Christhalla'. Now there is no doubt about what the ending means. *Halla* signifies not what it has become in the course of time, a hall, but a nook, a secluded place, and the village remains tucked away even today. But it is the first part of the name which is really surprising, for it seems to be none other than 'Christ'. In fact, this is so unusual in a place-name that one major authority, seeing no apparent reason for it, found it barely credible. He hazarded it must be a contraction of *cristelmael*, the Old English for 'cross'.

Even to call 'Christhalla' unusual does not do it full justice. It is all but unique. There are only three other places in the country with Christ in their names: Christchurch in Dorset, Cressage or 'Christ's oak' in Shropshire, and Christescroft at Coventry. Christow, Devon, does not qualify, for the original form meant 'Christian place'. I expect we shall never learn who gave Chrishall its name or why. In the Middle Ages there was a grange here farmed by the Cistercians of Tilty. Of all people they would have appreciated the significance of the name. Perhaps these lovers of solitary places chose the spot for that very reason.

In the south-west, on the fringe of what Cobbett derisively called 'the Great Wen', there are some very intriguing names to be encountered. Dagenham provides us with 'Whalebone Lane'. This was 'Beamsland Lane' in 1641, which indicates a bridge or beam. Very shortly after it took the name of the Whalebone Bridge, and 'Whalebone' was applied as well to the adjacent farm. The jawbones of a whale stood here as an arch across the road. Daniel Defoe mentions the tradition, now known to be incorrect, that they were set up in the year of Oliver Cromwell's death, 1658. The 'monstrous creature', twenty-eight feet long, was said to have been stranded by the Thames. The whalebones were there when Miller Christy's *Trade Signs of Essex* was published in 1887. The old 'Whalebone', a beer shop, had gone around 1870. Christy measured and drew the jawbones. Their height out of the ground along the curve was fifteen feet six inches. He quotes a Fellow of the Royal Society who doubted if the whale was the Greenland species 'which never visits our shores'.

I recently noted a Whalebone Cottage in Langham. Some years ago, while cycling through Lincolnshire, I came upon a whalebone arch over the drive to a house in Three Kingham. Yet another known to me is the whalebone arch gateway near the hospital on the main road between Arkley and Barnet in Hertfordshire. This folly-like use of maritime relics was once quite common. In *Moby Dick* Melville quoted Hawthorne's *Twice Told Tales*: 'I built a cottage for Susan and myself and made a gateway in the form of a Gothic Arch by setting up a whale's jawbones.'

'Collier Row', Romford, is from the Middle English for a charcoal burner, a collier. With the forest nearby, it was an appropriate spot for that occupation. Here stood one of the hatches or gates leading into Hainault Forest, hence the pub called the Bell and Gate. 'Gooshayes' in the borough is a 'goose enclosure'; 'Gooses' in a sixteenth-century will and in the journal of George Fox, who used to visit his son-in-law here.

'Gidea Park' is obscure. Once the site of Sir Antony Cook's fine mansion, it has been suggested it comes from a nickname, 'giddy'. In Sir Antony's will of 1576 it is spelled 'Guydyhall'.

Another mysterious name in this crowded corner of Essex is 'Hornchurch'. It was recorded as *'ecclesia de Haweringis'*, Havering church, in 1163 and first mentioned as 'Hornchurch' two hundred years later. The meaning is much in dispute. Although the horns fixed on the west front of the church date only from the late eighteenth century, these may have been replacements for leaden horns of an earlier date. Strangely, the horns get no mention in an article on the church in the *Gentleman's Magazine* in 1828, a magazine which rarely failed to overlook any notice of the peculiar. A horned bull's head figures on a seal of the fourteenth century. However, 'Hornchurch' could signify a church in the sense of one with horn-like gables. Such a shape could have been the origin of a popular name, with horns being appropriately placed on the building later. To complicate matters still further, in 1222 Hornchurch was referred to as a *'Monasterium Cornutum'*, the 'corn' being horn.

North Ockendon gives us 'Stubbers'. This is a house owned by Essex County Council and bears a local family name. In the preamble to a survey map of nearby West Thurrock prepared for the lords of the manor in 1645, a Peter Stubber is mentioned. He was one of 'Three of the most ancient Inhabitants of the same Lordship and Towne' who witnessed the survey's accuracy. It is doubtful if any part of the house today dates from the time of William Coys (1560–1627), a botanist who had a celebrated garden here. He was the first to get a yucca to flower in England, and his garden plants were the earliest to be classified scientifically.

'Thurrock' has several related meanings, denoting a small ship, the bottom part of a vessel and, sadly for the locals, its bilge. It is also a dialect word for 'chain'. This could be its sense here, although the bend in the river at Thurrock may have been seen as resembling the shape of a boat.

Of 'Purfleet' here there is a waggish opinion that it is so called from Queen Elizabeth's exclaiming at the time of the Armada, 'My poor fleet!' Perhaps Poor Fleet Farm, on a map of 1767, expresses or even gave rise to this popular belief. In sober fact the first element in the name is indeed 'pur'. It is obscure, but the 'fleet' means 'stream'. The place was 'Purteflyete' in 1285, becoming 'Pourteflet' a few years later.

While sampling names along the river, 'Thames' itself is not without interest. Meaning 'the dark water or river', it was mentioned by Julius Caesar in 51 BC. The name is akin to the Sanscrit 'Tamasa', a tributary of the Ganges.

If you think of 'Southend' and then stare at the name, doesn't it begin to look a little odd? The south end of what? The answer is Prittlewell, which is of far greater antiquity. The earliest reference to Southend occurs in a will of 1482 when it was a mere lane at the southern end of the parish. Earlier it was just 'street-end'. The lane ran from the priory at Prittlewell to Milton and the shore. It was primarily used to convey gain to Canterbury. In the eighteenth century Southend was noted for its oyster grounds, but from 1800 it was developed as a resort, at first very fashionable, called 'New Southend'.

Much further round the coast at Walton-on-the Naze (or promontory) you will find 'The Twizzle' and another at Burnham on Crouch where it is 'Twizzlefoot Bridge'. 'Twizzle' means 'fork', and at Burnham two streams fork to meet. This quaint word is a dialect one as well: 'to spin, to twist round and round'.

Up the creeks there are several strange double names. In Baring-Gould's *Mehalah* country there is Salcott cum Virley. The two parishes were at first one. 'Salcott' is 'salt cottage', well named in an area once noted for its salt pans. 'Virley' is from the Norman lord here in 1086, Robert de Verli, who came from Verley in Aisne, France.

'Moze' in 'Beaumont cum Moze' means 'marsh' and was joined with its larger neighbour in 1678. Originally Beaumont had the unfortunate name of 'Fulepet', 'foul hollow', but it was later christened with the French for 'fair or beautiful hill'.

This is the place to bring in poor 'Ugley' away in the north: Ucga's or Ugga's clearing. Jokes about the name persist, like the Ugley Women's Institute. And only the other day I read something from 1857 which gave this ditty:

Ugley church and Ugley steeple,
Ugley parson, Ugley people.

In his *Essex* Hope-Moncrieffe wrote of 'the name belying a place which by rights is Ockley or Oaklea'. Not so, I'm afraid. How the good people there must long at times for their village to be renamed, like Fulepet of old. But I expect they take it all in good part. Perhaps it is best, if inaccurate, to pronounce it 'Oojley'.

Another creek-side name is 'Goldhanger'. Although the land here is flat, the Domesday form of the name is *hangra*, a hanger or slope, and not *anger*, meaning grassland, as in Ongar. The only way to take it in the latter and admittedly more logical sense is to assume the Norman scribe made an error. It would certainly go with the 'Gold', the corn marigold, *Chrysanthemum segetum*.

Some names are far from what they seem. 'The Devil's Head Plantation' in Little Warley has a sinister ring, a place for black magic in the woods. It turns out to be very prosaic, named after a John Deville of 1327. Terling's 'Porridge Pot Hall' is a good example of popular etymology for it is a corruption of 'Porige', from William Porige in the late 1300s.

'The Easters' are similarly deceptive. Easter here is not the Church festival but the Anglo-Saxon *eowestre*, a sheepfold. Good Easter commemorates Godith or Godiva, an earl's widow who left her estate in Easter to the monks of Ely Abbey.

In High Easter 'Playstall', pronounced 'Plash'l', the village playground, is a variant of the eleventh-century 'Playstow' which is identical with Plaistow, a stow or place for play.

There are remote, or formerly remote, corners of farmland with names which may have been bestowed, often with irony, I feel, to denote their distance 'far from the madding crowd'. There are several to be found called 'World's End'. There is one at Pebmarsh. A 'Little London' can be seen at Berden, and there are others in the county. Egypt Farm at Rivenhall may not have enjoyed good harvests, named with the biblical famines in mind, but a former rector here drew attention to a type of wheat with the name.

A name in the parish of Alresford is 'Cockayne's'. It first occurs in records of the late thirteenth century. This could have been given in bitter jest, for Cockaigne is an imaginary land of idleness and luxury. Famous in medieval story-telling and poetry, it was particularly applied to Paris and to London, where it gave rise to 'Cockney'. To be cautious, it might have been a personal name, although no records for Alresford have revealed it. Cockayne Hatley in Bedfordshire gets its name from a Cockayne family there.

House names which tease, there are in abundance. I select here just three I have found of great interest.

Brazenhead Farm at Lindsell was recorded as 'Brasen Head' in 1558. Reaney noted a brass leopard's head on its outer gate but it seems it was Miller Christy who first drew attention to it back in 1892. He discovered this brazen head as a circular door-knocker on a then modern dwelling, the site formerly occupied by an ancient, moated farmhouse. The strange head, grotesque and heraldic, was certainly there in 1768 when Morant noted it. Christy tried to trace its ancestry but with no success, though he was told a peculiar anecdote of 'a certain old and half-crazed country woman,

Judy Boyett by name, who was said to have held it in superstitious reverence and to have come regularly at certain intervals to polish it. He thought the 'leopard' might have represented the crest of the Fitch family. That this was very likely can be deduced from a passage in Salmon's *History and Antiquities of Essex* (1740), where he tells us that a Thomas Fitch married Agnes, daughter and heiress of Robert Alyer of Brazen-Head. Salmon also mentions the object 'supposed to be a wolf's head'. This curiosity seems to have vanished without trace.

A house at Blackmore with the name of 'Jericho' recalls the time when Henry VIII used to visit the monastery here and his courtiers discreetly said, 'He is gone to Jericho.' The name was also colloquially used for a remote place of retirement and concealment. It was at Blackmore that Henry's mistress Elizabeth Blount gave birth to his son, christened Henry Fitzroy, 'son of the King', in 1518. She was married off to one of Cardinal Wolsey's retainers, Gilbert Talboys. The nearby River Can has often been called locally 'the Jordan'.

At Feering an unpretentious farmhouse has the name 'Maltbeggars'. (I'm told there is another as well in the county.) It was 'Mockbeggars' in the eighteenth century, and early in the next 'Mobbeggars'. Behind this there is an unusual explanation indeed.

Once in common usage in East Anglia, the word dates from the early 1600s, when rural gentry were going in ever-increasing numbers to the capital, either for entertainment or to newly acquired town houses. A consequence of this was that beggars found it harder to get their customary relief from the country estates. The word has also been found in field names. In Taylor's *The Water Cormorant* (1622) there are these lines:

> No times observed, nor charitable laws,
> The poor receive their answer from the dawes
> Who, in their cawing language, call it plaine
> Mock-beggar Manour, for they come in vain.

For quaintness, 'Snoreham' and 'Wendens Ambo' would prove hard to outmatch. Snoreham, a sleepy-hollow name, is at Latchingdon. Its meaning is unknown. Here Uleham's Farm is very fitting, for it means 'frequented by owls', as it must have been in 1086. Wendons Ambo, its village a delight, was once two villages with Wendons Lofts. 'Windon' or 'Wendene' seems to have been a 'winding valley'. 'Lofts' is after the family of a Robert Louhot in the thirteenth century. 'Ambo' comes from the Latin word for 'both (ways)' and is taken to indicate here the union of the two Wendons, at one time Great and Little. Should you go there, as I hope you will, you must not fail to see the church by a row of timeless cottages and a great tithe barn. Inside St Mary's, look on the bench-ends for a minute carving, a beast with its paw upon a 'mirror'. Variously described as a lion or tiger, it may well represent one of the Seven Deadly Sins, the one of Vanity.

'Layer Marney' and 'Layer de la Haye' make with 'Layer Breton' a prestigious trio. 'Breton' is clear, from the line of Lewis the Breton. 'Layer de la Haye' is also a manorial name. Maurice de Haia of Normandy held land here. This is the Layer with Blind Knights, which tradition tells us was granted by Richard Coeur de Lion to St Botolph's Priory in Colchester for the upkeep of maimed crusaders. Layer Marney is named after yet another knightly family, the de Marrinis from Marigny in France. The male line ended with the second Lord in 1525, and the remarkable house 'The Towers' was never completed. Lord Marney's death deprived Essex of a mansion which would have rivalled and perhaps surpassed Hampton Court.

One of the Layers, possibly Breton, was called 'Stokkenleire' in the thirteenth century. As *stoccen* in Old English means 'made of logs', this suggests that the original church may have been a timber one, as at Greensted.

Beauty, of course, lies in the eye (and the ear) of the beholder, yet I must draw my litany to a close with what are, for me, names of sheer loveliness regardless of their meanings. There's soft 'Shelley' which I am pleased to find a 'shelving lea'. Then 'Mellow Purgess' in Stondon Massey, and 'Mistley', the 'mistletoe wood' on the wide estuary of the Stour. 'Tolleshunt Knights', 'Flambards' at Cold Norton, 'Wynters' Armourie': I think of these as tapestry names, reminding one of lords and ladies.

The poet Edward Thomas was a lover of humble Essex places that had for him captivating names:

If I should ever by chance grow rich
I'll buy Codham, Cockridden and Childerditch.

Such names may not be the choice of you or me. Yet the range of Essex place-names with the power to strike poetic notes and to unlock the past is as rich as to be found in any other part of the country.

2

Weather Reports of Yesteryear

The vagaries of our island weather are our one unfailing interest, the perennial topic of conversation, a national and often tedious *idée fixe*. Extremes of heat and cold, of wind and rain, attract of course the keenest notice, particularly those which come upon us suddenly, out of season. Then there is that ever-present apprehension, in which we take an almost perverse pleasure, that the weather is getting worse, that things are not as they were. Like everyone growing old, I can 'remember' a procession of radiant summers the like of which have not been seen since childhood. Memories, however, are selective and were deceivers ever. There are plenty of experts as well who, gazing at their charts as at a crystal ball, can readily confirm our fears. It would seem the dreaded Ice Age always cometh, easy to believe with the raw, white winter of '81 still fresh in mind.

Records of the distant past, especially those of the more personal kind, often give us observations on impish weather long before official returns were kept. I have of late taken to jotting some of these down as they occur *en passant* while I read. They are entertaining in themselves, yet what is offered here mainly from old Essex sources may also serve to place our weather concerns in wider perspective.

Let us begin in 1579. This was the year, at least in south Essex, of 'the great snow'. Our witness is a troublesome parson of Langdon Hills, one John Goldringe, or rather the court records in which his name appears. Charged with keeping his sheep in the little church of All Saints, he pleaded his defence as follows:

A little after Candlemas last [2 February] his servants endeavouring to have his sheep saved from the covering of the

A winter scene

great snow, which at that time so greatly so did fall both by night and by day, and his servants being not able to bring them into any house and having a care to have them saved, having the key of the church door, near which his sheep were then pastured, they then locked the same sheep into the church ... then by great labour and pains his servants when the fall of snow was ended put them into another place and made clean the church again; which was done for great and extreme necessity and not in any contempt, all by his consent.

This sounds reasonable enough but although his plea was accepted the rector had to do penance, which amounted to a public confession of his fault and giving 6s.8d to the poor of the parish.

Moving into the next century, in the parish registers of Cold Norton for 1638 there is a note recording that the River Crouch froze so hard at Fambridge that ferry passengers walked across. Cold Norton certainly lived up to its name that year. Originally 'Nortuna' in the Domesday Book, it was later also known as 'Norton juxta Fanbrige'. By 1350 it had become 'Coldnorton', and it is even styled, oddly, 'alias Goldnorton' in 1605. There are some who think that the 'Cold' refers to its clay soil rather than to its exposed position by the marshes but this is, I feel, less likely.

The opening weeks of 1763 were very harsh. I haven't come across any references to their effects in Essex but two journals of the time tell of the sharpness of the cold. In that of Thomas Turner of East Hoathly, Sussex, since published as *The Diary of a Georgian Shopkeeper*, an entry for late January records that a severe frost was at last thawing after five weeks. The ice had been seven inches thick. Almost to the day the celebrated diarist James Woodforde, then a young man at New College, Oxford, skated down the Thames to Abingdon, a distance of ten miles, which he and his companions covered in an hour and a half.

On 1 July 1774 the *Chelmsford Chronicle* (now the *Essex Chronicle*) printed an account of a violent storm which had raged across the country a week before. 'Pitsea church had the spire (which was almost 20 feet above the tower) shattered to pieces and entirely destroyed, and the steeple otherwise much damaged. It is remarkable that one of the bell-ropes (which was new) was so violently forced against the wall as to be prest quite in two, the upper part stuck to the wall, and the timber appeared as though it had burnt, being very black and crockey. A gravestone in the churchyard was also fractured all to pieces.'

The January of 1776 was long remembered for its incredible severity. Late in the month the *Chester Chronicle* reported on Billericay that, 'The snow here affords the most amazing and melancholy scene ever known by the oldest man living.' For several days the roads were impassable, with coaches halted while gangs of men laboured to dig ways through. That month it was the same everywhere. Gilbert White down in Selborne noted: 'Rugged, Siberian weather', the snow 'driven into most romantic and grotesque shapes'. Writing on the 14th at Oxford, Parson Woodforde entered in his diary: 'Scarce ever was known so deep a snow as at present. Many carriages obliged to be dug out near Oxen.'

An eighteenth-century diary which deserves to be much

better known is that of John Crozier, a Maldon miller and farmer. (Edited, it can be found in J.F. Brown's *Essex People* published in 1972 by the Essex Record Office.) Among his entries for 1777 you will find this: 'Two remarkable hot days in the middle of March; the people worked without their coats, and two days after – it snow'd.' Nine years later, on 4 January 1786, he rode home from Bocking to write: 'I experienc'd the most severe night I ever remember; it snew very small and with the wind cut my eyes which caus'd some tears (which is frequently the case); but on alighting at Witham they were froze to my eyelashes, which the fire dissolv'd immediately.'

The final quarter of the eighteenth century was notable for extremes in the weather and not only in the winter. 'The climate in England', noted the *Chelmsford Chronicle* in February 1793, 'in the opinion of many has, of late years, undergone a considerable change. Formerly we used to have smart frosts in winter, and hot, sometimes dry, summers. For some years back both winters and summers have generally been wet, with so little ice, that luxury, by its agents, has been obliged to procure it from foreign parts. In the course of last year, those who kept a register of the weather tell us, there were but one hundred and three dry days. For the little that is passed of the present year, we have scarce had six dry days. The effects on men and animals in both years have been rather melancholy by increasing the number of sick and dead.'

Friday 5 June 1795 saw a remarkable hailstorm at Hatfield Broad Oak. Many of the stones were four inches in circumference. In places they covered the ground to a depth of five feet and remained there for a week. This is but one of a whole catalogue of disasters listed in a countryman's journal, extracts from which were given by Francis W. Steer in the *Essex Review* for July 1950. The spectacular storm of hail was also reported in the *Chronicle* at the time. Its readers were told that the storm, three quarters of a mile wide, drove across country for three miles, devastating the crops as it went.

Another Essex farmer who kept brief memoirs was Charles Hicks (1778–1865). They have the engaging title of *Annals of the Parish of Gt Holland by an Old Stager.* For

1802 he noted: 'Frost and snow from the 13th to the 18th of May.' At the same time, 17 May, a Fingringhoe farmer, Joseph Page, was writing in his journal: 'Another violent storm of snow and hail, so much so that it covered the ground completely and in many places, where it drove, it lay more than a foot deep and continued upon the ground for several days. Great damage was done to the fruit trees.'

In 1814 grim weather reappeared. Charles Hicks again: 'Frost set in on Christmas Eve and lasted 14 weeks. The Thames was frozen over and a bullock roasted on the ice. Wild fowl so numerous along shore they were frequently heard up at the Hall, the noise much like a pack of hounds at a distance.'

The Prittlewell doctor Jonas Asplin kept a diary for the years 1826 to 1828. On 12 May 1826 he entered: 'The weather here has been and still is so cold that nothing grows.' He added ten days later: 'The first morning we have sat down to breakfast without a fire.' The summer was fine when it came in. A year later, on 10 April, he observed the weather on a poetic note: 'Drove to Wakering. Morning very fine, something of a white frost. After the blustering weather we have had lately, it was something to see the smoke from every chimney of the village ascending tranquilly in a direct line.' Incidentally, Great Wakering gets the lowest average rainfall in the whole country, 19.2 inches annually.

1832 saw the destruction of a familiar landmark in the Rodings, for on 15 May during a tempest the wooden spire of High Roding church was struck by lightning. It was later replaced by the present bell-cote. An account of the fire appeared in the *Kent and Essex Mercury*. The Dunmow fire-engines were sent for but the blaze, which had threatened the whole church, had been controlled by the time they arrived.

On 29 November 1836 a great wind roared over mid-Essex the like of which had not been experienced since 1795. A month before there had been a heavy fall of snow.

This run of abysmal years had one to go before it spent its course. Farmer Hicks began his notes for 1837: 'Violent colds and influenza generally prevailed throughout the kingdom during January. Nearly half the inhabitants of

London from illness could not attend to business ... One hundred and thirty clerks at the Bank of England absent one day.' This is no doubt from newspaper reports of the time, but he is soon commenting on the weather he could see and feel about him: 'On the 20th January ten men and two boys were absent from their work at Gt Holland Hall from influenza. March the 25th was the coldest day experienced this winter. Very cold weather from the 3rd to the 9th April. On the 4th the frost was so severe the pumps were frozen up. The ground was covered with snow on the morning of the 6th, 9th and 12th of April. Great demands for all kinds of food for cattle and sheep from the backwardness of the season. The brook would not run and timber could not be felled in Hall Wood before the 1st of June. The wheat ears just began to show themselves on the first of July.' However, by the end of 1838 he was able to record 'a capital crop of every description'. It would be some years before he noted a bad season again.

Francis Steer's countryman tells of 'A Heavy Tempest and a great flood' at Chelmsford in October 1853, killing sheep and cattle. And a very dry summer in 1858 ended dramatically on 22 October when 'It set in Whet wich Caused a Verry Great Flood.' In his untutored language he also gives another great wind for the last day of February 1860, 'such a one as has not been knowne in the memory of man'. It 'blue down thousands of trees in Parks about the Cuntry'.

1860 proved to be another dismal year throughout. Charles Hicks, giving the last of his weather entries in his diary (except for remarking on the damage by a high wind to a windmill), wrote of it at some length: 'An unusual quantity of rain fell, both winter and summer. The land was so wet even in summer the horses could not be got on the land to plough or cart sometimes for days. The corn grown was never known of so bad a quality; it told seriously on all heavy lands ... some farmers were entirely ruined and others so bent they never got straight again. The following year was nearly as bad, the quality better. The heavy land farmers had cause to remember the years 1860 and 1861.'

Hicks did not live to see that these years were a portent of what was to come a decade or so later. The closing years of the century saw the great agricultural depression which was such a marked feature of late Victorian and Edwardian England. A contributory factor was the blight which descended on the countryside through a succession of wet harvests.

Those dark, hard days on the land have been well researched and documented on a national scale. Not so well known are the little volumes on the country life of the time, books which brim over with local colour. In limited editions, some are long out of print, though copies are to be found here and there in second-hand bookshops, lying in wait for the collector of rural literature. One of these is *No Rain in Those Clouds* written by the late David Smith of Broomfield (published by Dent in 1943 and reprinted the following year). The book is a delight to read, charmingly written and rich in the personal reminiscences of David's father, John Smith, and the keen observations of the author. Apart from being a fine country book, it is of great value to the local historian, for it deals in the main with the life and farming in West Hanningfield from the second half of the nineteenth century until around 1918, all seen through the eyes of a family whose parochial roots went back for 130 years at Link House Farm. (John Smith died at Broomfield in 1955 a few days before his ninety-third birthday.) In the present context David Smith's book is of no mean value, for its numerous references to the weather and its local consequences. In the main they read as a litany of misfortunes.

The beginning of the great decline in farming can be dated with fair precision to 1879. The weather was so bad that wheat was still being drilled in January. Many fields of wheat and barley yielded only three sacks to the acre. It was 'the beginning of the end for the real old-time farmer'.

On the first day of 1880 a savage thunderstorm hit Essex, leaving a sea of mud everywhere. However, the rest of the month was fine. The following year there was a phenomenal snowstorm on 18 January which went on for twenty-four hours. Drifts were still lying in April. August was a very wet month.

Throughout the rest of the eighties the weather seems to have been normal, although there was flooding in Chelmsford in 1888 which carried away the bridge over the

Can. Winter flooding was not unusual in the county town, but this one occurred in July after a series of thunderstorms. The damage was immense. The last serious flood in Chelmsford was in the late 1950s, which led to the implementation of a major flood-prevention scheme.

1840 and 1892 were two black years for crops. Then from March to November in 1893 there was a prolonged fall in the already low farm prices.

The day after Queen Victoria's Diamond Jubilee, in June 1897, West Hanningfield was struck by a great hailstorm which scythed its way across country on a narrow front. Although the parish was not at the centre of its path, damage was extensive from the hailstones, 'big as walnuts'. The locals felt it was a retribution for their not having publicly celebrated the Jubilee, the farmers failing to agree on the best way of keeping it. A public fund was raised to help out those whose crops had been flattened.

1902 was the third of three wet seasons in succession, and 1904 also had a sodden harvest. But 1911, the year of King George V's coronation, was a vintage year with 'a roaring hot summer'.

It seems fitting to conclude this little resurrection of old weather tales with the last lines in David Smith's tribute to his father, headed 'Epilogue'. His father, then in his seventies, is depicted talking to a soldier on his farm at Broomfield in the war years of the forties.

A light wind sprang up, and the sentry
looked up at the sky
'Is it going to rain, sir?', he asked
Father glanced up before he replied:
'No, boy. There's no rain in those clouds.'

3

Old Epitaphs and Inscriptions

One of my more curious pursuits, curious that is to my friends, is an interest in the lives of the obscure or, rather, in the remnants of them.

I delight in reading old wills and in turning the pages of parish registers. Equally 'in serious humour' I like to browse in country churchyards and contemplate the memorials in churches to the long-since dead. These sepulchral tastes are not so eccentric. They are widely shared. But I suspect as well that there may be a deeper motivation than just curiosity in our visitations to such grave places as 'the several regions of the dead'. As more than one headstone to be found puts it:

Whoever ye be who passes by
Stop here, and read, and breathe a sigh.
Look such as we are, such shall ye be,
And such as we were, such be ye.

Although Weever's *Funeral Monuments* of 1631 shows that much of great interest has gone, here in Essex we have numerous churches with epitaphs displaying what Charles Lamb fondly called 'the oddities of authorship'. In brass and stone many of these texts embalm the sentiments and now rare doctrines of a more theological age. And yet the greatest pleasure in deciphering the old words surely comes from the antique modes of the language, with many a 'ye' and every other word it seems Exalted with a Capital Letter. Then there are the variations in the spelling, happy experiments before all was finally standardized.

Most of the deceased commemorated are solely names, simply recorded for posterity with their entrances and exits.

In Addison's fine words after walking among the tombs of the great: 'I could not but look upon these registers of existence, whether of brass or marble, as a kind of satire upon the departed persons; who had left no other memorial of them, but that they were born and then died. They put me in mind of several persons mentioned in the battles of heroic poems, who have sounding names given to them, for no other reason but that they may be killed, and are celebrated for nothing but being knocked on the head.'

Many of the names are long out of fashion and might themselves be said to be deceased. Some of these can give an unexpected merriment. A particular favourite of mine, on a splendid small tablet in Little Baddow church, is Mercymight Springham.

Out at Willingale in St Andrew's, the older of the two churches keeping company side by side in the churchyard, there are two small floor slabs with quaint inscriptions. They lie at either end of the chancel rails and cover the graves of two young children. Sadly, the diminutive brass figures have not survived. One of the inscriptions reads:

> This happy child adorned wth gifts of grace
> His choice was dissolution
> His song wth Simeon to depart in peace
> Unto Christ's heavenly mansion.

> Here lyeth Joseph Kello being XIII yeares
> Of age departed this life ye last day of Sep
> tember 1614. He was sone to Mr Bartholomew
> Kello minister of Christ Evangell & Parson
> of this parish of Willingale Spayne.

The other memorial, comparable in form, reads:

> This godly child knew his originall
> And though right young did scorne base cells of earth
> His soul doth flourish in Heavens glistening hall
> Because it is a divine plant by birth.

> Here lyeth Isaac Kello being IX years
> of age departed this life the 13 of July

1614. He was sone to Mr Bartholomew
Kello minister of Christs Evangell

The last line of this second text, when compared with the final line of the first, can be seen to be incomplete, the craftsman having run out of space.

Although the verses are awkward in their scanning, they are interesting if modest examples of the metaphysical poetry in vogue at the time. Both express the pious and, for us, ludicrous conceit that these little unfortunates chose their early end, which came within such a short time from each other. Perhaps they died from an infection, victims of the ever-present smallpox or the plague.

A moving little inscription to another child can be found in the parish church of Woodham Mortimer:

> To the memory of Dorothy
> daughter of Giles Alleine
> that died 1584
> aged 3 years
> A little impe here buried is
> Whose soul to Christ is fled.

In striking contrast to the near-total obscurity of these children, we can pass to the more substantial if still shadowy figure of Stock's benefactor, that man of valour Richard Tweedy. In the will of this local Elizabethan worthy we can read that he wanted to purchase a plot of land in Stock 'as near the church as I can' for the erection of almshouses 'for four poor men to dwell in' from the parishes of Stock and Boreham. His almshouses have graced the scene until today. He was buried as he requested in the lovely All Saints and is remembered in a most engaging way on a tablet which is probably a *mensa*, the pre-Reformation altar stone. The memorial, incised with five crosses, bears an eight-lined rhymed inscription:

> The corpse of Richard Twedye esquire lyeth buried here in
> tombe
> Bewrapt in claye and reserved untill the Joyfull Dome
> Whoe in his lyffe hath served well against the Ingleshe foes

In fforen landes and eke at home his countreye well yt knowes
The prince he served in Courte full longe a pensioner fitt in
personage
In his countrye a Justice eke, a man full grave and sage
Foure alms-houses here hath he built for foure poor knights to
dwell
And them indowed with stipends large enogh to keep them well
      In ffiftye eyghte years his course he ran
      Occidens ye 28 Januarye 1574.

What a Chaucerian tone that has, although it came two
centuries later!

At East Donyland in the nineteenth-century parish
church of St Lawrence, 'Quite remarkably original', there is
an imposing monument to Elizabeth Marshall, who died in
1613. Below her seated figure her daughter kneels with two
babies cradled. The memorial inscription is lengthy, in three
parts and highly ingenious.

Clotho: In tender armes thy tickle rock I beare
        Wherein consists of life this hemisphere
        Frayle flyinge fadeinge fickle slipereye
        Certaine in nothing but uncertaintye

Lachesis: From of thy rocke her slender thred I pull
        When scarce begun but yt my spoole is full
        Then tyme begetts brings forth & with her haste
        Makes after tyme tymes former workes to waste

Atropos: I with my knife have cutt that thred in twayne
        And loosde that knott not to be knitt agayne
        What two wer one my knife hath both opposd
        In heaven her soule in earth her corpes inclosd.

These verses are thought to have been composed by the then
vicar, Gilbert Longe. Clotho, Lachesis and Atropos were the
three Fates of Greek mythology. Clotho presided over birth,
drawing from her distaff the thread of life; Atropos cut the
thread, and then Lachesis watched over the soul between life
and death. The expression 'rock' in the verses means
'distaff'.

In the church of St Margaret of Antioch at Toppesfield there can be found one of those epitaphs which more than most tease us into wanting to know more. It is both sad and enigmatic, commemorating the death of one Sarah Howlett, aged eighteen, in 1793:

> Enriched with uncommon extent and variety of attainment,
> of which she was so far from making an ostentatious
> display that she seemed unconscious that she possessed them.
> Nay, the degrading conception she unhappily formed of her
> own virtues, moral and intellectual, were probably the
> cause of unsupportable suffering.

Behind these sonorous words there must lie a poignant drama of corrosive self-doubt and accusation, a dark night of a gifted soul.

Death is farewell, and many a stone testifies to the anguish of the final parting. For some of those who are left behind it proves too much. In Margaretting church there are these lines of 1666 to Peter and Julian Whitecombs:

> She on this clayen pillow layd her head
> As brides do use the first to go to bed
> He missed her soone, and yet 10 months he trys
> To live apart, and lykes it not, and dies.

An aura of solemnity, of course, is what we expect and find with the great majority of epitaphs. In Chelmsford Cathedral the colourful monument of Sir Thomas Mildmay and his wife provides a good example. Its final words are awesome.

Here are seen graven the effigies of Thomas Mildmay and Avice his wife, but within their remains lie in peace He was a renowned Esquire, she a daughter and lovely branch of William Gunson, Esq, and they had fifteen pledges of their prosperous love: seven whereof were females, eight were males. Afterwards in the year of our Lord 1557, and in the morning of the 16th day of September, Avice returned to that dust from whence she originally sprung, and on the 10th day of the Kalends of October in the 9th year following, the unrelenting King of Terrors triumphed over Thomas.

But there is a solemnity of a different order to this, a gentler gravity and less ostentatious. I think of these memorials which pay tribute to simple piety and quiet good deeds; fond remembrances where death as a spectre does not hover. One of these can be seen at tranquil Tilty, once famous for its Cistercian abbey 'beautiful and opulent ... in which religious observance and prudence rivalled each other'. All that remains of it now are tell-tale markings in the soil, a series of humps and hollows, and the lovely 'Chapel without the Gate' which mercifully survived to become the parish church of St Mary the Virgin. Here on the south wall of the nave, lit by the splendid tall five lights of the medieval east window, is a sole biographical reminder of a great monastic past. This is the unfigured brass to Abbot Thomas de Takeley, one of the long line of abbots from the foundation of the abbey in 1153 until its suppression and closure almost four hundred years later. On the brass plate there is a rhyming Latin epitaph which begins 'ABBAS FAMOSUS, BONUS ET VIVENDO P'BATUS'. The little guidebook to the church by Philip Dickenson translates the text as follows:

An abbot, renowned, good and of excellent life,
Born in Takeley, is buried here.
He was called Thomas, may he be numbered in
the fellowship of Christ.
Right well he governed and he greatly loved this place.

Thomas was the abbot here from 1459 to 1475, and I find something very satisfying in the fact that the good Father of romantic Tilty was a local man.

The repute of the Mildmays and the Abbot Thomas was largely confined to Essex, but in the churchyard at Black Notley there lie the remains of a man whose life and work have been of far wider importance. This is the botanist John Ray, son of the village blacksmith. The great Linnaeus owed him no small debt. On the obelisk which marks Ray's grave the Latin inscription, a lengthy one, leaves no one in doubt of his greatness. Among the declamatory lines are these:

Hid in this narrow tomb, this marble span,

Lies all that death could snatch from this great man.
His body moulders in its native clay,
While o'er wide worlds his works their beams display,
As bright and everlasting as the day.
To those just fame ascribes immortal breath,
And in his writings he outlives his death.

But not all is a solemn music. There are memorials in lighter vein. In the church of St Augustine at Birdbrook there are two with a marital theme which are almost competitive. Both are inscribed on the same tablet, an oval one erected late in the eighteenth or early in the nineteenth century:

MARTHA BLEWIT
of the Swan Inn at Bathorne End
in this Parish
buried May 7th 1681
was the Wife of nine Husbands succefsively
But the ninth outlived her.
The Text of her Funeral Sermon was
"Last of all the Woman died also."

ROBERT HOGAN
of this Parish
was the Husband of Seven Wives succefsively
he married Ann Livermore his seventh wife
January 1st 1739

For a commemoration of sheer numbers, a tablet in St Peter-ad-Vincula's at Great Coggeshall would be hard to match. Put up to the memory of Mrs Mary Honeywood, it was originally to be seen in the old parish church of Markshall, St Margaret's, demolished in 1932. Mary Honeywood, who died at the age of ninety-three in 1620, was one of that grand old family of Honeywoods who lived for generations at Marks Hall. Their house, of Tudor date and with a deer park, also went from the landscape in 1951. The tablet records that she bore sixteen children, from whom came 144 grandchildren, 228 great-grandchildren and 9 great-great-grandchildren, making a phenomenal total of 367!

Many memorials have disappeared, either through thoughtless 'restoration' or wantonly reaved. No church can have suffered more from this brand of vandalism than St Clement's at Leigh-on-Sea, where the alterations of 1838 were said to have been 'singularly destructive to monuments'. In the previous century Morant noted that it contained 'more sepulchral monuments than are to be found in the whole Hundred besides'.

Many naval worthies lie buried here. The Haddock family alone provided nine. There is a brass to Richard Haddock, his two wives and their children, of 1453, but the marble tablet commemorating Admiral Nicholas Haddock was destroyed. Three framed oaken panels 'with inscriptions and devices curiously illuminated in gold and colours, and richly emblazoned with armorial bearings' also vanished after the restoration. One of these read as follows: 'Near this place lyeth Capt. John Rogers, who after several commands at sea, executed with great courage and fidelity, was made Captain of his Majesty's ship the "Unicorn", in which he behaved himself with incomparable valour and conduct in three bloody engagements with the Dutch in the year 1672, for which remarkable services he was advanced to be Captain of the "Royal Charles", and then of the Henry. He was buried, to the great grief of all who knew him, Nov 30, 1683, after he had lived in this town 36 years. He died 65.'

It seems the three tablets were stored in the vestry. From there they were filched by the sexton, one Thorpe, who defaced the wording and arms of the Rogers memorial and, cutting it up, made it into a cupboard door! Eventually he was dismissed when he was found committing what must have been thought a graver offence, namely stripping the lead from the church roof and taking the pipes from the gutters.

Another act of folly in 1838 was the breaking-up of the tomb of John Sym, a seventeenth-century theologian and rector of the parish. The brass inscription plate of Robert Salmon, Master of Trinity House, who died in 1641, was torn from its matrix, but his half-length effigy survives.

As a final offering from the diverse range of inscriptions to be encountered throughout Essex there is 'The Dumb Animals' Humble Petition'. In white cast-iron and of the last century, this is at Langham, kept in the porch of the church of St Mary near Gun Hill. Although not strictly *'in memoriam'*, it does serve to keep us in mind of the common bond of mortality between man and beast:

Rest drivers rest on this steep hill,
Dumb beasts pray use us with good will.
Goad not, scourge not, with thonged whips,
Let not one curse escape your lips.
God sees and hears.

Lady Dean's memorial, Great Maplestead

4

In Memory of Lost Churches

Among the many 'secrets' concealed in our countryside are its missing places. Modest houses and grander halls, highways, even entire villages have vanished from the landscape down the ages. Here and there a few physical traces can be found for their previous existence – perhaps a ruin, an overgrown site, an outline in the soil. Place-names, sometimes on old estate maps which are themselves virtually lost from public view, are often the only clues we have that they have ever been.

Many churches figure in the phantom scenery of the past, and some have so completely disappeared that they have even fallen out of local memory and tradition. Records of these are sparse and there are few details to go by, so brief recitals must suffice.

The twelfth-century church of St Stephen in Cold Norton is one of these, demolished in 1855 to make way for the High Victorian one there today. This hilltop church preserves a sole reminder of its forerunner, a brass to a lady of about 1520. It also has a pulpit and a reading desk said to be made from the old oak timbers.

This is but one of a number removed by Victorian zeal. At East Donyland the church of 1838 stands on the site of the old church. As we have seen, a striking monument of 1613 with a long inscription fortunately remains. In Cranham the original All Saints went in 1874, the newer building being erected on the spot, while at Aldham St Margaret's dates from the mid-nineteenth century but contains some material in its structure of the previous church. Only the porch is medieval.

The three Chignalls once had a church apiece. That of Chignall St Mary has long gone. Its location is marked by ditches and became a garden called St Mary's Croft. The three parishes were merged into one in 1888.

On Canvey the old church was burnt by the Dutch fleet when it came up the Thames in 1667. This was not done as an act of vandalism, for the towers of the Thameside churches were used as beacons and look-outs. A wooden church dedicated to St Catherine was built in its place.

The little church of St Nicholas at Hazeleigh in Purleigh was pulled down in 1922. From a photograph in Woodham Mortimer church, it appears to have been a chapel of ease. Of timber and plaster, it looked like a cottage and was in part Elizabethan. Prior to its demolition it was used in its final years as a mortuary chapel.

St Andrew's at Langenhoe was dismantled as recently as 1962. Severely damaged in the Essex earthquake of 1884, it was granted a further lease of life when it was rebuilt two years later.

By its name Lee Chapel on the edge of Basildon New Town indicates what once stood there in the Middle Ages. In the parish of Laindon it was, however, extra-parochial under the constable of that parish. Earlier this century a few traces were still visible on the farm. From chalk footings found in 1964, the chapel seems to have had an apse.

In Coggeshall the Chapel Inn stands where an old chapel was pulled down in 1795. It was built in the sixteenth century, from money left by a Thomas Hall in his will. Probably Chapel Hill in Braintree also took its name from a church.

At High Beech until late last century the little brick chapel of St Paul stood deep in the forest. It was of no age, being built in 1836, but it soon fell into disuse. It was replaced in 1872 with the Church of the Holy Innocents, designed by Bloomfield with a commanding spire, an Epping landmark. In a lovely setting, that tormented poet John Clare knew it well when he was an inmate of Fairmead House, with London 'nothing but a guess among the trees'. Of the chapel by Fern Hill he wrote:

How beautiful this hill of ferns swells on
   So beautiful the chapel peeps between
The hornbeams, with its simple bell; alone
I wander here, hid in a palace green.

Another category of lost churches are those which lie in ruins. The old church of Little Holland is in pieces by the sea. Four centuries ago it was a mile inland. A small iron church, St Bartholomew's, replaced it here in 1893.

Brentwood's vestigial Chapel of St Thomas Becket was founded from St Osyth's Abbey in the year 1221. Since Becket was canonized in 1178, three years after his murder in Canterbury Cathedral, the date of the chapel testifies to the early growth of his popular veneration. It was here that Hubert de Burgh, chief minister to Henry III, fled naked to take sanctuary after being warned at the last minute of his impending arrest. And it was here, too, that the young Brentwood martyr, John Hunter, was examined on his heretical beliefs, for which he paid the penalty at the stake the following year.

Old St Mary's at Little Birch is in ruins, standing in the park by Birch Hall, a villa of the last century which has gone. The church has an ivy-covered tower. It had fallen into disuse as long ago as 1598. No services were held there at that time, when attempts were made to evict a local squatter.

Another fragmentary church is All Saints in the grounds of the Hall at Stanway. Its end came during the Civil War, when the roof was removed and its timber and lead were sold. The tower and nave are medieval, from the reign of Edward I, although there are a few seventeenth-century additions.

Other churches which can be styled as 'lost' are those which have become redundant, victims of the conflict between Faith and Economics. Three I know of have been converted into houses.

Shellow Bowells delights with its odd name although it has the unfortunate suggestion if mispronounced of 'shallow bowels'. It has an Essex rarity, a red-brick church completely of the eighteenth century, bearing the date '1754' above the door. Once dedicated to St Peter and St Paul, it stands on the Roxwell Road. It is now a house, which I discovered to my consternation by walking up the path through the churchyard, just spotting in time a line of washing.

There was another church here before the present one, for its registers date from the sixteenth century. John Wright was the rector from 1564 to 1573, with a parsonage and fourteen acres of glebe. The benefice of Shellow Bowells went to nearby Willingale Doe in 1798. The bell of the church now hangs in the tower of St Christopher.

St Mary and All Saints on Langdon Hills has also been secularized. Like the old church of Hazeleigh and that at East Hanningfield, it was used towards the end solely for funerals. It lies hidden away down a lane. It is mainly of sixteenth-century brick, and Pevsner found it 'a surprise in these bungalow surroundings' although modern estate housing is taking over. Its chief eye-catching attraction, which I assume is still *in situ*, is the lovely coat of royal arms painted on the tympanum, with the date '1660'. It was not there when John Goldringe was the rector, a character introduced in a previous chapter.

Goldringe was not only in trouble over his sheep. Like not a few Elizabethan parsons of the lower ranks, he was a lusty, disorderly fellow. In 1589 he was accused of adultery with the wife of one of his parishioners. The case, which proved involved, ran into several sessions, one of which was held at the old St Thomas' Chapel, Brentwood. There, although he had found several men of local standing as character witnesses, the woman unexpectedly confessed to having 'lived incontinently' with him. The case was adjourned to be heard in the Romford chapel. Further complications developed when the husband claimed he had been persuaded by the rector through a bond to remain silent about the relationship. Another was an allegation by the rector of Cranham that Goldringe had neglected his parochial duties, not giving sermons and failing to aid the poor. In the end John Goldringe was found guilty of adultery and had to do public penance in his church on two Sundays. He is also on record as being a drunkard and a quarreller.

Another ancient church at Langdon Hills stood somewhere on Westley Heights in the vicinity of the Hall. Five centuries back it marked a separate parish belonging to St Paul's. Already in decay in 1297, it was finally joined with Langdon in 1432 but Mass continued to be said there once a year on the feast day of its dedication. By tradition the old barn contains timbers of this forgotten church.

Out in eastern Essex, towards the marshes and the creeks,

there are several lost churches of especial interest.

South of the Blackwater the village of Latchingdon today boasts two churches. One is early Victorian. The other, St Michael's, is set on a hilltop. However, quite recently this church, too, has been sold off as a house, with its new god, a TV set, in the chancel. The churchyard is still used for burials.

But there used to be a third in nearby Snoreham. Although for purposes of local government Latchingdon-cum-Snoreham is now one, they remain separate ecclesiastical parishes. The site of old Snoreham church can be found on the Chapman map. It is marked as a ruin and shown opposite the Hall, in the stockyard in fact, on the road linking the two parishes. Dedicated to St Peter, there is no vestige of it now. According to Scarfe's *Shell Guide*, at one time a sermon was preached each year beneath a tree on the spot. The church seems to have been abandoned as far back as 1656, for in that year the parishioners were being petitioned at Quarter Sessions to contribute towards the

Old Mundon church

repair of Latchingdon church and its churchyard.

Just a mile or so to the north is Mundon, mentioned in the Domesday Book as having a vineyard. The old church by Mundon Hall is a revelation and not only because it is totally hidden from the world at the very end of a long, narrow and no-through lane. To visit it is likely to give you a very rare experience, a mixture of melancholy, elevation and delight, for this church is a gem and yet utterly unused and derelict. It is on the very edge of the abyss of time into which all must tumble in the end. Those readers who know the letters of Charles Lamb may well be reminded at this spot of the lone church he stumbled across at Hastings. Writing to his Quaker friend Bernard Barton, his words are very appropriate to what you will find here: 'There it stands like the first idea of a church, before parishioners were thought of, nothing but birds for its congregation, or like a Hermit's oratory (the Hermit dead), or a mausoleum ... like a church found in a desert isle to startle Crusoe with a home image; you must make out a vicar and a congregation from fancy, for surely none come there ...'

Mundon's old church is very small but with a lovely hexagonal Tudor wooden tower which has been renovated, the work of the Friends of Friendless Churches, who are taking a close interest in the building. Inside there is a simple nave without aisles. Amid the desolation of rubble, dust and flaking plaster there is a complete set of box pews, eight on either side. The chancel walls have faded 'sentences' of the Lord's Prayer and the Creed, while on the arch a painted inscription proclaims 'Behold the Lamb of God'. The Georgian east window is of plain glass, broken in places, with a webbed half-circle above rather like a large fanlight. The tie beams in the roof are splattered with bird droppings. Until very recently the large window on the north side was completely open to the elements, and the church for so many years has been a little sanctuary for birds. The south wall has a lancet window and one in the Perpendicular style. The Norman font, noted in Arthur Mee's *Essex*, has gone. A carved wooden porch, also of Tudor date, is on the north side, an unusual position. Its finer detail, foliage and small faces, has been worn away by decades of wind and rain. When I was last there, the churchyard was all but completely overgrown. Among the few tombstones to be more easily found are several dating from the 1930s and forties.

This church, which has been here for six hundred years, was in use in the last century and apparently more recently still, judging from a wall plaque of the 1920s inside. But its troubles began long ago. In 1572 it was in 'great decay'. A few years on, in 1598, the glass in the east window needed repair and the pavement of the chancel was broken. The church then had a layman as its rector. In the eighteenth century the chancel was rebuilt but the history of the church since then has obviously been one of make-do and mend and then finally abandonment. This little church is a sorry vision of mortality. It is concealed by trees as though to open it up to a wider view would prick the uneasy conscience of our age. (If this was done, as of now the vista would be dominated by a huge black dump of worn-out tyres!) And yet the church is not beyond a resurrection. It awaits the funds which perhaps can come only from a superlative act of faith and generosity.

A few miles further east lies the quaintly named Beaumont-cum-Moze. Moze, which means 'marsh', was joined with its larger neighbour in 1678, when its population of eleven farmers was no longer able to meet the cost of up-keeping of the church. The location of the church near Old Mose Hall is shown by a couple of oaks and a concrete cross. Materials from the church were used in repairs to Beaumont's St Leonard's.

Archdeacons' Court records of the 1590s have preserved for us the trials and tribulations of two local characters. One was charged with attending a service drunk. His punishment, laughable now and probably then, was to sit on his knees in the porch of Moze church with a white wand in his hand and three empty cups in front of him. Then, after the second lesson of the service, he had to enter the church and publicly say the words of penance ordered by the minister. The other had been accused by the churchwardens of not attending church, an offence for which the fine in Elizabethan England was 12d. But he was not so intimidated as his neighbour. He replied to the charge in an uncouth and no uncertain manner: 'He coming by them very irreverently and contemptuously farted unto them and said "Present that to the Court".' That could have come straight out of the pages of Chaucer or Rabelais.

A third place with a double 'cum' name in these remoter parts of Essex is Salcott-cum-Virley which is off the low road which skirts Abberton reservoir. Salcott's present church was one of those, like Langenhoe's, to suffer from the remarkable earthquake a hundred years ago. The former church of St Mary at adjacent Virley is now only ruins in the rector's garden. It was certainly still in use in the seventeenth century, and Chapman depicted it with a spire or steeple. Baring-Gould described it in his marshland romance, *Mehalah*.

I suspect one could fill a small book alone with tales of old churches. But there remains one group to touch upon, those which came to a sudden and dramatic end. Of these a prime example is the medieval church at East Hanningfield. Its tragic fate was closely reported in the county Press at the time.

The church the visitor sees today is only just short of a hundred years old, a Victorian building of 1885, standing well screened by trees off the spacious village green, the Tye. But there was an earlier church, the original All Saints, brick-built and in the Perpendicular style of the fifteenth century. This was on another site, well away from the village a mile to the south. Behind the Hall, it is now only ruins, the broken shell of a nave and chancel, for shortly after the Christmas of 1883 it was gutted by fire which broke out around 1 p.m. after the morning service on Sunday 30 December. As the church had been locked and the keys were not readily to hand, the flames spread rapidly and within minutes there was a major conflagration. The fire seems to have begun in either the roof or the wooden steeple. Amid showers of sparks, burning timbers crashed to the pine furniture in the nave below. An elderly parishioner was sent dashing into Chelmsford for the fire brigade. Although they were on the scene in well under an hour, there was nothing they could do to quench the blaze, despite a good supply of water in the local pond. They stood by while it burnt itself out. Through the day and the following night the towering flames lit up the sky for miles around. The thoroughness of the destruction has been equalled locally only by the terrible burning of Downham parish church in recent years.

A few items were saved by two acts of daring. Very soon after the outbreak was discovered, bystanders broke a window, allowing a boy to climb through, one wonders if with reluctance, and he was able to recover the church plate and clerical garments. Much more surprisingly he managed to get out the Communion table! Later a fireman, at great risk to himself, saved the sixteenth-century painted glass of the east window. A few books were also removed. Fortunately the parish registers, which date from 1540, were at the rectory.

Eyewitness accounts differ as to how the fire started. Some of those first on the spot claimed they saw smoke rising from the roof near the flue of the stovepipe from the burner in the nave. Others, however, said they had first seen smoke rising from the belfry. In fact, during the morning some boys had been caught playing there. An allegation that they had been striking matches was strenuously denied. But the cause of the fire, whether due to negligence, careless accident or what we now call vandalism, was never satisfactorily resolved. The destruction of the church must have greatly saddened the rector, the Rev. J.T. Fowler, who had only just been appointed and had that very day 'read himself in' before his congregation. It was small comfort that the main body of the church had been insured for £1,000.

The decision to build a new church closer into the village was clearly in response to local wishes, for since Tudor times the population of East Hanningfield had become much more centralized. The ruins of the old All Saints stood open to the elements for many years. They underwent some demolition in the 1930s, and the site, being on farmland, is no longer readily accessible to the general public. But it was not until about 1940 that the chief treasure of the old church, a wall painting, was removed to safety. This fine late-medieval work, six centuries old and one of the few church mural paintings in the county, escaped both the fire and years of exposure. It depicts Adam and Eve and St Catherine with their traditional emblems: spade, spindle and wheel. The painting is now at the Victoria and Albert Museum in South Kensington.

An equally dramatic end came to the massive Norman tower of another fine All Saints, the parish church of Writtle. The church endures, though very much restored, with the tower rebuilt 'in a tasteless fashion'. The ancient base also remains, with dominating buttresses and masonry $4\frac{1}{2}$ feet thick. Its mighty fall was vividly penned on the very day of the disaster, 4 April 1800, and printed in the *Gentleman's Magazine*, that valuable source for so much in old Essex a century or two ago. I quote it here as a spectacular close to this little survey of our churches 'bent to the hand of Time'.

This day, at noon, the north-west corner of the venerable tower of Writtle Church, Essex, which had shown for some time past evident marks of decay, and had been at times very injudiciously repaired, came down with a most tremendous crash. The remainder of the tower, having lost the support of this corner and its buttresses, opened to the eye of the astonished beholder a scene which imagination alone can form. The bells were seen hanging in the steeple, suspended in the shattered and momentary crumbling fragments, of the then still venerable pile; the clock revolved in an unusual manner; and thus rested the scene till twelve at night, about which time the north part of the east and the whole of the west side bent to the hand of Time, hurling in its course the bells and clockwork, and converted in an instant that once majestic fabric into ruins. The jangling of the bells was to the inhabitants a sure sign of its total destruction. The body of the church previous to that moment had received no damage, but a part of the east side of the tower falling upon the roof, forced its way through to the singing-gallery, carrying in its course vast sheets of lead, the weight whereof, and the immense force of the stones from the tower (which was about 28 yards in height), dealt destruction in their course, crushing to atoms the gallery and seats beneath, but left the church fit, and still used, for divine service. The humble residents of a cottage near the church very reluctantly quitted their dwelling ten minutes before the fall of the ruins, which levelled it to the ground.

5

'Strange News out of Essex'

Many odd stories have gone on record from what were formerly remote corners of the county, tales of quirky characters and curious events. No doubt there are others waiting to be collected. I could add several to the number from my own first-hand experience, but the privacy of the living ought to be respected at least until 'the tolling bell'.

To begin with, as a curtain-raiser, I turn yet again in these pages to that most fascinating of our Essex diarists, John Crozier. This is what he gives us among his entries for December 1787: 'Came into Maldon a building on Wheels, wherein a man, his wife and six children liv'd. By the side there was another large building in the form of a Tea Kettle. This was shown for a sight. You first was shewn into the house where every thing, tho' useful, was in miniature; thro' which you was usher'd into this Tea Kettle, which form'd a complete little parlour hung with red baize, a fire place, table and complete seats; these being wholly the work and contrivance of this poor man. Great numbers went to see it and gave something, by which means, travelling from place to place, they procur'd a lively hood.'

'There was an old lady who lived in a shoe' – I wonder if this gave them their ingenious notion.

Crozier noted the death of 'Thos. Fytche, esq,' of Danbury Place in 1777 but not the remarkable discovery made in the church there two years later, a find occasioned by the burial of Mrs Frances Fytche ...

The church on Danbury Hill is particularly famed for the three oak effigies of knights which lie in recesses there. They are thought to represent members of the St Clere family who owned the manor (there were also St Cleres at Tilbury). The figures date from the thirteenth and early fourteenth

246

The Goat Woman of Havering (from an old print)

centuries. With their feet crossed and resting on lions, a crusader posture, they are carved in different attitudes. The younger-looking knight is shown in prayer. When, in 1779, workmen began to uncover the floor slabs in the north aisle to receive the body of Mrs Fytche, they came upon a leaden coffin. The rector being sent for, the coffin was opened in his presence and that of the churchwarden. Another witness was a Mr S. White who later gave an account of what was found. Because of its fascinating detail I am giving it here in full as it appeared in the *Gentleman's Magazine* in 1789:

On October 16, 1779, as some workmen were digging a grave for the interment of Mrs Frances Fytche in the north aisle of the parish church of Danbury, Essex, just beneath a niche in the north wall, wherein is placed the effigy of a man in armour carved in wood, in a cumbent posture and cross-legged, they discovered, about thirty inches from the surface of the pavement, beneath a very massy stone, a leaden coffin without any inscription thereon, or marks where any had been affixed. Judging that this coffin enclosed the body of the Knight Templar represented by the effigy, I communicated my opinion to the late Rev. Mr De L'Angle, the then very worthy rector, and Lewis Disney Ffytche, of Danbury Place, churchwarden, who, concurring in the same idea, resolved to open the coffin, but deferred it a day or two to avail themselves of the company and information of the late Rev. Dr Gower, of Chelmsford, an eminent physician and antiquary, who was requested to attend on the Monday following.

Some professional engagements deprived us of the doctor's company and observations; however, the workmen proceeded to open the coffin. On raising the lead there was discovered an elm coffin inclosed, about one-fourth of an inch thick, very firm and entire. On removing the lid of this coffin it was found to enclose a shell about three-quarters of an inch thick, which was covered over with a thick cement of a dark-olive colour and of a resinous nature. The lid of this shell being carefully taken off, we were presented with a view of the body, lying in a liquor or pickle, somewhat resembling mushroom catchup, but of a paler complexion, and somewhat thicker consistence. As I never possessed the sense of smelling, and was willing to ascertain the flavour of the liquor, I tasted, and found it to be aromatic, though not very pungent, partaking of the taste of catchup and of the pickle of Spanish olives. The body was tolerably perfect, no part appearing decayed but the throat and part of one arm. The flesh everywhere, except on the face and throat, appeared exceedingly white and firm; the face was of a dark colour, approaching to black; the throat, which was much lacerated, was of the same colour. The body was covered with a kind of shirt of linen, not unlike Irish cloth of the fineness of what is now usually retailed at three shillings per yard; a narrow, rude, antique lace was affixed to the bosom of the shirt; the stitches were very evident, and attached very strongly. The linen adhered rather closely to the body; but on my raising it from the breast to examine the state of the skin more minutely, a considerable piece was torn off, with part of the lace on it. This I have in my possession for the inspection of the curious; it is in good preservation, and of considerable strength.

The coffin not being half-full of the pickle, the face, breast, and belly were, of course, not covered with it; the inside of the body seemed to be filled with some substance which rendered it very hard. There was no hair on the head, nor do I remember any in the liquor, though feathers, flowers, and herbs in abundance were floating, the leaves and stalks of which appeared quite perfect, but totally discoloured. The appearance of the feathers helped us to discover the cause of the dark appearance of the face and throat. The coffin was not placed in a position exactly horizontal, the feet being at least three inches lower than the head, the greater part of the liquor consequently remained at the feet; the pillow which supported the head in process of time decayed, and the head unsupported fell back, lacerating the throat and neck, which with the face appeared to have been discoloured from the decay of the cloth or substance that covered them. The jaws when first discovered were closed, but on being somewhat rudely touched expanded, owing, as was supposed, to the breaking of some bandage that bound them together; when the jaws were opened they exhibited a set of teeth perfectly white, which was likewise the colour of the palate and all the inside of the mouth.

Whether the legs were crossed or not must for ever remain a doubt, though I am strongly of opinion that they were; for one of the gentlemen pushing a walking-stick rather briskly from the knees to the ankles, the left foot separated from the leg somewhere about the ankle.

The limbs were of excellent symmetry: the general appearance of the whole body conveyed the idea of hearty youth, not in the least emaciated by sickness. The whole length of the corpse very little exceeded five feet, though the shell which enclosed it was five feet six inches within. After the above remarks were made the church doors were opened; and the parishioners and others having satisfied their curiosity, the shell and wooden coffin were fastened down, the leaden coffin was again soldered, and the whole left, as near as circumstances would admit, in statu quo.

A few years before this, another mysterious corpse had caused a stir, this time at Thorpe-le-Soken.

In June 1752 Customs men boarded a vessel which had been set for Harwich but had gone off course in a storm. Looking for possible contraband, they searched the luggage of a passenger calling himself Williams, a merchant of Hamburg. He protested vehemently at the action. When they found jewellery and costly female clothing, their suspicions were aroused. Among the cases was a large chest which Williams refused to open, but he gave way when one of the officers made to run it through with a sword. Upon the lid being opened, the body of a woman was revealed inside. Williams, who appeared unable to understand English, was placed in custody and lodged with the body in the little church on the Hythe below Colchester.

Soon all was made clear and a strange story disclosed. 'Williams' was in fact Lord John Dalmeny, son of the second Earl of Rosebery. Four years before, he had met and married in London a Kitty Canham, the daughter of a wealthy farmer who lived at Beaumont Hall in Thorpe-le-Soken. Kitty, unbeknown to Dalmeny, was already married and had left her husband, the Rev. Alexander Gough, the vicar at Thorpe. She had found her life with him an unhappy one; so one day she upped and disappeared, leaving no trace of her whereabouts. John and Kitty went abroad. It was while on their travels, at Verona, that Kitty's escapade of romance and excitement came to an abrupt end, when she fell ill and died. She was only thirty-two. Just before her end she wrote a brief confession which ended, 'My last request is to be buried at Thorpe.' Dalmeny had her body embalmed and chartered a ship for England.

The burial was a very poignant one, both 'husbands' in deep mourning standing by the grave. John Dalmeny lived on four years. Henry Gough survived his wife by nineteen.

Early last century Havering-atte-Bower was noted for a living curiosity, a hermit, Elizabeth Balls, who became known as 'the Goat Woman'. She was the subject of a painting once in the possession of the great sea captain Earl St Vincent, himself 'a character', who passed his final years at Rochetts in South Weald. A now rare lithograph of the painting, first offered for sale in 1824, was reproduced in the *Essex Review* of July 1935. It shows the old woman in her hut surrounded by animals: seven goats, a dog and two playful cats. A century or so earlier they would have been seen as 'familiars'. Elizabeth Ogborne, who wrote a *History of Essex* in 1814–15, was one of the fortunate few to get near to her, but none was allowed inside the hut. She would only permit someone to enter her hovel twice a year to clean it out.

The short account tells us she was born in Hemel Hempstead, her father being a respectable farmer. Her dwelling at Havering was close to the green. At one time she kept as many as fifty goats along with some sheep and chickens. The picture leaves one in no doubt they literally lived in with her. But she did venture forth from her plot occasionally with a horse and cart, driving to collect hay from Romford market.

At the time of the painting she was judged to be around sixty years of age. The artist depicts her as a bulky figure well wrapped in a shawl and ragged clothes, her face large and worn. Her right hand looks withered. She looks every inch an earth-mother. She was no ogre, however. The face is kindly and she was described as mild-mannered. Nor could she be said to be destitute, for her annual income was reckoned to be nearly £150.

'It is said,' Ogborne wrote, 'that a disappointment in her affections, either from the death or defection of her lover, was the original cause of her whimsicality of conduct, and seclusion from all human society.'

This, of course, is a common enough explanation for anyone who retreats from the world, whether vanishing into a convent or a tent. The villagers of Great Canfield certainly thought so of Jimmy Mason, a rural hermit much closer to our own time. The remarkable story of this recluse has been admirably told in close and fascinating detail by Rayleigh Trevelyan in his book *A Hermit Disclosed*, published by Longmans in 1960.

The story is a complex one and can be only baldly outlined here. There are several good reasons why Trevelyan's book should be read. It narrates a patient, thorough and determined quest to resolve a mystery – namely, why it was that Jimmy Mason withdrew so completely from the eyes of all around him – a quest which involved some two hundred interviews with mainly local people and which lasted for nigh on two decades. That the essential mystery remained at the end was no fault of the author's. His research also took him into a rural world which has all but gone; to go to Canfield now is to be in another country. But above all his book gives us what it gave him in its making, the very rare opportunity of drawing close to the soul of an unseen solitary.

Alexander James Mason died in 1942 at the age of eighty-four, having been a hermit for over forty years. At first he lived in a hut in the grounds of his parents' house, Sawkins. Later he retreated further, to a copse a mile away. The hut here, densely concealed by a tangle of bushes, wire and corrugated iron, was his fortress home for the greater part of his adult life. Only a very few people ever glimpsed him. His brother Tommy took him food but was hardly a real link with the outside world. For a while Jimmy exchanged little notes and gifts with village girls, one in particular; the articles were left in the screen of branches. He also 'spied' on passers-by, sometimes with a telescope.

Trevelyan's interest in the hermit began in the year of the old man's death. (He had finally succumbed to cold and exposure, and probably cancer of the stomach.) The author's family were then living at Sawkins. That winter the pipes froze. Trevelyan, then eighteen and just about to go into the army, climbed into the loft to check the water tank. Here in the rubbish of former years he came across a pile of rotting papers. Among them were the remains of a diary, short and fragmentary entries kept by Jimmy from 1895 to 1897. With this chance discovery Trevelyan began his long and increasingly obsessive search.

The 'jilted lover' theory for Mason's strange behaviour was widely shared, not least by the popular Press, but Trevelyan's book shows this to be far too simplistic. Jimmy's father had been a hard and brutal man and must have played a decisive role in his son's decision to live alone, an irrevocable step taken in 1882. This was the year he cryptically marked as that of the 'Earthquake'. Jimmy also suspected that his brother was trying to poison him; his dog had died in dubious circumstances. He also had strong religious fixations and at least one 'revelatory' experience. His bedroom in the hut where he was at last found dead, an emaciated figure with a long grey beard, was packed with copies of the *Christian Herald*, 'a paper cocoon'.

He was, says Trevelyan, 'a man in a mental mask'. Unlike Elizabeth Balls, his rejection of the world and its values was uniquely extreme, the secular equivalent of a medieval anchorite or the life-style of the Desert Fathers. He lived towards the end solely in communion with himself.

The melancholy spot of his retreat has changed beyond all recognition, every trace eradicated of his image. As one by one the witnesses to his being there pass on, the enigma of old Jimmy now lies sealed in a country churchyard, and in a book.

Had Jimmy Mason been born a few score years earlier, he might have been regarded as a witch. This was the fate of a poor deaf and dumb Frenchman who in 1863 was living alone in a miserable shed at Sible Hedingham. Eighty years old, he was known in the vicinity as 'Dummy'. His true name does not seem to be on record. The only way he could communicate was by grotesque gestures which in themselves marked him out as weird and 'other'. He was held in some awe and seems to have been consulted as a 'cunning man' for telling fortunes and the like. Had it not been for his tragic end, we should probably be quite unaware of this village oracle today. A long newspaper cutting of the time kept at the Essex Record Office tells the bizarre story.

On 3 August 1863 Dummy went to the Swan Inn in Sible Hedingham. There, in a crowded room, he was approached by one Emma Smith, the wife of a beershop-keeper at Ridgewell. She began to complain loudly that Dummy had put a spell on her and she tried to persuade him, with the inducement of several sovereigns, to go home with her and remove the curse. However, he would not be moved. Later, outside the pub, she tried again. On his further refusal she dragged him, with the aid of Samuel Stammers, a master carpenter, to a nearby brook. A crowd had gathered, estimated between sixty and seventy people, many of them straw-plaiters by occupation. In the affray which followed, Stammers took Dummy by the heels and threw him into the stream. When he tried to clamber out, he was cast back. It has been surmised that perhaps his assailants were attempting the old ritual of the ordeal by water. (Such a 'ducking' took place as late as 1751 at the Gabblecote cross-roads at Tring. The victim, Ruth Osborne, was believed to be a witch. She died as a result and one of her attackers, found guilty of murder, was hanged near the spot. Another attempt in 1770 on an alleged witch at Ivinghoe was aborted at the last moment.)

In a state of collapse Dummy was carried to his hut and later transferred to the Halstead Infirmary, where he died on 4 September. The medical evidence was quite clear that his death was due to the vicious treatment he had received.

Giving her testimony in the police court, the woman, speaking in a peculiar voice, claimed that Dummy had cursed her with illness some months before and had spat at her when bewitching her. He had also, she said, put up a note on a door to let others know what he had done. She had been ailing ever since. She went on to accuse others who had gathered of actually manhandling him. Both Emma Smith and Stammers were placed in Colchester Gaol to await trial at the Assizes. Charged with unlawful assault, each was sentenced to six months hard labour.

Another story from north Essex which is 'rich and strange' is the legend of the Flying Serpent or Dragon of Henham. I first came across this in Herbert Tompkins' *Companion Into Essex*, a classic of old-world charm published in 1938 but alas no longer in print.

The tale originally appeared in a rare pamphlet of 1669. There is a copy in the British Museum, and a facsimile was produced at Saffron Walden in 1885. The title page is suitably wondrous, the wording lengthy, as so many titles were in that word-spinning age. It announces THE *Flying Serpent or Strange News out of Essex, BEING a true Relation of a Monstrous Serpent which hath diverse times been seen at a parish called Henham-on-the Mount within four miles of Saffron Walden, Showing the length, proportion, the bigness of the Serpent, the place where it commonly lurks and what means hath been used to kill it.* Signs and wonders may change from age to age but it seems that, like things from out of space in our own science fiction fantasies, such alien creatures must be killed – simply because they are there.

The tract is given a semblance of authenticity with a list of 'witnesses' on the title page. They include a churchwarden, a constable and an Overseer of the Poor. It should be a relatively easy thing to do but I don't know if anyone has put their names to the test. Suspiciously, the author is unnamed, but this could well be the work of William Winstanley, alias 'Poor Robin', for the almanac which bore his *nom-de-plume* and which was very popular in the nineteenth century, has frequent references to the Serpent. An Essex man, Winstanley was known as 'the Barber Poet'. He also turned out chapbooks, little books containing ballads, anecdotes etc which were hawked around by chapmen or traders. His best-known work was *Poor Robin's Perambulations from Saffron Walden to London*. He was related to the Winstanley who built the first, and ill-fated, Eddystone Lighthouse and who had no mean reputation as a practical joker, especially demonstrated in his house of tricks at Littlebury.

The Serpent was no marvel of the distant past, for ostensibly it had appeared in the year before the pamphlet. The lair of this 'venomous creature' was a birch wood where it had been spotted basking in the sun. The narrative gives brief accounts of several sightings. The beast is described as eight or nine feet long and with small wings. It had large, penetrating eyes, like a sheep's, and sharp, white teeth. A crude, fierce drawing accompanies the text.

It was first seen by a man riding along 'a Gentleman's way'. (In her history of the village Joyce Winsmill pointed out that the way in still there, a path by Lodge Farm and the field called Birch Wood.) Numerous attempts were made to slay the dragon, all of them it seems half-hearted, but it proved elusive, which kept the story going. A shy and docile creature, it did no damage. Apparently, it was as frightened as its pursuers.

A natural explanation which has been advanced is that it may have been an outsize diver-bird, but I should think that even superstitious country folk would have had more nous than to confuse a bird with such a phenomenon. Whatever it was, if ever it was, it must have been a mighty entertainment in those unruffled parts.

The pamphlet adds a further spice with an account of a cockatrice. As few of my readers are ever likely to meet one of these in the flesh, I ought to tell you, although I cannot explain, what it is or rather was. It should be of sufficient warrant that it was around in Shakespeare's time; look in *Twelfth Night*. It is even in Isaiah. It is a fabulous and heraldic beast, a composite creation with the wings of a fowl, the tail of a dragon and the head of a cockerel. Also styled a basilisk, from its crest, it takes its name from a cock's egg hatched by a serpent. Much more importantly, it could kill by sight. 'If looks could kill' was only too true of the cockatrice.

According to our jovial pamphleteer, one had terrorized Henham and the surrounding land in days of yore. It was finally put down by a knight in armour of crystal glass. 'In memory whereof his sword was hung up in Walden Church, the effigies of the Cockatrice set up in Brass, and a Table hanged close by wherein was contained all the story of the adventure; but in these late times of Rebellion, it being taken for a monument of superstition was by the lawless souldiers broken in peices, to show they were also of a venemous Nature as well as the Cockatrice.' I like the moral, for so much of Merrie England withered beyond recall under the cold Puritan gaze of disapproval.

The legend of the Serpent and other nasties of the pit may have been well rooted in the whole area from time immemorial. There is a carving of a dragon, of fourteenth-century date, in the north arcade of Henham church. Another indication lies in place-names. One of these some miles further to the south at Felsted is Gransmore, otherwise Grinsmore and Grismal Green. The name means 'Grendel's mere' or 'pool' and seems to recall none other than Beowulf's monster of the fens.

These darkling things are well suggested in the poem of an 'Essex rhymer', quoted by Tompkins in his book but the source apparently unknown. Conjured up on the seashore, the first and last of its verses run:

> What time I take my pipe in hand
>   I see the oddest things,
> This side and that, on sea or land
>   With legs and fins and wings;
> And some there be – a wicked band –
>   Armed, in their tails, with stings.

Dragons and other brutes roved there,
　　I scorn to sing their praise;
Nor would I rouse them in their lair,
　　Or watch their wicked ways;
Yet these, and more besides, I swear,
　　Lived in the good old days!

Among 'the oddest things' to be found in the history of
the county are more natural monstrosities. Of these the
foremost must surely be the figure of Edward Bright. I use
the expression 'figure' quite literally, for as 'the Great Man
of Maldon' he would have held the record for his weight in
any eighteenth-century *Guiness Book of Records*. Entries in
the parish registers of All Saints and an engraving of around
1790 celebrate his incredible size.

Edward Bright was a tallow chandler and grocer in the
town: 'a very honest tradesman, a facetious companion,
comely in his person, affable in his temper, a tender father
and a valuable friend'. As a post-boy he had gone to
Chelmsford each day on horseback, riding there and back.
When he died in 1750 at the early age of twenty-nine, he
weighed, in the words of the burial register, 'upwards of 42
stone (horseman's weight)'. His coffin was huge, six feet
seven inches long and three feet six over the shoulders. To
get it out of his shop near the corner of St Peter's
churchyard, a way had to be cut through the wall and
staircase. It was drawn on a carriage to the church and then
moved on rollers to the brickwork vault. Then it was
lowered into place by means of pulleys. The spot is marked
in All Saints by a grave-slab near the font. The shop leased
by Bright, now called Church House, can still be seen in the
High Street.

His enormous girth was the subject of a memorable bet.
Round the chest he measured five feet six inches and round
his stomach six feet eleven. 'A Wager was proposed between
two Gentlemen of that Place & determin'd December the first
1750, which was that five Men at the age of 21 then resident
there could not be button'd within his waistcoat without
breaking a stitch or straining a Button, wch when come to
tryal, not only ye 5 propos'd but 7 Men were with the
greatest ease included.' This happened barely three weeks

after Bright's funeral. It would be good to know what became of the prestigious relic.

On his death his widow was expecting her sixth child. Forty years later his son Edward was interred in the family vault. He, too, was vastly corpulent, reckoned to be half the weight of his father and of unusual size. Another prodigy in the family was Sarah, the sister of Edward Bright Senior. She died in 1765 at Thaxted. Her weight was around twenty stone, and her coffin had to be lowered from the window.

From these beguiling observations let us turn to something lighter, some happy eccentricities.

At Fairlop, now an urbanized sprawl, there once stood a famous oak, one of the oldest and grandest in the land. A late eighteenth-century work, Gilpin's *Forest Scenery*, records it was thirty-six feet in circumference and had a spread of eleven vast arms.

It was to this ancient tree that around 1730 Daniel Day, a pump-and engine-maker of Wapping, came with some friends to picnic. He had a small estate in the district and much admired the spot close to Hainault Forest. From this time on for over thirty years his visits became an established custom, with him returning on the first Friday in July and dispensing from the hollow trunk a largesse of bacons and beans and drink to all who gathered there. He came in a colourful procession, drawn by six horses in a large, wheeled boat of the dug-out variety. The genial, Dickensian Mr Day died a bachelor in 1767, aged eighty-four, and was buried at Barking. He was interred, it is said, in a branch of the tree. It had fallen to the ground, which Day took as a portent. The tradition has it that he tried it for size and, thinking the section a bit too short, remarked, 'Just ask my executors to cut off my head and tuck it between my legs.'

The summer visitations did not cease but grew into a full-scale Cockney festival with musicians and a whole variety of booths around the oak, including gingerbread stalls and puppet shows. A watercolour by Rowlandson pictures the crowded scene on 7 July 1815, showing the arrival of a cavalcade of carts and wagons. But by then the oak had virtually gone, burnt down ten years before by flames from the kitchen of a gypsy encampment. Some of its wood went into the making of the pulpits for the new St

Pancras' parish church and that at Wanstead.

The fair became disorderly and 'low', too much a thing of the people, it seems, and was suppressed soon after 1850. The Forest authorities took the lead in ending it. But for long the setting remained an attraction. Among its frequenters was an archery club, the Hainault Foresters. Early this century King George V, when Prince of Wales, planted a new oak on the site, which had become a recreation ground.

Fairlop Oak was one of a number of legendary trees which stood as sentinels in wooded Essex. Its closest rival was the Doodle Oak at Hatfield, giving the village the added name of 'Broad Oak'. Another was at Hempstead. It was noted by that indefatigable traveller Arthur Young: 'Seven wagon-loads of hay have stood under its shelter at one time.' It was ninety feet high and had a spread from north to south of well over a hundred feet. This was probably Turpin's Oak, which has gone. The highwayman was born in the village alehouse, now the Rose and Crown. Opposite, behind the war memorial, is Turpin's Ring, a close circle of stout trees said to have been used for cock fighting.

A fine tree with a magnificent span virtually covers the green at Sandon. Surprisingly, it is of no great age. A very rare Spanish oak, it was planted to commemorate the Diamond Jubilee of Queen Victoria.

For rustic eccentricity of a truly woolly kind, old Coggeshall has pride of place. Few people in the county appear to have heard of those delightful absurdities 'Coggeshall jobs'. Exactly when or why these follies were attributed to 'Coxall' folk remains a mystery. They are akin to the stupidities of the Wise Men of Gotham, a collection of which was published in the reign of Henry VIII.

Brewer gives two brief examples of Coggeshall jobs, but by far the best account is to be found in C. Henry Warren's *Essex*, first published in 1950 by Robert Hale as one of their fine County Books series. They first seem to have appeared in print in 1871, when a Kelvedon Quaker, James Hurnard, made them a subject in his ten-thousand-line poem 'The Setting Sun'. Warren quotes at length the story of the hay-straw volunteers. Like all the others from 'the City of Wisdom' it is marked by 'Blunders absurd and misadventures various'.

One of my favourite tales is that of the Coggeshall Town Band. They were rehearsing in the upstairs room of a house when someone came in to tell them how good the music sounded in the street below. So they all filed out to hear it! In another of these anecdotes a wheelbarrow was bitten by a mad dog, whereupon the villagers locked the barrow in a shed.

Then there's the one about the two men drinking in the Woolpack. Well in their cups, they decided they did not like the position of the church and went off to move it. They found they were pushing against the wind, so taking off their coats and leaving them on the ground, they walked round to the other side. Again they pushed to no avail, so they returned to the original spot. Finding their jackets had gone, one of the men exclaimed, 'Dammit, if we ent shoved the owd chu'ch right over our coats!' – which seems to me to be a merry note on which to end.

One lifetime alone will not suffice to perambulate old Essex. No matter, for this thought should make us happy.

For there is good news yet to hear and fine things to be seen,
Before we go to Paradise by way of Kensal Green.

Select Bibliography

Some of the books listed below are currently out of print. Among them are a few very rare volumes and these are marked with an asterisk. However, they are all well worth seeking out either in major public libraries or in second-hand and antiquarian bookshops.

*The History and Antiquities of the County of Essex, (2 vols), Philip Morant (1st ed. 1768, 2nd ed. 1816)

*The History and Topography of the County of Essex, (2 vols) Thomas Wright (1831-36)

*History, Gazetteer and Directory of the County of Essex, William White (1848)

A Companion into Essex, Herbert W. Tompkins (Methuen, 1938)

Shell Guide to Essex, Norman Scarfe (Faber and Faber, 1975)

*Essex: A Dictionary of the County Mainly Ecclesiological G. Worley (Bell, 1915)

The Buildings of England: Essex, Nikolaus Pevsner (revised Enid Radcliffe) (Penguin 1979)

The King's England: Essex, Arthur Mee (Hodder and Stoughton, revised ed. 1966)

*Essex, A.R. Hope-Moncrieffe (A. and C. Black, 1st ed. 1909, revised 1926)

*Romantic Essex, Reginald Beckett (Dent, 1901 and 1907)

Essex, C. Henry Warren (Robert Hale, 1950)

Little Guide to Essex, J. Charles Cox (revised C. Henry Warren), (Methuen, 1952)

Essex, Marcus Crouch (Batsford, 1969)

Essex People: 1750-1900, A.F.J. Brown (Essex County Council [ERO Publications No.59], 1972)

Essex Eccentrics, Alison Barnes (Boydell Press, 1975)

Essex Worthies, Sir William Addison (Phillimore, 1973)

The English Country Parson, Sir William Addison (Dent, 1947)

Elizabethan Life, (5 vols), Dr. F.G. Emmison (Essex County Council, 1970-80)

No Rain in Those Clouds, David Smith (Dent, 1943)

Mary Rich, Countess of Warwick (1625-1678): Her Family and Friends, Charlotte Fell Smith (Longmans Green, 1901)

A Hermit Disclosed, Rayleigh Trevelyan (Longmans, 1960)

The Countess of Warwick, Margaret Blunden (Cassell, 1967)

My Darling Daisy, Theo Lang (Michael Joseph, 1966)

Mrs Hurst Dancing and Other Scenes From Regency Life 1812-1823, Diana Sperling, with text by Gordon Mingay (Gollancz, 1981)

Coastal Adventure, James Wentworth Day (George Harrap, 1949)

Index